Intentions

Literature and Philosophy

A. J. Cascardi, General Editor

This series publishes books in a wide range of subjects in philosophy and literature, including studies of the social and historical issues that relate these two fields. Drawing on the resources of the Anglo-American and Continental traditions, the series is open to philosophically informed scholarship covering the entire range of contemporary critical thought.

Already published:

J. M. Bernstein, *The Fate of Art: Aesthetic Alienation from Kant to Derrida and Adorno*
Peter Bürger, *The Decline of Modernism*
Mary E. Finn, *Writing the Incommensurable: Kierkegaard, Rossetti, and Hopkins*
Reed Way Dasenbrock, ed., *Literary Theory After Davidson*
David Haney, *William Wordsworth and the Hermeneutics of Incarnation*
David Jacobson, *Emerson's Pragmatic Vision: The Dance of the Eye*
Gray Kochhar-Lindgren, *Narcissus Transformed: The Textual Subject in Psychoanalysis and Literature*
Robert Steiner, *Toward a Grammar of Abstraction: Modernity, Wittgenstein, and the Paintings of Jackson Pollock*
Sylvia Walsh, *Living Poetically: Kierkegaard's Existential Aesthetics*
Michel Meyer, *Rhetoric, Language, and Reason*
Christie McDonald and Gary Wihl, eds., *Transformation in Personhood and Culture After Theory*
Charles Altieri, *Painterly Abstraction in Modernist American Poetry: The Contemporaneity of Modernism*
John C. O'Neal, *The Authority of Experience: Sensationist Theory in the French Enlightenment*
John O'Neill, ed., *Freud and the Passions*
Sheridan Hough, *Nietzche's Noontide Friend*
E. M. Dadlez, *What's Hecuba to Him?*
Hugh Roberts, *Shelley and the Chaos of History: A New Politics of Poetry*

Intentions

Negotiated, Contested, and Ignored

Arabella Lyon

The Pennsylvania State University Press
University Park, Pennsylvania

A portion of Chapter 2 will appear in *New Perspectives on Rhetorical Invention* (Tennessee, forthcoming).

Library of Congress Cataloging-in-Publication Data

Lyon, Arabella, 1951-
    Intentions : negotiated, contested, and ignored / Arabella Lyon.
       p.   cm. — (Literature & philosophy)
    Includes bibliographical references and index.
    ISBN 0-271-01797-X (cloth : alk. paper)
    ISBN 0-271-01798-8 (pbk. : alk. paper)
    1. Literature — History and criticism — Theory, etc. 2. Literature —
Philosophy. 3. Intentionality (Philosophy) in literature.
I. Title. II. Series: Literature and philosophy.
PN49.L86   1998
801'.95 — dc21   97-49173
                                                                           CIP

Copyright © 1998 The Pennsylvania State University
All rights reserved
Printed in the United States of America
Published by The Pennsylvania State University Press,
University Park, PA 16802-1003

It is the policy of The Pennsylvania State University Press to use acid-free paper for the first printing of all clothbound books. Publications on uncoated stock satisfy the minimum requirements of American National Standard for Information Sciences— Permanence of Paper for Printed Library Materials, ANSI Z39.48-1992.

Contents

	Acknowledgments	vii
	Introduction: Intentions Assumed	1
1	Literary Rhetorics, Ethics, and Cultural Orthodoxies	27
2	Intention, Invention, and Interpretation: Rhetoric at the End of the Twentieth Century	55
3	Kenneth Burke on Form, Motive, and Purpose	81
	Hinge/Acknowledging Prejudices	105
4	Just Say No: Intentions Ignored	113
5	Wittgenstein's Stories: Desiring Less and Accruing More	143
6	Metaphors as Enthymemes: The Evolution of Language-Games and Form of Life	169
	Works Cited	197
	Index	211

Acknowledgments

In writing about conflicting intentions and the nature of understanding, I have become especially aware of the vagaries of communication and the necessity of listening to one's audience. Whatever useful meanings I present here would not have occurred without conversations with legions of interpreters, audiences, and friends. Whatever useful meaning you take away, gentle reader, is a reflection of your intentions, interests, and interpretive efforts. For that, I thank you.

Research for material included in this book was supported by grants from Temple University, University of Illinois-Chicago, and the Dartmouth School for Criticism and Theory. I thank the staff and administrators of these institutions as well as Donald Marshall, Ned Lukacher, and Lynne Tribble. Stanley Cavell and Dominick LaCapra were very helpful during my summer at Dartmouth.

Many individuals read portions of the book in draft and/or discussed its ideas with me. I am grateful to the various members of my writing group whose timely tolerance of mess or requirement of rigor helped me think my way through a series of impasses: thanks to Lisa Downing, Abe Rothman, Frank Sullivan, and Kathleen Wright. I also wish to thank Sue Wells for her very careful reading of an early draft of the manuscript, and Tony Cascardi for the broad vision of his suggestions, which helped to unify the final project. The manuscript benefited from the generous comments of Charles Altieri, Sheldon Brivic, Carol Colatrella, Jeanne Fahnstock, Robin Grey, Stephen Mailloux, Sally Mitchell, Alan Nadel, George Pullman, Paula Robison, Jack Selzer, Alan Singer, Robert Wess, and Jim Zappen. Finally, I am eternally indebted to my muses, the lovely members of BWP, Laura Downing, Lisa Downing, and Jack Meszaros.

I dedicate this book to the memory of Joanne Wagner. Her comments would have added to both the book's logic and humor.

Introduction:
Intentions Assumed

(21) I have by means of speech removed disgrace from a woman; I have observed the procedure which I set up at the beginning of the speech; I have tried to end the injustice of blame and ignorance of opinion; I wished to write a speech which would be a praise of Helen and a diversion to myself.
—Gorgias, "Encomium of Helen"

In its sophistic origins, rhetoric toyed with authorial intention and its significance for interpretation and evaluation. Gorgias, having given a speech in praise of the defamed harlot Helen of Troy, in his last four words, explicitly supplements his earlier stated intention, and so renegotiates the meaning of his speech and forces his audience to revise their responses to his argument and their understanding of the author's purpose. Is this really an argument about Helen's innocence, or is this simply a diversion for a bored sophist, or is it both (as Gorgias claims)? The encomium's ambiguous meaning is commonly discussed, but there is more here. In addition to explicit play with the relationship between authorial intentions and meaning, Gorgias also toys with the audience's intentions or purposes. Any audience hearing or reading the piece is called on to revise their interpretation, to analyze what is a proper understanding of the text as a whole, to voice their prejudices, and to discover their relationships to the purposes of the argument and the desire for diversion. In effect, the speech calls on the audience to foreground their intentions in listening and interpreting. Gorgias's probings are still more complicated: he also plays with a second audience, one within his speech, Helen. Unlike the living audience trying to make sense of Gorgias, she is totally passive. Her voyage to Troy has no basis in her actions and intentions, but rather is dictated by fate, violence, persuasion, or love. Unlike the audience, who is called to active and troubled interpretation by Gorgias's last line, Helen is the purposeless receiver of forces to which she responds, but is not responsible for resisting. Her lack of intentions and lack of resistance to the intents of others is remarkable not just because it increases her vulnerability, but because it demonstrates the correlation between active intentions and ethical behavior (even human behavior) and because it illustrates the necessity of deliberating on the speeches and intentions of others and deciding a course of action carefully. If one is human—as opposed to a despised mythical figure—one seemingly should have complex, multiple purposes that at least occasionally require one to struggle against fate, violence, persuasion, love, and sophists.

I

Despite this early demonstration of the complexity of intentions within rhetorical situations, rhetorical theory has evaded developing theories of intention.[1] While the rhetoric-related disciplines of literary criticism and hermeneutics debate issues of intention, and while they often successfully argue that intention is too elusive as a criterion of accuracy in interpretations and comparative evaluations of interpretations, contemporary rhetoricians rarely mention intention, let alone analyze the interactive relationships between the rhetor's intentions and the audience's intentions. Rhetoricians sometimes write of authorial motives and purposes and are concerned with the negotiation of meaning, but they have not sustained a discussion that allows them to theorize the interactivity of conflicting intentions. Hence they have little sense of what theorizing intention would add to rhetoric. The conception of intention now in the discipline is very little evolved from the questions raised by Gorgias. This is

---

1. Of course there are exceptions, ancient and modern, that I do develop: for example, Plato's *Phaedrus* in this chapter and Burke in Chapter 3. Katherine Eden in *Poetic and Legal Fiction in the Aristotelian Tradition* discusses the origins of the concept of intention in Greek law and its development in Aristotle, particularly in his forensic rhetoric (39–61). Rita Copeland in *Rhetoric, Hermeneutics, and Translation in the Middle Ages* discusses the rhetorical origins of the concept of *intentio* in medieval *enarratio* or hermeneutics.

a strange omission in view of rhetoric's conflicted relationship to postmodernism, a conflict in part constructed by rhetoric's assumption of intending subjects, an assumption that a few (such as Mailloux and Gaonkar) willingly abandon for the insights gained by using the textualist, interpretive theories of hermeneutics and literary criticism, but one which a majority of rhetoricians still embrace.

In any system of thinking, the most difficult sites to critique are assumptions, assumptions so deep and intrinsic as to structure the whole enterprise. Consequently, to identify agent and intention as concepts in need of discussion is a shift that is evidence of a revolution in American rhetorical thinking; the textualism of postmodernism and tropology of Continental rhetoric have given us alternative approaches which demand that we articulate what was safely and simply assumed. As a commonplace, traditional rhetoric's response to sophistry is to posit an ethical, purposeful subject, "the good man speaking well."[2] This traditional move away from sophistry privileges expressible purpose and intention and places them at the core of rhetoric, in the rhetor's first word and not in a sophist's final, teasing phrase or a moment's play with craft and trickery. Despite the debates in interpretive disciplines, intention remains basic to rhetorical practice for many contemporary rhetoricians. In responding to a discussion about the modern subject and agency in traditional rhetoric and hermeneutical aspects of rhetoric, John Campbell writes, "Of course there has to be an agent and purposes and talk of strategies and intentions—these terms are part of the basic lexicon of the craft, and are part of the store of suggestive distinctions and terms that has made rhetoric so invaluable and traditionally attractive for historians" (314). In fact, Glen H. Stamp and Mark L. Knapp go so far as to write that "intent also lies at the heart of theory, assumptions, and practices of research and methods of teaching in communications" (282). In considered response to the assumption of intention, I contend that, despite the current lack of carefully articulated reasons for intention's inclusion, there are good reasons for us to continue to use and to develop further the concept.

Rhetoric's assumption of intention, especially authorial intention, has been supported historically by at least four aspects of the discipline. One, unlike poetics and philosophy, rhetoric emphasizes communication—functional, instrumental, persuasive communication—over the art, truth, interpretation, or play of language. From Aristotle's taxonomy onward, if rhetoric emphasizes art, it moves toward poetics; if rhetoric emphasizes

---

2. Jan C. Swearingen in *Rhetoric and Irony* and Susan Jarratt in *Rereading the Sophists* provide useful, historical approaches to the premise of the ethical orator.

truth, it moves toward philosophy; if it emphasizes play, it moves toward sophistry. Rhetoric's boundaries have kept it concerned with, though not limited to, instrumental discourse, and within instrumental discourse, purpose, motive, and desired effect are defining aspects. Two, Western rhetoric originates in oral practices and the presence of a speaker who can articulate at least a few of her intentions and the presence of an audience who, in turn, is quite capable of enacting its intentions. Hence, in most rhetorical situations, the presence of competing interlocutors increases their sense of difference, including different intentions, and the need for negotiating difference is so apparent that the *process of negotiations* dominates any analytic response regarding the possibility of truly knowing one's intentions. Three, historically, rhetorical theory has considered actions and effects rather more than interpretation and its grounds. By normal definition, there is intention within action (as opposed to mere motions). Action, like rhetoric, has a public dimension, a demonstrated, sensate effect. Four, traditional rhetoric emphasizes *kairos* or occasion. The analysis of the particular highlights a more singular, specific use of discourse, a response that addresses a single situation with particular people for definite reasons. This specificity encourages the belief in limited intentions, beliefs, and purposes. Alternatively, interpretive activities such as reading and rereading over long periods of time diminish the specificity of any single situation, the aspect of conventional and institutional context, and the immediacy of effect, and instead emphasize the text as discursive space rather than discourse as temporal progression. Obviously, there is more to the underlying assumption of intentions within rhetoric, but these are the most basic explanations as to why rhetoric still tends to privilege intention at the end of the twentieth century.

These reasons in themselves, however, do not explain why intention has not been theorized. I would hypothesize that the defining place of a rhetor's and audience's intentions within rhetoric placed them outside controversy, or did so at least until the new theories of interpretation and a heightened awareness of the place of interpretation within rhetorical situations entered the field in the late twentieth century. As a consequence of not theorizing intention, and in response to institutional pressures, disciplinary rhetoric has taken an interpretive turn that diminishes its historical emphasis on practice, negotiation, and deliberation. Given rhetoric's increasingly common institutional placement in English and the nature of humanistic disciplines, rhetoric is likely to continue as a predominately interpretive field. Interpretive rhetorics, however, cannot continue to ignore issues of deliberation and intention *and* claim a particularly political nature or, for that matter, a significant connection to the practices of speaking and writing. In fact, if the field of rhetoric is going to reengage the public sphere, interpret popular and civic discourses, and articulate appropriate models for multicultural deliberations, its practitioners need to study deliberative processes and develop research questions that address these particular concerns. Ultimately, contemporary rhetoric's relationship to discourse in the public sphere is complicated by rhetoric's own duplicity: it is both a practice and a theory, and so always engaged and yet not quite engaged in public deliberations. Whether the discipline itself can aspire toward public deliberation and textual production and remain an analytic tradition very much will depend on how we are able to engage and analyze the nature of deliberation.[3]

The questions of other fields, by themselves, will not promote rhetorical projects and, in likelihood, may hinder them. Specifically, the questions asked about intentions in literary criticism, hermeneutics, aesthetics, philosophy of mind, and computer science do not reflect a rhetorical tradition of civic concerns and actions. Literary criticism, aesthetics, legal theory, and hermeneutics discuss authorial intentions within a frame that acknowledges the difficulties of recognizing intentions and then using them as criteria for evaluating interpretations and, in some instances, judging the aesthetic value of a text. These fields ask such questions as, Can we know authorial intentions? How do we know authorial intentions? Can they define or aid correct interpretation? Can they be used as criteria for evaluating competing interpretations? What constitutes evidence of intentions (consistency, context, biography, cause, effect/end, introspection)? Overall, these fields accept that the author's (and the audience's) complete intentions are unknowable and difficult to use as criteria for interpretation, but they continue through these questions to seek or deny a grounding for interpretation and aesthetic evaluation.[4] The interpretive questions about intention look back in time and seek a means of weighing present interpretations, using time much in the manner of forensic practices and in a manner very unlike Aristotle's description of deliberation.

---

3. In defining deliberation, I am comfortable with slightly adapting Lani Guinier's definition in *Tyranny of the Majority* by adding rhetorical elements (my additions in brackets): "the process of [articulating and] framing issues to be resolved, proposing alternative solutions, examining the reasons for and against the proposed solutions, [advocating for specific solutions, recognizing and responding to the concerns of others,] and settling on an alternative [action]" (256). In her brief discussion, Guinier provides a useful bibliography on the term from a legal-political perspective.

4. Gary Iseminger has edited a useful collection, *Intention and Interpretation*, that provides both a history and analyses of the concept of intention by literary critics and aesthetic philosophers. P. D. Juhl's *Interpretation* outlines seven major theories of interpretation and then argues for a connection between intention and meaning, the author as a historical person, and one and only one correct interpretation which may not be knowable.

Philosophy of mind and action also are concerned with intention, though in a variety of ways, or rather in a progression of related questions. At times, philosophy of mind discusses intentionality as part of an examination of the nature of our mental states, such as beliefs, desires, and intentions.[5] Other times, philosophy of mind discusses the specific mental state of intention from the perspective of planning an action.[6] The broader approach to intentionality might be called *aboutness*, inquiry into how thinking, feeling, and knowing are *about* the world. In a tradition of inquiry following Edmund Husserl and Franz Brentano, John R. Searle, for example, defines intentionality as "that property of mind (brain) by which it is able to represent other things" (*Intentionality* 24). Questions of aboutness might start with the question, How are mental states (beliefs, desires, intentions, emotions) about the world? Or, more simply, How are our thoughts about the world? The broad inquiry may be supported by such narrower questions as, What is the relationship between mental states and the objects or things they are about? What is involved in having beliefs, desires, or intentions directed at objects that may not exist (God, mermaids, honest men)? How are mental phenomena causally efficacious?

From this larger approach to mental states arise questions specifically concerning intention as possibly one of our mental states. Concerning the mental state of intention, one might ask: How is the mental state of intention different than those of desire and belief? What is an intentional action? What are the relationships among intentional attitudes, linguistic entities, and intentional objects? What is the relationship of an intentional action to purpose as opposed to a reflexive action or an action that is a side effect, not the primary intention? How do the differences between actions that are intentional, reflexive, or incidental affect theories of ethics?

In developing concepts of intentionality, philosophy of mind and action and some artificial intelligence research describe intention as a specific mental state with a distinctive role leading to planning, a role not shared with desires and beliefs. These fields link intentions to the making of formalized plans, which in turn are conceived of as systems of intentions. Philosophers of mind see both plans and intentions as being future oriented; intentions here are unlike those in aesthetic research, concerned

---

5. Daniel C. Dennett gives a quick overview of this in *The Intentional Stance*, and while he does favor his own position in the discussion, he offers as quick and clear an account of the positions as I have read. Also helpful is Roderick M. Chisolm's encyclopedia entry, "Intentionality." For distinctions among positions, see Donald Davidson, Michael E. Bratman, Robert Audi, and Alfred R. Mele.

6. Bratman, who is very influential in describing intention as planning, actually marks the break slightly differently, calling the other school "desire-belief."

with past actions of an author, or research on belief or desire, concerned with the present state within a mind. Inquirers focusing on intentions as plans might ask: How do future-directed intentions influence later conduct? What is their influence on choice and practical reasoning over time? What is the difference between knowing a plan and intending to act on it (I know how to cheat, I intend to cheat)? What are the components of plans? Is a plan a collection of actions an agent will undertake, or is it a collection of an agent's intentions and beliefs? Superficially these questions have relationships to communicative actions, but in explication they veer from communication between people. Philosopher Michael Bratman, for instance, connects intention as planning to *deliberation* and *practical reason,* terms commonly connected to rhetoric. His sense of both words, however, is removed from their rhetorical meanings. Practical reason entails solely rationality, and deliberation is limited to the individual making choices (Which breakfast cereal?) rather than political deliberations among parties in the tradition of Aristotle. What is helpful about Bratman's focus on planning is that thinking of intention as planning explicitly involves a future-oriented approach to action very different than the retrospective act of looking back before the existence of a text and reconstructing an author's original plan. A planning model of intention focused on action gives one a way of thinking that is not forensic and past-oriented, but rather concerned with future effect.

While other inquires into intentions may be useful to some rhetorical projects, rhetoricians concerned with understanding the place of intentions, so long assumed in rhetoric, need to formulate approaches that address concerns within their own field. This book develops and explores questions that are concerned with textual production and the negotiation of meaning and action between an author and an audience. In doing so, it attempts to stay within the historical domain of deliberative rhetoric (insofar as rhetoric ever stays within a domain) because this gives a stronger sense of planning and action. It is concerned with the differences between a rhetor and an audience (not his interpreters), their texts and context, and the actions that arise or fail to arise from their conjunctures. The questions this book asks and answers, consequently, are significantly different than those of other disciplines.

Do an audience's intentions affect interpretations and thereby affect deliberations about meanings and actions?

How do audiences negotiate meaning when faced with a rhetor's competing, alien, or unintelligible intentions?

When do the negotiations of meaning fail to satisfy the writer or another reader, and what is the resulting outcome?

How can we define or understand intention within rhetorical situations and in pluralistic communities?

Is the negotiation of intentions played out differently in different discursive forms (genres, tropes)?

What is the relationship between the description of interpretive process and the positing of an ideal interpretive process? Does positing an ideal process affect practice?

Can the concept of intention help rhetorical theory understand deliberation?

Can we find some interpretive patterns that allow rhetorical theorists to predict the effects of discursive events?

Undoubtedly there are many more questions tacitly asked and answered here, and there are questions that might be asked and are not. Still, this particular set of questions should help our understanding of the nature of deliberation, its relationship to competing intentions or purposes, its effect on making meaning, and the nature of rhetorical action within our rhetorical culture, or rather our evolved and pluralistic democracy.

II

Within contemporary rhetoric, and following interpretive theory, intention is most commonly conceived as *purpose,* occasionally taking a turn toward the broader structures of motivation or a more public process of deliberation and planning but consistently linked to purpose and the instrumental aspect of rhetoric.[7] For example, Michael Leff, in delineating the difference between rhetorical criticism and critical rhetoric (ideologi-

---

7. J. L. Austin in "Three Ways of Spilling Ink" (*Philosophical Papers*) works out many of the nuances among acting "intentionally," "purposefully," or "deliberately." Despite some useful distinctions, he ends the essay with a warning: "there are overriding considerations, which may be operative in any situation in which I act, which may put all three words out of joint, in spite of the other standard conditions for their use being satisfied" (286). Certainly general distinctions about time, process, and relationship to action can be made, but the distinctions are blurred in everyday usage.

cal critique), writes of an intentional and extensional dimension of rhetoric. According to Leff, in focusing on "the *purpose of the rhetor* as he or she composes a discourse designed to persuade an audience" (emphasis added), the intentional dimension "stresses artistic integrity of the discourse" ("Things" 223). In contrast, extensional rhetoric, focusing on the effect on the audience, emphasizes social impact. Leff's placing of intention within the aesthetic frame and away from ideological critique diminishes the dynamic between authorial intention and audience response in formulating an action. Instead, he makes intention a textual issue rather than an issue concerned with social position, conflicting purposes, and the why of action. This characterization of rhetorical criticism within textual and potentially aesthetic frameworks blocks thinking about a political rhetoric, even if one maintains a dialectic between critical rhetoric and rhetorical criticism, as Leff proposes.

The conception of intention found in contemporary rhetorical theory unfortunately is much more like that of literary criticism, which focuses on authorial intention in relationship to the interpretation of a text and the evaluation of the significance—meaning and worth—of art. Since W. K. Wimsatt and Monroe C. Beardsley's 1946 essay, "The Intentional Fallacy," literary debates have assumed intention to mean an author's purpose or plan; the debates themselves, following from Wimsatt and Beardsley's repudiation of the role of intentionality in evaluating the meaning and value of literature, have considered whether authorial intention can be known, whether it is helpful in determining meaning, and whether it is necessary for evaluating a work's success. Neither Wimsatt nor Beardsley propose that intentions do not exist, only that they are inadequate for judging meaning or aesthetic value. For that matter, within any discipline, it is difficult to find denial of the existence of intentions.

While literary questions about and approaches to intention often are not helpful to rhetorical concerns, I do find Michael Hancher's description of three aspects of authorial intention useful for understanding the multiplicity of concepts within intention and for thinking about the process of producing rhetorical discourses.[8] Hancher argues that the author's intention has three elements: (1) a generic or *programmatic* intention to use a particular linguistic form rather than another, (2) an *active* intention to be understood by an audience as acting in some way or meaning some thing, and (3) a *final* or perlocutionary intention to achieve a specific effect. In Hancher's analysis, these parts of an author's creative activity have different significance for aesthetic evaluation and interpretation. As he writes in

---

8. Donald Davidson develops a similar taxonomy in "Locating Literary Language" (298-99).

criticism of Wimsatt and Beardsley's discarding of the critical functions of authorial intention, "to challenge the bearing of programmatic intention on evaluation is not to challenge the bearing of active intention on interpretation" (834). That is, to say that an author's (programmatic or formal) intention to write a comedy is not related directly to evaluating the play's worth is *not* to say that an author's (active) intention to be ironic is irrelevant to the interpretation and basic meaning of the play. Nor are these two claims the same as saying that an author's (final) intention to make the critics rage is irrelevant to evaluating the persuasiveness or effectiveness of the author's text.

Hancher is most concerned with active intention and its use in the interpretation of literature, a concern not detached from rhetoric; what the audience comes to believe of the author and her work is important to both rhetoric and literary criticism.[9] Final or perlocutionary intention, however, is a concept more familiar to rhetorical criticism and is often used to evaluate and interpret rhetorical texts. We may cringe when the freshman student writes that Lincoln's first inaugural address was a failed speech since it did not stop the Civil War, but we recognize that the achievement of a final intention is a measure, one of the criteria of rhetorical success when we read Martin Luther King Jr.'s "Letter from Birmingham Jail" and consider the history of the civil rights movement. Gorgias's "Encomium of Helen," with its stated final intentions, requires us to stop and wonder if the speech was meant to praise Helen or to divert Gorgias or to accomplish both, and we wonder further if it succeeded in its stated purposes and how much in which of its stated purposes. Obviously few texts have stated or easily demonstrable final intentions, though I would argue rhetorical texts tend to be defined and, in fact, often are defined by the dominance of the final intention. As well, in subtle ways to which I will return, the author's choice of form (programmatic or generic intention) and its intended effect have significant rhetorical influence and show us how cultural conventions, such as genre and trope, effect our understanding of authorial purpose.

In borrowing a literary concept of purpose, limited to the author and

---

9. In *Interpretive Conventions,* an analysis of the editor's relationship to authorial intentions, Steven Mailloux actually expands on Hancher's concept of active intentions. He posits an operative intention that combines the author's understanding of his action during writing and his understanding of the effects of the acts on a projected reader. This concept seems rather introspective for study, but his second addition, inferred intention, is more useful because it focuses on the critic's description of the author's understanding of his effects on the projected reader. While there seems to be a infinite regression of intention interpretations here, the critic's description of attribution allows us to understand how understandings about intentions are conventionalized.

evolved to describe interpretive activities, rhetoric borrows a concept that needs expansion to describe the intentions of an audience and the relationships between an individual and a community's purposes. It also borrows a concept of purpose that is weak in the connotation of worldliness, if strong in pleasure and artistic effect. While Hancher's distinctions are helpful in outlining the productive aspects of an author's intentions, they do not tell us much about the process of deliberating on a course of action, nor do they hint at the ferocity with which we hold on to our intentions.

For a model more related to rhetoric's specific concern with action, one that builds some connections between philosophy of mind's intention and literary intention, I turn to Charles Altieri's concept of intentionality (beliefs, desires, and intentions). Rather than seeing intentions as purposes or mental states or actions in prospect, Altieri sees intentionality as a "means of characterizing the dynamic processes by which first-persons determine aspects of the world as 'mine' " (*Subjective* 26). This is a valuable definition in that it incorporate the aboutness intentionality of philosophy of mind with the process-oriented aspects of individual purpose included in rhetorical production. Intentions are "about" things in the world, our conception of them and our relationship to them, but also intentions are about our relationship to ourselves. Intentions define what we see as ours. Altieri's idiosyncratic definition highlights the significance of intentions for the subject's control of the world. That is, he conceives intentions as basic to personal identity, power, and the life-world. They are not artifacts behind the text or processes locked in the mind; rather, intentions are our engagement in the world, an engagement characteristic of both rhetor and audience. Rhetorical actions create personal identity, power, and the life-world: rhetorical intentions are not aesthetic considerations, nor are they simply concerned with textual meaning, but rather they form the basic realm of our differences, coins in our barters, where we join and come apart. Intentions are about the world, but more than that, they confer meaning on the world and help to constitute our relationship to the world and to each other.

In a manner similar to G. E. M. Anscombe and Quentin Skinner, Altieri develops a grammar of intention to differentiate its aspects. Altieri distinguishes between the *intention to* do something and the *intention in* an action (44). According to Altieri, in speaking of intention to, we are referencing a state of mind; in effect, we speak in a way reminiscent of the concept of intention within philosophy of mind: intention to is related to planning and consciousness about aspects of the world. It is the action that is to happen, a way of thinking appropriate to both perlocution and the forward-looking aspect of deliberative rhetoric. When instead we speak of intention in, we speak of intention within the action or practice itself and so within the present. Here intention is "not a cause, but as what Kant called a purposive process" (44): one might say that my intention in speaking is to educate. In the temporal present of intention in, the intention and the speech act are together; in the moment of practice, they do not separate out, but are integral. Altieri's concept of intention in helps to emphasize the present/presence of the rhetor and the situation, thereby defining a moment where intention is an observable part of the meaning, rather than an elusive mental state (meaning in the author) or an extractable part of the text (meaning in convention). The concept of intention in places the three elements of authorial intention in close proximity; it returns Hancher's analytic tool to the synthetic practices of the speaking subject, embedded in discourse. It is the reverse move in what is a necessary, constant dialectic between intention defined by purposeful action and intention analyzed into its parts.

III

I undertake the project of theorizing intention from a rhetorical perspective in response to a larger concern in the discipline, the repeated calls for a revitalized public sphere, the recognition of public discourse as multicultural, and a wider but different literacy.[10] In the context of these calls, I am puzzled by the interpretive turn within rhetoric. Interpretive rhetorics are obviously essential both to the discipline and to democratic practices in a pluralistic society, but I wonder if interpretation's place in public discourse and democratic practices cannot be theorized in other disciplines while rhetoricians focus on rhetoric's familiar areas of expertise, such as the production of texts and their relationship to political action. Rhetorical criticism has demonstrated value within the field, but establishing the relationship of that value to actions of deliberation in a pluralist

10. Nancy Fraser outlines the issues surrounding the concept of public sphere in *Justice Interruptus* (69–120). See Thomas B. Farrell's *Norms of Rhetorical Culture* for an introduction to the rhetorical literature calling for a renewed public sphere. Susan Wells's *Sweet Reason* provides a very thoughtful connection between Habermas's concept of the public sphere and rhetorical approaches to literacies. See Andrea Lunsford, Helene Moglen, and James Slevin's *The Right to Literacy* and Eugene Kintgen, Barry M. Kroll, and Mike Rose's *Perspectives on Literacy:* Either is a good starting place for understanding the literacy debates. Jan Swearingen's *Rhetoric and Irony* is a historical approach to the relationship between rhetoric and literacy.

democracy needs careful argument, analysis, and recognition of its limitations.[11] I take up the methods of rhetorical criticism, but with some core suspicions. I am ambivalent about characterizing rhetoric—as a theory, let alone a practice—as predominantly interpretive.

Instead I see the calls for a renewed public sphere as calls to be answered in rhetoric by a resurgent understanding of deliberative rhetorics and political theory. Rhetoric has many traditions (belletristic, tropological, pedagogical, sophistic, etc.), but in describing the language of the public sphere, rhetoric has been theorized inadequately beyond Aristotle's investigations of the deliberative, forensic, and epideictic.[12] Postcolonial nations have needs that are both similar to and different than those of the polis. Postmodern subjects have capabilities both similar to and different than those of citizens in the polis. If our mass media leads a public to expect and to act on snappy one-liners, rhetoricians can have four responses. We can theorize the effects of snap, crackle, and pop culture; we can produce more snap, crackle, and pop; we can theorize alternative public spaces; or we can develop and promote alternative public spheres and voices. The traditional theories based in Aristotle can only provide a starting point to any of these actions because the culture of late capitalism includes more voices, technologies, suspicions, and opportunities than the prior cultures where rhetoric has been theorized.

In *Aristotle's Rhetoric: An Art of Character*, Eugene Garver reads Aristotle richly, but fully acknowledges the limits of Aristotle for contemporary thinking.[13] Garver specifically notes that Aristotle's sense of the polis

---

11. The difficulty of understanding the place of rhetorical criticism in rhetoric is well argued in the literature. See, for example, the forums in *Quarterly Journal of Speech*. In volume 77, see Maurice Charland, Robert Hariman, and Raymie E. McKerrow. In volume 78, see Henry David, Michael Leff, and Barbara Warnick.

12. While I will outline a different set of issues, I still believe Benjamin Barber's *Strong Democracy* offers productive, though alternative points for considering what a post-Aristotelian deliberative theory might include or reject. After a critique of liberalism, Barber offers a model of participatory (not representative) democracy and includes a brief, though useful discussion of "political talk" (163–212). Political talk, unlike speech or systems of signs, is characterized by (1) listening no less than speaking, (2) emotion as well as reason, and (3) engagement in worldly action (174). While Barber includes simple persuasion as one of its nine functions, I see the other eight ("agenda setting," "exploring mutuality," "witness and self-expression," etc.) as pieces of what rhetoricians traditionally call persuasion (178–79). Still, his analysis of political facets of persuasion extends the vocabulary for discussing deliberation.

13. While Garver feels obligated to describe Aristotle's *Rhetoric* first as a "philosophical inquiry" to be judged "by philosophical standards" (3), I instead find it, like Garver, a "political inquiry" (18), but as well that most suspect of inquiries, a rhetorical inquiry. My point here is that while Garver responds to the *Rhetoric* with more thought and care than anyone else in this century, he does so from a philosophical framework that, despite the significance of his under-

as natural makes his theory less than applicable to our political institutions, given the contemporary sense of the unnaturalness of our lives (26-27, 12). Ultimately, however, Aristotle raises problems for us to think through, problems about the relationship of activity to art, the relationships among civic character, reason, and emotion, and the centrality of argument and enthymeme (logical form) within rhetoric.

Garver argues that Aristotle's innovation is defining connections among rhetoric, artificial proof, and persuasion and that with this innovation, he places the character of the civic speaker—the orator and legislator—as essential to rhetoric. According to Garver, Aristotle's emphasis on rhetorical argument, rather than simply argument, involves the civic enactment of an interaction of dialectic (logic or faculty) and politics (ethics), and this makes rhetoric accountable to two standards, not independently, but simultaneously (77). Rhetoric is not just about conflict, but about *the dialectical means of finding justified action.* Garver's reading of Aristotle also asks us to attend to two themes. In the first theme, Aristotle offers a picture of practical reasoning and rhetoric that bears a complicated relationship to the character of the rhetor. Ethos alone is inadequate for citizenship as citizenship requires logos, too, and the integration of logos and ethos is not a given, but like the integration of art and civics in rhetoric, it is an achieved harmony, a labor of language. The second theme describes reason and form in rhetoric as tied to purpose and matter. In Aristotle, the form of a rhetor's response is dependent on the rhetor's purpose and subject.[14] Together these themes, based in the agency of the rhetor, allow Garver to make some strong assertions about the nature of Aristotle's rhetoric, including the assertion that deliberation is "the center of rhetorical activity" (52).

Granted, it is not always easy to follow these themes throughout the *Rhetoric* or even Garver's argument, but they intersect productively in Garver's discussion of the differences between the sophist and the rhetor. Aristotle writes, "What makes a man a 'sophist' is not his faculty, but his moral purpose. In rhetoric, however, the term 'rhetorician' may describe either the speaker's knowledge of the art, or his moral purpose" (*Rhetoric*

---

taking, reveals a repressed reluctance to respect rhetoric. Leaving this problem aside (fascination with philosophical inquiry seems to go hand in hand with a terror of sophistry and a suspicion of rhetoric), Garver develops Aristotelian rhetoric in ways productive for disciplinary rhetoric.

14. The formal nature of rhetoric and its relationship to purposes and culture reappears in my discussion of Kenneth Burke who is sometimes described as a structuralist for, among other things, his concern with form and structure. That classification of Burke has less weight when form and structure are seen as limits and dictates within the tradition of rhetoric.

I.1.1355b17-19). Garver reads this section, supported by other sections in Aristotle, as making a crucial distinction (despite its brevity). Aside from a difference in moral purpose between the sophist and the rhetor, they have a difference in practice as rhetoric is an art, and Aristotle requires arts to have an *internal* or guiding end (internal standards of success) as well as an *external* or given end. Rhetoric's external (or given) end of persuasion is shared with the profession of sophistry, which might well persuade and succeed by specious argument, but rhetoric—as an art, a civic art—has an end not of persuasion alone, but as well has its internal (or guiding) end of finding the available means of persuasion in each case (I.1.1355b10-12). An art has a limited means and ends, and artistic proofs (logos, ethos, and pathos) are the limited means of rhetoric. Rhetorical, artistic method requires knowledge of the art. Success does not correlate with external standards of persuasion alone, though the rhetorician pursues persuasion as well as an internal standard available "through the exercise of practical intelligence" (220).

There is an inside and an outside intention or purpose within the citizen's speech; each with separate criteria of evaluation. Persuasion is the outside purpose, the end that will affect the audience's actions. Practical reason is the inside, moral purpose, the end that guides the formation of an artistic speech. While each is public in that it is accessible enough to be judged by a rhetor's standards, they are not judged by the same standards. According to Garver's Aristotle, the speaker's intentions and the audience's intentions should converge, but only within the practice of artistic proofs. As Garver writes, "From the outside, the audience is the measure of successful rhetoric; from the inside, the art of rhetoric can criticize the judgments of the audience" (221). It is easy to extend Aristotle and say that the potential conflict is, in part, because the rhetorical situation arises from competing intentions, values, and criteria.

This statement of the conflict defines a problem that is not so different from the concerns of many contemporary thinkers—feminist, post-Marxist, postmodernist—who, in addition, see some innate value in the differences and debates between a speaker and an audience and who find a single standpoint of judgment difficult to assess and claim, let alone ground. Though historically he defines conflict within a rhetorical situation, conflict was less a problem for Aristotle, who did not have a contemporary sense of deliberation, citizenship, revolution, and democracy, nor our understanding of difference, coalition, and social inequality. This difference in sensibility contributes to Aristotle being most commonly understood as taking for granted shared ends within the polis (or successfully repressing the differences within the polis).[15] In the polis, the *ideal* polis, citizens shared a common sense of the good. The good, such a funny, old Greek concept, was evident to citizens within the culture; only the alternative routes to the good were in debate.[16] While this is far from the only way to read him, in the prevalent, communitarian readings Aristotle's deliberative theory does not address our deep need to consider alternative ends, multiple interpretations, ruptures in communication, differences between cultures, and too often the possibility of incommensurable discourses.

This is a key point—the assumption of shared social meaning within much of classical rhetoric—that makes old-fashioned theories of deliberation inappropriate for contemporary rhetorics. While figures as diverse as Wayne Booth and Richard Rorty struggle to offer better (more pluralistic) models of community and consensus, their results are not significantly different than Aristotle's in that there is a community and an end, and their accounts are weaker for not addressing explicitly the rhetorical basis of deliberation.[17] After all, long ago Aristotle observed that human nature is

15. Alasdair MacIntyre's *After Virtue* and Hannah Arendt's *Human Condition* are two prominent sources of reading Aristotle as a communitarian. MacIntyre, who refuses Enlightenment concerns with rule-based virtue and Nietzsche's will-to-power virtues, seeks to sustain Aristotelian ethics, read as communitarian, based in the life of the city. MacIntyre's major criticism of Aristotle is that he doesn't understand "the centrality of opposition and conflict in human life" (163). Arendt's reading emphasizes Aristotle's polis as the guarantee of immortality over "the futility of individual life" (56) and his concern with telos as finding the "means to achieve the end" as already in the end (206-7).

In "Deliberation and Practical Reason," David Wiggins provides an overview of the textual controversies around deliberation within the *Nicomachean Ethics;* using careful translations he argues that Aristotle has a wider sense of what choice, deliberation, and practical reason are. Martha Nussbaum in *The Fragility of Goodness* reads Aristotle as seeing deliberations as based in means and focused "towards" ends, and so as more than simply instrumental (296-97).

16. Aristotle's concept of telos fosters this understanding. So, for instance, the communitarian MacIntyre reads telos as "the essential final and completing ingredient in the life of the man who is *eudiamon*" (158), the man who has "blessedness, happiness, prosperity" (148). It is a token of the divine.

In his reclamation of Aristotle's political thought, Stephen G. Salkever understands Aristotle's teleology to be less than absolute. He argues that Aristotle is well aware that the diverse character of human happiness is a problem requiring deliberation; he reads Aristotle—"the purpose of politics is not to make living together (*suzen*) possible, but to make living well (*eu zen*) possible" (*Politics* 3.1280b39-1281a4)—as arguing that human happiness is the site of deliberation and that living well varies with human diversity and within multifunctional political organizations. Though with less focus on telos, Bernard Yack and Arlene W. Saxonhouse also read Aristotle as concerned with and tolerant of diversity and conflict.

17. As I argue in "'The Good Man Speaking Well,' or Business as Usual," pluralism can be dangerous to less central, less powerful, and less numerous voices, and tolerant (vs. cooptive) pluralism is at best a momentary position. Pluralism is no kind answer. See also Chicago Cultural

defined in discourse, with its dialectical logic, and language both enables and impedes communication, practical reason, deliberation, and democratic action. In his *Politics,* Aristotle—just after declaring that man is the political animal, more so than other gregarious animals, since man alone has language—writes of how language "declares" difference: "language serves to declare what is advantageous and what is the reverse, and it is the peculiarity of man, in comparison to other animals, that he alone possesses a perception of good and evil, of the just and the unjust, and other similar qualities; and it is association in these things which makes a family and a city (*polis*)" (1253a16-17). It is our ability to speak that explains and justifies our nature, forms and deforms our attunements and associations, and makes our politics. Understood in a discourse of difference, the human potential for extremes looms large, even in the polis. Aristotle, concerned with the internal and external purposes of rhetoric and cognizant of the dialectical imperative in language, acknowledges the necessary tension between consensus and difference in deliberation, for to study politics and rhetoric is to contemplate associations, hierarchies, and instabilities. Difference is the norm for both ancient and contemporary politics and rhetoric; consensus, if it exists, is fleeting.

In response to models that either assume the virtue of common ends or the privilege of a pluralism controlled by a majority (albeit with constitutional constraints), there are many political theorists to whom rhetoricians might turn; much of contemporary political theory converges on the problem of tolerating and utilizing diversity rather than simply valuing consensus building.[18] Most suggestive are radical democrats, who seek

---

Studies Group, Lani Guinier, bell hooks, Catherine A. MacKinnon, Ellen Rooney, and responses to Annette Kolodny's celebration of pluralism in *Feminist Studies*, especially those of Elly Bulkin, Judith Keegan Gardiner, and Rena Grasso Patterson.

18. The following discussion focuses on Laclau and Mouffe's model of radical democracy, which emphasizes the discursive nature of declaring difference, politics as struggle and transformation, and, most significantly for my (feminist) purposes, the expanded dominion of what is political. Among my reasons for taking this focus, Laclau and Mouffe are the radical democrats most familiar to those in discursive studies.

Other models of democracy, some more focused on deliberation, are available. Radical democrat Benjamin R. Barber's *Strong Democracy* is one of this century's earlier examples of a political theorist engaging rhetorical concerns. Neoliberals Amy Gutman and Dennis Thompson offer an excellent orientation to the literature in their *Democracy and Disagreement* where they argue for "deliberative democracy" as an approach to moral disagreement. The core idea here is that citizens should reason together and reach mutually acceptable conclusions through conditions of "reciprocity," "publicity," and "accountability" on the content of "basic liberty," "basic opportunity," and "fair opportunity." My concern with their argument is the limiting of deliberation to moral disagreements in a narrowly defined public sphere. The model, despite its development

not to repress difference and conflict, but to redefine and embrace it, for the complete achievement of community and a final moment of equality and democracy are impossibilities. At its most basic, radical democracy means the valorization of the process of participatory democracy and the expansion of the realm of politics into what has been considered other socioeconomic arenas. In expanding the realm of politics, radical democrats join feminists in refusing a unified public sphere, identifying as political what had been deemed private (family, household, sexual relationships), and seeking a proliferation of new and different political spaces.

In much of the humanities, radical democracy is most commonly associated with the work of Ernesto Laclau and Chantal Mouffe.[19] In their version of radical democracy, Laclau and Mouffe, post-Marxists who rethink socialism for the postmodern condition, repudiate the essentialist and positivist strands in Marx and recognize the plurality and indeterminacy of the social, the nonessential character of social relationships (i.e., class does not determine politics), the discursive nature of all practices,[20] the construction of certain privileged discursive points (nodal points) that partially fix meaning, and the subject as "ambiguous, incomplete, and polysemical" discursive identity. The plurality of meanings, nodal points, and subject positions is the plurality of identities that fuels the new (democratic, polysemantic, and pluralistic) political struggles. Laclau and Mouffe see political action as "a type of action whose objective is the transformation of a social relation which constructs a subject in a relationship of subordination" (*Hegemony* 153). This definition broadens both what

---

and usefulness, proceeds very much in the liberal tradition, setting out fair terms of consensus building without adequately critiquing the assumption of consensus. In *Democracy and Deliberation*, responding to the direct majoritarian nature of U.S. politics and trivialization of democratic power, James S. Fishkin offers three approaches (the deliberative opinion poll, the representative voucher, and the constitutional moment) as a means to more adequate deliberation in the mammoth nation state. In *A Civil Tongue*, Mark Kingwell optimistically argues for civil dialogue as a means of achieving justice.

19. While literary theorists associate radical democracy most strongly with Laclau and Mouffe, in part due to their linguistic turn and theoretical complexity, political theorists also associate the concept with the work of Benjamin Barber, Samuel Bowles, Herbert Gintis, John Keane, Douglas C. Lummis, Susan Moller Okin, Carole Pateman, Joseph Schwartz, Michael Walzer, and Iris Marion Young.

20. The relationship between linguistic acts and extralinguistic acts is clarified in Laclau's *New Reflections on the Revolution of Our Times* and "Politics and the Limits of Modernity." In what might be called rhetorical realism, he defines the totality of acts as discourse, analyzes the interpenetration of meaning and action (discourse and social relationship), and follows an explicitly Wittgensteinian theory of language.

constitutes a political act (initiating sexual harassment proceedings) and where political action can take place (in the military).[21] In this broadened definition, politics is struggling against inequalities, inequalities of both recognition and distribution.[22] Laclau and Mouffe emphasize struggle, dialectical process, and the ineradicability of antagonism as a response to liberal democrats whose explanations are dependent on individualism, reason, progress, and coming to consensus in traditional forums. They argue that Enlightenment values, values that evade or at least modulate the political, have poorly prepared contemporary democrats for understanding the new ethnic, religious, and national antagonisms. On the other hand, radical democrats understand human beings as political and politics as difference. To quote Mouffe, "This 'agonistic pluralism' is constitutive of modern democracy and, rather than seeing it as a threat, we should realize that it represents the very condition of existence of such democracy" (*Return* 4). Within a vital democracy, consensus and unanimity are dim illusions, not ideals: in fact, they may well be the signs and symptoms of democratic turpitude, apathy, and death.

Laclau and Mouffe's approach to democracy offers a concept of politics compatible with the rhetorical tradition and an emphasis on pluralism, complex subjectivity, and the symbolic useful for theorizing postmodern deliberation. Their model, however, suffers from an inadequate engagement in social, economic, and historical injustices (the contingencies upon which rhetoric is based), an undertheorized political subject whose agency is in doubt, and a failure to strategize effective means of redress beyond the extension and radicalization of democratic struggles.[23] In offering an underdeveloped agent, inadequate strategies for redress of

---

21. This definition obviously makes much, if not all, of human life political, and it also emphasizes the hierarchies in human life. In doing so it evades the issue of authority (who authorizes the values and the transformations?), and political institutions are specifically about authorizing. While there are problems with the expansion of politics into all domains and a fixation on subordination, limiting politics to certain, visible institutions and cultural practices misses too many aspects of the political and of authorization, especially for a project on theorizing intentions.

22. Our need to integrate both the politics of recognition and of distribution is developed in Nancy Fraser's *Justice Interruptus*.

23. These criticisms are related to a common feminist critique of poststructuralist political theory, that it deconstructs but gives us no means for constructing. For an introduction to the issues as related to post-Marxism, see Rosemary Hennessy's *Materialist Feminism and the Politics of Discourse*, Barbara Epstein's "Why Post-Structuralism Is aDead End for Progressive Thought," Nancy Fraser's *Justice Interruptus*, or Ann Travers's "Radical Democracy's Feminist Potential." Marxists (such as Norman Geras, Allen Hunter, and Eli Zaretsky) offer similar critiques of the theory's limited political application and eliding of material injustices as do Donna Landry and Gerald MacLean, who in addition critique Laclau and Mouffe's use of deconstruction. Robert

injustice, and no means of transforming nodal points or discourses, the model leaves open for rhetoricians the Herculean task of theorizing the rhetor and her audiences, the rhetorical situation, and deliberative strategies. There is work to do. After all, Laclau and Mouffe offer a political theory, not a political practice nor a rhetorical theory.

The problem of deliberation (or its lack) in contemporary political practice is a complex one. Obviously, writing deliberative theory exceeds the task of analyzing competing intentions in rhetorical situations, but I hope this study of specific negotiations of meaning, negotiations fairly removed from the frame of identity politics and distributions of wealth, will begin to revitalize rhetorical study of deliberation (be it conversational or confrontational) and political action. A developed rhetorical criticism and critique from the perspective of conflicting intentions potentially can aid in later elaborations of how contemporary deliberations arise from differences of meaning, what is the nature of responses to diverging interpretations, and which theories would support both a recognition of and respect for difference while providing a space for action. The aim of the book is to illuminate how we understand each other, despite our differences; the hope is to catch a glimmer of how we come to action.

IV

This project is framed in the need for new models or, at least, new perceptions of rhetorical deliberation, and it is undertaken with a nagging understanding of the political nature of interpretation, political in that my interpretations are situated and nagging in that interpretation and its forensic aspects do not leave the study of deliberative rhetoric despite their different time orientations. While in our daily life we interpret constantly, unconsciously, seamlessly in the present, in analytic work, interpretation is backward looking, forensic, and the connection to future action is weakened. I presume that intentions—conceived as competing purposes and determinations of aspects of the world as "mine," both embedded within discourses and invented by individual rhetors and audiences—initiate deliberative moments, future-looking, planning moments. In studying intentions and their plans for future action, we begin to know

---

Wess is unhappy with Laclau and Mouffe's desire to make all political struggles equivalent. Clearly, the left's political agenda is in disarray.

how we proceed from texts, what comes from our interpretations. My purpose in this first excursion into a rhetorical theory of intention is predominately descriptive, and descriptive of understanding rather than of deliberation. To that end, in the book's first section I describe what has been the nature of intentional theory within twentieth-century rhetoric; in the second section I describe negotiations over meaning in three narrow discussions within the discipline of philosophy.

In Chapter 1 I examine the discussions of intention by three rhetoricians frequently associated with literature, I. A. Richards, Wayne Booth, and Stanley Fish. While Richards and Booth found meaning in authorial intention and Fish in the interpretive community, both approaches evade issues of power differentials, argumentation, and deliberation and demonstrate deep suspicion of ordinary language and everyday practices of meaning-making. The study of literature, innately a canonical activity, emphasizes a culture's historical values and existing systems of meaning, ethics, justice, and education. When rhetoric—a potentially revolutionary study concerned with diversity and change—is allied with literary study, institutional placement mutes the study of argumentation, deliberation, radical democracy, and diversity within communities. While we need not ignore the formalist insights of literary rhetoricians, we should look elsewhere for models of intention. If used as exemplars, literary approaches that limit interactivity are detrimental to theorizing an active public sphere and the constant negotiations necessary in a pluralist society.

If literary rhetorics tend to evade deliberation by placing the control of meaning on one side or the other of what should be a dialogue between rhetor and audience, then hermeneutical rhetorics, as discussed in Chapter 2, attempt to acknowledge a dialogic nature to meaning-making without acknowledging competing purposes or power-laden rhetorical debate. They imply that rhetors and audiences are interpreters, though in fact rhetors and audiences are not interpreters; they have different approaches to meaning-making than hermeneuts. Contemporary ontological hermeneutics, which, unlike Romantic hermeneutics, avoids psychological engagement, redefines the meeting of intentions or purposes within interpretations in terms of prejudices and traditions and so removes deliberation from directly concerning issues of agency and conflict and claims to the world. In its concern with the negotiation of meaning, hermeneutics further minimizes the activity of textual productivity to promote reception. While it may be useful, kind, and necessary to read Gadamer's fusion of horizon as an alternative form of deliberation based on listening—though a form that requires audiences to risk their intentions—it is a form of deliberation that ignores the dangers of others' texts and the importance of protecting one's claims to the world. In response to the increasingly common move to collapse hermeneutics and rhetoric by theorists such as Stephen Mailloux, I argue that while hermeneutics and rhetoric are interdependent practices and theories, they are not synonymous, and I demonstrate their differences in the concept of invention to delineate the place of authorial intention in the production of discourse.

Kenneth Burke provides a vocabulary for discussing intention within postmodern rhetorics. Chapter 3 describes how Burke's three concepts—*form, motive,* and *purpose*—provide vehicles for thinking about intention. His unique definitions of and reliance on form, motive, and purpose allow intention to be both analyzed and integrated with the concepts of structure, situation, culture, authorial ends, and audience interpretation. This chapter examines the nature of form in dictating or controlling purposes and desires. It develops the implications of motives broadly defined as "shorthand terms for situations," showing how Burke understands motives, cultural and universal, as both defined by and defining our world view and so limiting our intentions (*Grammar* xv). Form and motive develop aspects of intentionality that address the cultural and discourse-based aspects of intending to mean. To understand intentions in the negotiating of specific meanings in specific situations, I turn to Burkean drama where many of the terms (act, scene, agent, agency, purpose) implicate intentions; that is, intention can be indicated by act, agent, agency, and purpose. I specifically develop Burke's discussion of purpose and mysticism to highlight problems with interpretive models that place purpose outside the agent, act, scene, or means. In this chapter, I begin to describe the public nature of intentions as embedded in the culture and individual action.

Having developed an analytical frame for discussing rhetorical intentions, in the second part of this book, I describe what happens when people who may share motives, or cultural purpose, read different forms and interpret with different purposes. After an interlude, "Hinge/Acknowledging Prejudices," where I describe my ordinary language prejudices, I look at a variety of philosophers reading Ludwig Wittgenstein's negativities (reversals in his arguments), narratives, and metaphors and find that the form of the discourse affects the nature of deliberations on and responses to Wittgenstein's texts. I describe how two of Wittgenstein's texts are read by philosophers and how his audiences know and acknowledge, or fail to know and to acknowledge, forms, cultural motives, and subjective intentions, or purposes. In focusing on philosophy, a small disciplinary community, I pretend to be able to control the infinite expanse of context, agents, and motive necessary to describe any practice of interpretation. Part of what I demonstrate in limiting the scope of debate, the power differentials, and the range of differences is how each factor permeates any discourse.

Wittgenstein's *Tractatus Logico-Philosophicus* is an odd book, written as three reversing or negating arguments: one about limits of naming, one about the tautological nature of logic, and one, unnegated and ultimate, about the value of ethics and mysticism in their unworldly, unphilosophical aspects. It repeatedly defines these issues in terms of what they are not. Wittgenstein, apparently pursuing the ineffable, chose a form that asserted and denied. Chapter 4 analyzes how philosophers Bertrand Russell and Rudolf Carnap when reading Wittgenstein's *Tractatus* limit their engagements to the parts that meet their prejudices, preunderstandings, and intentions. Despite the fact that the *Tractatus* is finally concerned with ethics and aesthetics, Russell, whose disciplined purpose is the development of a logically perfect language as a regulatory ideal, defines Wittgenstein's concern as "the conditions for a logically perfect language" (Introduction 7) and dismisses the last argument despite his inability to refute it. Carnap interprets the book in a similar frame and manner, though he assumes his intention is Wittgenstein's. When Wittgenstein places value (ethics and aesthetics) outside the world, Carnap interprets this as a dismissal of the significance of ethics, which fits his prejudices as Carnap sees ethical statements as "value statements" with "no theoretical sense" ("Ethics" 206). While one cannot know exactly Wittgenstein's intended meaning for ethics, using the trope of negativity I demonstrate the facility with which even disciplined readers utilize pieces of an argument, even if those pieces are later negated. Readers can ignore other pieces of an argument that do not meet their purpose, and so evade the difficulties of deliberation and, in fact, feel little obligation to negotiate authorial intention.

An author's intentions represented in other forms seem less easily subsumed or ignored. The meaning of Wittgenstein's narratives and metaphors are less ignored and more negotiated than those of his negatives. Chapter 5 describes how Wittgenstein's small stories, told with the likely intention of resisting metanarratives in philosophy, become metanarratives through accrual of analysis, repetition, and counterinstance. While the meaning of the stories has more social consensus, the effect of responding to the stories and deliberating on their significance changes, renegotiates authorial intention. I examine this effect both in Norman Malcolm's telling of imitative stories, told to support and build his theory allied with Wittgenstein's work, and in more normal disciplinary practices where narrative is more embedded in the disciplinary discourse and less strikingly fictive. In "Thinking," Malcolm tells six brief tales in response to paragraph 93 in Wittgenstein's *Zettel;* the effect of his cumulative telling gives insight into speaking and thinking and develops a taxonomy of relationships between speaking and thinking, while the purpose of Wittgenstein's single paragraph apparently is to demonstrate the problem of distinguishing their differences. The 1989 American Philosophical Association symposium on Wittgenstein discussed his work with fewer fictive tales, but the same effect of accruing purposes to create metanarrative; the very last sentence of the program can be read as a normalizing narrative that subsumes Wittgenstein's work within a philosophical tradition.

In the process of examining accrual, Chapter 5 begins to delineate a relationship between desire and intention that is both sparser and less essentialist than the models of psychoanalytic criticism and analytic philosophy as well as suggestive of ways to understand the multiple changes in audiences affected by narratives told for different purposes. Open or partial narratives told for purposes of deliberation create a different relationship between rhetor and audience than does a forensic narrative told to justify a judgment. Wittgenstein's narrative works to create a critical audience, and the second set of narratives, as told by philosophers in a disciplined debate, works to control a reader in ways described, by some psychoanalytic theorists, as sadistic, but that may be more simply explained as taking pleasure in judgment.

Of the three forms of discourse I examine, metaphors are the most successful at initiating deliberation; that is, readers are less likely to ignore divergent meanings and the concept of authorial intention. Chapter 6 presents a model of the metaphor not as generative, but rather as enthymemic and as a site of deliberation. Adapting work by John Searle, I argue that the missing terms that connect a metaphor's tenor and vehicle function enthymemically to reveal cultural values. Wittgenstein's metaphors *language-games* and *form of life* are borrowed from earlier texts; they are not his genius, nor are they innately revolutionary. Instead their disciplinary significance is in how philosophers argue over their interpretation and what those interpretations mean for catachresis (filling gaps) within the discipline. The chapter examines the deliberations on the meaning of form of life in the work of Stanley Cavell, Lynne Rudder Baker, Gertrude Conway, and Newton Garver and on language-games in the work of Jean-François Lyotard and Terry Eagleton, and it shows that Wittgenstein's intentions most concern his readers in metaphors.

In concluding, I show that negotiations of meaning are the product of intentions made public in cultural contexts, authorial purposes, reader purposes, and the form of discourse. Despite the rhetor's intentions and rhetorical strategies, audiences have multiple tactics (conscious and unconscious, inventive and formal) for resisting unwanted intentions. They refuse meanings, contest meanings, and transform meanings. Even within the narrow framework of a discipline and among like-minded scholars, understanding is dynamic, sometimes aesthetic and sometimes instrumental, but always a fragile, partial process subject to the restraint of forms and motives and purposes. We keep, share, negotiate our intentions, always at great risk to our claims to the world, and yet sometimes we willingly risk our worlds.

1

Literary Rhetorics, Ethics, and Cultural Orthodoxies

> *In this typology, the category of intention will not disappear; it will have its place, but from this place it will no longer be able to govern the entire scene and the entire system of utterance.*
> —Jacques Derrida, "Signature, Event, Context"

Intention is a concept that will not disappear from either the concerns of literary criticism or from the concerns of literary rhetorics.[1] The discursive overlaps between literary criticism and literary rhetorics influence the thinking of rhetoricians, who often are inclined to assume authorial intention; literary criticism nuances their rhetorical discussions of intention, but does not erode the assumption of intention. Consequently, even if W. K. Wimsatt and Monroe Beardsley are accurate in their 1946 argument that "the design or intention of the author is neither available nor desirable as a standard for *judging the success of a work* of literature" (3, emphasis added), literary rhetoricians still tend to believe that authors have intentions, that works come about through purposing or designing mental states, and that an understanding of authorial intentions is necessary for interpreting irony, satire, and parody and helpful for analyzing, in part, the politics, ideological predispositions, and historical conditions to which a text responds. While few

---

1. See Denis Dutton's "Why Intentionalism Won't Go Away."

rhetoricians are likely to join E. D. Hirsch in either his 1967 or 1976 argument for the need of a concept of authorial intention as a criterion for interpretive correctness, most of us recognize that some interpretations are at odds with authorial intention, outside the purposes and experiences of the writer; we recognize this even if we cannot *prove* the divergent interpretation is wrong. In effect, the complexity of authorial intentions and of interpretation's dependence on historical situations (including those of the author and reader) guarantees that literary critics and literary rhetoricians will continue to discuss the concept of intention in critical enterprises, even if they have to live with the uncertainty of interpretation and be less concerned with the concept's use in assessing aesthetic value or with the valorization of individual author's lives.

When discussing intention, the scholarship in literary rhetorics tends to follow the pattern of literary theory, emphasizing theoretical issues of interpretive control and seldom considering authorial biography or the historical placement of the author; certainly these issues are limited in the work of I. A. Richards, Wayne Booth, and Stanley Fish. And in contrast to rhetoric's historical fascination with authorship and the production of specific, effective texts, literary rhetorics seldom puzzle over the best means of communicating one's purposes or how to control the audience's interpretations and future actions. Rather, scholars of literary rhetorics more typically focus on the ethics or rightness of reading another's intentions. That is, their concerns are analytic rather than productive, and they struggle with the implications of interpreting texts that have been created with or, at least, informed by authorial purpose. Still, despite this concern—seemingly ethical—I argue that they tend to focus on canonical texts, the stability of interpretive traditions, and the limits of interpretation rather than on agents, agency, and the dynamics of meaning-making in pluralistic communities. Consequently, while many of the rhetoricians who work the sharp edge between poetics and rhetoric claim to desire a balance between the text and the ethics of negotiating meanings between rhetor and audience, they ultimately diminish the audience and give primacy to the author, the text, or the established values they find inscribed therein; or, with an equally heavy hand, they diminish the author, the text, and the historical values in the text to give primacy to the audience. Literary rhetoricians avoid the discussion of negotiating intentions between author, text, and audience because it opens up a confusion of rightness, goodness, and correctness as well as the acknowledgment of politics, social change, and the chaos of cross-cultural interpretation. Their push is to transcend the nitty-gritty dirt of meaning and to find an ideal outside of and safe from pluralistic forces.

Rhetoric has a long, recognized tradition of avoiding charges of sophism by representing itself as a decent, even ethical, enterprise and appealing to the true and good. But the engagement with ethics enacted by literary rhetoricians is not a simple response to potential charges of sophism; rather, as I will show, it is the result of a subtler concern with determining who controls meaning within a culture and thus who controls the possibilities for action. That is, a rhetorical theory, when not sophistic, is not a simple honesty but rather an ideology too often glossed as a theory or ideal concerned with intellectual matters. I. A. Richards, for example, balances his concern for democratic negotiation of purposes with an equal concern for order, value, form, and the cultural hierarchy. While Wayne Booth engages, at times, more clearly with rhetorical situations and the pluralistic nature of democracy, his desire for an ethics of discourse and a more open society also falls before his need for *assent* to order and hierarchy. Finally, in contrast, Stanley Fish appeals to the discourse community as the source of meaning, but, in doing so, also creates an alternative *author*ity that limits interpretive practices.

I

I. A. Richards, by his own announcement as well as the announcements of countless rhetoricians who have followed him, is the initiator of the New Rhetoric, including its epistemic and interpretive concerns, though his arrival in the field of rhetoric is only a piece of the sequence of interdisciplinary studies of meaning and communication that he undertook.[2] In countermovement to Plato's arrival at philosophical rhetoric after disdaining poetics and political rhetoric, Richards' progression seemingly is from clearly philosophical concerns with language to concerns with poetics and rhetoric in both their theoretical and pedagogical manifestations.[3] His engagements with multiple perspectives and disciplines make any attempt

---

2. He is the first rhetorician discussed in Foss, Foss, and Trapp's *Contemporary Perspectives on Rhetoric*, and the second represented in the twentieth century of Bizzell and Herzberg's *The Rhetorical Tradition*. See also Ann E. Berthoff's introductory essay in *Richards on Rhetoric*, Stuart C. Brown's "I. A. Richards' New Rhetoric," and *Rhetoric Society Quarterly*, vol. 8 (1988), which devoted a section to the significance of Richards.

3. Richards followed an interesting course to his concerns with literacy and rhetoric. As an undergraduate he studied philosophy; in fact, he spent seven years studying with G. E. Moore. He followed that with work in medicine before he turned to literary theory, followed by literacy and rhetoric, and finally poetry. See John Paul Russo's biography.

to classify him doomed from the outset. Still, because of his continual efforts to bridge rhetoric, poetics, philosophy, textual production and interpretation, public discourse, pedagogy, and tropes (in more than twenty-five books and innumerable articles), Richards' work is a telling place to begin a discussion of the relationship between contemporary literary rhetoric and intention, a relationship that has worked historically to inscribe stability despite the dramatic social changes of this century.

As Richards develops his theories over decades, his sense of meaning as experiences shared between interlocutors gradually becomes offset by a deep concern that too frequently these experiences are mismatched and that misunderstandings dangerously growl and grow. In response, he seeks a firmer founding and grounding of meaning and works to thwart misunderstanding through appeals to order, form, and correctness. While he understands misunderstanding as a necessary feature of communication, he sees it as sabotaging meaning, not creating desirable possibilities of new meaning or opportunities for negotiation.[4] The resulting drive to shared meaning, form, and order ultimately restricts Richards' sense of the dynamics of rhetoric and, over time, reduces his sense of rhetoric to "a somewhat chaotic collection of observations made on the ways of lively venturesome speech and writing" (*Speculative* 159). However, before I demonstrate these limits to his rhetoric, it is requisite to understand his definitions of intention and communication as well as to appreciate his commitment to mutual understanding within a complex but ordered society.

Richards obviously is a thinker most concerned with the transfer of meaning, a man obsessed with translation and most haunted by fears of misinterpretation and misunderstanding, and so, he is generous in defining his terms. While his definitions of intention and purpose vary among his texts, from his earliest work on, Richards recognizes the potential problems of competing purposes between audience and author. Perhaps because of his concern with the multiplicity of intentions within a meaningful act, Richards' use of *intention* seems ambiguous, shifting from context to context. As W. H. N. Hotopf has noted, Richards uses intention to signify both *use* and *meaning* (*Language* 250–52). Intention, for Richards, can signify an authorial aim, conscious or unconscious, as seen in basically the use, action, or purpose of the author's communication, or it can imply the interpretation of the speech act itself, the meaning of an

---

4. Much earlier than Richards, Friedrich D. E. Schleiermacher accepts that misunderstanding is more natural than understanding, and that the harder task of understanding needs a studied approach.

utterance as apprehended. On occasion, we can see this blurring within a single paragraph. For example, in laying out four points of view on a speaker's meaning (sense, feeling, tone, and intention), Richards writes:

> Finally, apart from what he says (Sense), his attitude to what he is talking about (Feeling), and his attitude to his listener (Tone), there is the speaker's intention, his aim, *conscious or unconscious*, the effect he is endeavoring to promote. Ordinarily he speaks for a purpose, and his purpose modifies his speech. The understanding of it is part of the whole business of apprehending his meaning. Unless we know what he is trying to do, we can hardly estimate the measure of his success. (*Practical Criticism* 176)

While the slippage here is small, it is clear that, for Richards, authorial intention functions in both the author's utterance ("his aim" or desired "effect") and an interpreter's understanding of meaning (that is, apprehending authorial intention is part of meaning). In these few lines, intention is implicated in use and meaning. Furthermore, use and meaning are collapsed into the more common "purpose" or "aim" (clearly used interchangeably). The slippage implies and is productively indicative of Richards' conception of communication as dynamic, a whole made up of but not divisible into use, meaning, and purpose. Purpose, aim, and intention are all but synonymous, and a key part of meaning and communication.

Richards' concerns with and definition of communication (and intention) shift with time in telling ways. To demonstrate these shifts, I will travel from his first to his last book-length inquiries, looking at texts from *The Meaning of Meaning* (1923) to *Beyond* (1974). Even in his early philosophical phase, a phase that coincided with and responded to the rise of positivism, Richards privileges communicative aspects of language. *The Meaning of Meaning*, written between 1910 and 1922 with philosopher C. K. Ogden, demonstrates their mutual commitment to and anxieties about public communication and education. The preface promises a book addressed to a new world order. In premising a world politic in which "new millions of participants" are in "the control of general affairs," Ogden and Richards set forth the problems of symbolism and communication that will drive much of their lives, and they articulate their commitment "to raise the level of communication through a direct study of its conditions, its dangers and difficulties. The practical side of this understanding is, if communication can be taken in its widest sense, Education" (x). While this can be read as democratic commitment to educating a world citizenry, their word choices of "control," "dangers," and "difficulties" clearly express anxiety, perhaps not undeserved, about the possibility of not communicating at a sufficiently effective "level" in a diverse and changing world. In the service of raising the level or quality of communication, a very necessary goal and one that Richards and Ogden will pursue in their development and promotion of Basic English in future decades, they critique both positivistic theories of philosophy that connect words to things and superficial theories of aesthetic emotion, calling each set of theories guilty of minimizing the communicative function of language.[5] Richards and Ogden, instead, theorize that words, reflective of thoughts and emotions, have meaning only in context. They write, "It is only when a thinker makes use of them (words) that they stand for anything, or, in one sense, have 'meaning.' They are instruments" (10). Despite Ogden and Richards' training in philosophy, even this early position can be read as rhetorical for its vision of meaning as always context-dependent and words as malleable tools.[6] They posit language as being used by thinking, intending individuals "as an instrument for the promotion of purposes," including deception and misdirection (16).

After grappling with the inadequacies of no less than sixteen definitions of *meaning* (including the inadequacies of defining meaning as "intending to refer to"), Ogden and Richards move to defining communication as "a use of symbols in such a way that acts of reference occur in a hearer which are similar in all relevant respects to those which are symbolized by them in the speaker" (205-6). This first definition is clearly a psychological (internal) as opposed to social (external) model. The speaker's purposes and utterance control the symbol situation (the situation acknowledged only as it is referenced in the utterance) and impact the hearer who is not quite passive. The hearer is acknowledged as involved in the manipulation of symbols, though meaning only happens when the hearer approximates the speaker's referencing in the symbols.

This definition of communication shifts significantly over Richards' life. In *Principles of Literary Criticism* (1925) and *Practical Criticism* (1929), he begins to develop the counterpart to the speaker's production of communication: an interpretive theory based on written aesthetic texts. In this critical turn, Richards continues to assume a speaker's intentions as

---

5. In *Language and Philosophy,* Max Black connects *The Meaning of Meaning* and several of Richards's early books with inadequately supported behaviorist and empiricist theories, but this minimizes the complexity of the interpretative process imagined by Ogden and Richards *within the context of the early twenties and the rise of literary criticism.* Jules David Law, in *The Rhetoric of Empiricism,* gives a better sense of the complexity of Richards's relationship to empiricism (238-43).

6. This is also discussed in their chapter "Sign-Situations."

the major factor in the development of meaning, but, as well, he begins to develop an ethics of interpretation, focusing on the human response to stimuli and its potential for "conflict, suppression, and interplay" (*Principles* 112). He shifts his definition of communication from the earlier one in which a speaker's use of reference is the source of a similar response in a hearer to a definition of communication as occurring "when one mind so acts upon its environment that another mind is influenced, and in that other mind an experience occurs which is like the experience in the first mind, and is caused in part by that experience" (177). The later definition, while resembling the definition of *The Meaning of Meaning*, locates the cause in the environment: still, one mind acts and the other is influenced, but the place of the rhetorical situation has evolved from a referencing of reality to an environment, a word choice suggesting both its own dynamics and an impact on its inhabitants. Richards continues his explication of communication and claims that "the active communicator's gift" lies in her "use of past similarities in experience and the control of these elements through the dependence of their effects upon one another" (180). Authorial intention, with the addition of strategic control, remains the dominant factor in communication: the hearer's mind is imprinted with the experience of the active communicator, but this second definition acknowledges the openness of experience, the dynamics of environment, and the interplay between authorial intention and experience and the audience's experiences. While his new definition seems simple, even positivistic to postmoderns, Richards is beginning to articulate a dynamic between environment, author, and audience. This, however, is more dynamic than he likes.

Richards moves away from authorial intention as the control of meaning and comes to posit the limits of meaning within a discourse's history—a safer limit than the individual author, who might intend any sort of corruption. In the essay "Toward a Theory of Comprehending" in *Speculative Instruments* (1955), twenty-six years later, Richards seeks a means for comprehending comprehension and in doing so, develops a very different model of communication; he gives up the model of communication as an authorial gift of experience and acknowledges the historical embeddedness of discourse. Richards now begins this inquiry into the nature of our historical and cultural inscription by "devising a system of instruments for comparing meanings" (19) even though by his own admission the instruments themselves are representations of a position, a regression, which is inescapable. Still, to speculate on comprehending, he designs "the simplest system" that would "compare meanings" in the service of "a translator's purposes" (21). That is, to understand comprehension, he uses translation with its interpretive problems as a site for studying communication.

Richards begins with the stark, reductive engineering model of communication, the one where a message travels from a source to a destination, but he elaborates this model of communication, somewhat more complexly, by including "comparison fields," a conceptual vehicle for comparing the new message with old messages. The units of comparison fields are the similar utterances used in similar situations that a "source" and "destination" employ to comprehend a new utterance. Having articulated this stark model, Richards defines a comprehending as "an instance of a nexus established through past occurrences of partially similar utterances in partially similar situation—utterances and situations partially co-varying" (23-24). While intention, the speaker's purpose, was *a*, if not *the* controlling factor in meaning before, now Richards diminishes the significance of the individual utterance and, in exploring translation, emphasizes the historical ("past occurrences") and situational aspects of interpretation. From *The Meaning of Meaning* to *Principles of Literary Criticism* to *Speculative Instruments,* the roles of situation (environment) and utterance increase. Richards still acknowledges "purposing"—in all utterances—as never lapsing, but in moving his focus from communicating to comprehending, he has subsumed authorial purpose to the overall, larger activities of comprehending in a changing culture (27-28).

In fact, in his discussion of comprehending via the comparison of utterances, in addition to "purpose," he describes the six other "sorts of work" that an interpreter or translator needs to do and presents them (indicating, characterizing, realizing, valuing, influencing, controlling) in more detail, apparently assuming purpose or "policy" as a given less in need of explication. In fact, in the last paragraph of the essay, of the seven tasks we must perform for comprehension, he privileges controlling, naming us "guardians" caught in a paradox: "we must derive our powers, in one way or another, from the very forces that we have to do our best to control." Over time, Richards shifts the focus of his project on meaning from communication to comprehension and interpretation, and in doing so, he diminishes the roles of agency and purpose. This diminution of speaker and hearer intention may be related in part to the addition of critics and translators, and so the creation of a more complex negotiation of meaning, yet the shift is a telling one.[7] The addition of history signals shifts, not just from a too simple sender-receiver model, nor from a model

---

7. See a discussion of the third-person attitude as opposed to the performative attitude of an interpreter in Jurgen Habermas's *Moral Consciousness and Communicative Action.*

that equates comprehension with the re-creation of an utterance (*Meaning of Meaning*), but rather to a model that acknowledges communication as bound by its culture and situation in a way that diminishes the possibility of new meanings. In effect, Richards argues for a paradigmatic model of meaning, a prison house of language. In conceptualizing the act of interpretation as being equal to and as significant as the creation of situations and speech acts, and in allowing prior utterances and existing meanings to control the interpretation and extension of cultural discourses, Richards has moved away from a model of communication that would enable "new millions of participants" to invent their meanings and promote their purposes and toward a model that emphasizes reception in the context of existing utterances, the utterances made before the "new millions" could participate. "Participants" are rewritten as "guardians," and the model of communication both seeks "better mutual comprehension" and limits and controls the nature of participation. His concern with the control of meaning is especially startling within the frame of his emphasis on "past occurrences" as necessary for comprehending.

Richards' desire both to control meaning and to emphasize the static aspects of community and communication actually is articulated earlier. Issues of control and stasis are evident in his texts on literary criticism, but since the desire for control is less clearly stated and these books are less often read by rhetoricians, his conservatism is less apparent to rhetoricians than literary critics.[8] Because we know best *The Philosophy of Rhetoric* with its interactive and generative theory of metaphor, rhetoricians rarely consider the conservatism of his work and its desire for stasis. Still, this drive to control the making of meaning, to expel misunderstanding, and to anchor the intentions of readers and hearers in either the words of the authoritative speaker or the cultural tradition is apparent once he moves from a generalized theory of speech in *The Meaning of Meaning* to explications of written words and canonical texts in *Principles of Literary Criticism* and *Practical Criticism*. Richards slides away from agent-based models of communication toward textual models of exegesis, and while

---

8. William V. Spanos and Paul A. Bove are articulate on this problem though from different perspectives. Spanos analyzes the conservatism ("ontological logocentrism," "ethnocentrism") of Richards's work on the Harvard General Education Program from a posthumanist perspective; his point is that the history of humanistic education is the repeated response of logocentric pedagogy to ruptures that reveal its reactionary, bourgeois ideology. Bove looks at Richards's place in the development of literary criticism, arguing that he is not an originary subject but a subject function of institutional structures. His work then is normative, producing a best combination of poetry and science in a way that disciplines the student and legitimates the humanities in the early-twentieth-century university.

his move to exegesis is useful to critical understanding and initiates New Criticism, it ironically minimizes the possibilities of interpretation and the diversity of activities for undisciplined audiences.

In *Principles of Literary Criticism,* Richards posits a masterful poet unlike "the ordinary man" who "suppresses nine-tenths of his impulses" and "goes about in blinders" (243). The poet "through his superior power of ordering experience" can create an aesthetic experience. In some unconscious way, the artist orchestrates "a welter of disconnected impulses into a single ordered response" (245) and creates an "equilibrium of opposed impulses" (251). The artist has powers, unique and unavailable to the masses, who still somehow respond to the work, but as followers.

More allied to the creator of art, the good critic as the exemplary reader must experience, "without eccentricities, the state of mind relevant to the work of art he is judging," distinguish experiences subtly, and be "a sound judge of values" (114). This critic represents normality, not in the sense of average or ordinary, but as a standard of experience (194). The emphasis on shared normality—in itself not alien to the concept of communication—prefaces the development of an ideal interpreter who few can emulate. Furthermore, the recipient's failure to reach that standard is not simply a return to average, but a moral threat to cultural values. Richards writes, "Bad taste and crude responses are not mere flaws in an otherwise admirable person. They are actually a root evil from which other defects follow" (62). Slightly later, in *Practical Criticism,* he worries about "the threat" posed as "our everyday reading and speech now handles scraps from a score of different cultures" (318). As a result, our utterances and interpretations deteriorate, become "less faithful to the thought, less discriminating with the feeling, cruder in the tone and more blurred in intention" (318-19). All our utterances are endangered by heterogeneity. He fears, "The result of this heterogeneity is that for all kinds of utterances our performances, both as speakers (or writers) and listeners (or readers), are worse than those of persons of similar natural ability, leisure and reflection a few generations ago" (318-19).

His terms of terror—"scraps," "fears," "heterogeneity"—have become terms of honor in postmodern discourses, but Richards is a man concerned, throughout his career, with the normative aspects of language. In *Speculative Instruments,* he argues against linguistics' tolerance of "all varieties" of discourse and asserts that the broader study of symbolic forms, "the over-all study of language, its services, and its powers . . . is, I am insisting, inescapably normative . . . concerned (as every speaker and every listener is always concerned) with the maintenance and improvement of the use of language" (124). According to Richards, what might constitute legitimate data collection for linguistics has no place in "education or criticism." The criteria for improvement are implicit in his privileging of the patriarchal traditions of Britain, and they are disquieting, not simply quaint because he goes so far as to extend "normalcy" to the concept of justice, arguing "a just man is a sane man—nothing out of order or unbalanced about him" (108).

At his better moments, Richards allows for the multiplicity of plausible interpretations through "the ambiguity of thought" (*Coleridge* 201), but the multiplicity is of rich, developed, critical interpretations, not of motley, hybrid, plebeian copiousness. His drive to control the standards of interpretation as well as education, justice, dialects, and the language of a "score of different cultures" undermines any liberal analysis of his interpretive process and reduces the sense of communication as a dialogue between writer and reader. Of course, the later Richards fervidly hopes and works for democracy and broad-based education (despite his growing love of Plato and fascination with the "justice" of the Republic), but his *desire* is to create a just—that is, communitarian—society where "all serve, not their own aggrandizement, but the commonwealth" and where "no faction, no pressure group, no self-interested power-seeker, can push the rest of the citizens around" (108). Two world wars lead him to believe that commonality is the effective approach to difference, a means for eradicating misunderstanding and subsuming individual intention under his tradition.

The tension between his interest in justice and his drive to normalize is evaded in his discussion of rhetoric, not as public discourse, oppositional or consensus building, but rather as trope and form. *The Philosophy of Rhetoric* (1936) is the book that both places Richards at the start of twentieth-century rhetoric and identifies him in the discipline of rhetoric. What is so startling about this book—especially in the context of Richards' avowed commitment to world literacy—is that it totally refuses traditional rhetoric's fascination with the agora, public discourse, legislation, and persuasion. He denigrates the old rhetoric and its preoccupation with the "debater's interest" (64) and, in defining rhetoric as "the study of misunderstanding and its remedies" (3), sets a standard of interpretive correctness as the ends of rhetoric: while his worldly activities, trips to China, and promotion of Basic English might seem concerned with speaking across differences, he refuses the more traditional rhetorical ends of actions in the world.

Escaping from a deliberative rhetorician's worldly purposes and moving to a literary rhetorician's analysis of morphemes, the interanimations of words, and tropes, Richards culminates the lecture series with a new theory of metaphor. While tropes have historical precedence and Richards' work on metaphor is groundbreaking, in effect, virtually half of the New Rhetoric is devoted to the workings of metaphor, and, for that matter, the workings of metaphor in poetics (from *Othello* to "Jabberwocky"). As Sue Wells has commented, "Richards' use of metaphor as a paradigm of discursive understanding canonizes his distrust of argument, of dispute, of the explicit project of persuading" ("Richards" 64). Indicative of his fears of argumentation, the ambiguity of discourse, and the potentially plebeian power to persuade is his use of canonical poetry as paradigm for the interanimation of words and metaphor in *The Philosophy of Rhetoric*. While some might argue for the generative effect of metaphor in society, Richards' limited examination of poetic texts circumscribes his sense of the social dynamic of metaphor and contains his fears.

The limited scope of the New Rhetoric denies rhetoric as a creative force for change in social structure: there is no author who intends and argues to change a community's power structures, meanings, and actions and no audience who sanctions or refuses the changes or the power structures, meanings, and actions. Richards' relationship to rhetoric, a field where he might have opened the existing aesthetic value system to argumentation, alternative discourses, or simple dialogue, is not so positive as many introductions to rhetoric suggest.[9] Quite possibly due to his fear of debate and concern for existing power structures, Richards' conception of rhetoric is limited for one raised in the Anglo-American tradition. Despite his repeated focus on language as an instrument of communication, Richards rejects a rhetoric conceived as a purposeful tool of persuasion or an instrument of creating social identities. Richards, from *The Philosophy of Rhetoric* onward, sees rhetoric as a complex connection between metaphor and human knowledge, a position more typical of French and belletristic rhetorics than of the rhetorics of persuasion and deliberation. When Sue Wells writes that Richards' rhetoric "abstracts the audience from its experience, its history, and its social location" (64), she is being generous. Richards abstracted rhetoric itself from experience, history, and social location. While he can acknowledge environment and experience in *Principles of Literary Criticism,* an exploration of high culture's texts, he moves from intention, experience, and environment when theorizing the dangerous activity of rhetoric. In *Speculative Instru-*

---

9. See Ann E. Berthoff's *Richards on Rhetoric* and Stuart C. Brown's "I. A. Richards' New Rhetoric."

ments (1955), arguing against a connection between Shakespeare's art and his training in rhetoric, Richards goes even further in his dismissal of disciplinary rhetoric, writing that " 'rhetorical theory in its entire scope' is after all no more than a somewhat chaotic collection of observations made on the ways of lively venturesome speech and writing" (159). Arguing against writers who connect qualities in Shakespeare's writings to a rhetoric education, he espouses suspicion of "pedagogical relations between precept and example" (159). In fact, he resists the notion that classical training in rhetoric is useful for students of his age, a position not unlike the recent one of Cy Knoblauch and Lillian Brannon in *Rhetorical Traditions and the Teaching of Writing*. Surprisingly, while Knoblauch and Brannon have been criticized at length for such a position, perhaps in part because they wish to open rhetorical education to heterogeneous forces and change the tradition of education, Richards' resistance remains unquestioned, unacknowledged by his proponents in rhetoric.

Richards, no simple figure, is no simple hero for the rebirth of rhetoric nor the emancipation of "new millions of participants in the control of general affairs" (*Meaning* x). His difficulties in acknowledging a rhetoric that could allow for cultural change beyond the play of metaphor are symptomatic of a distrust and a resistance to the masses, their potential for power, and the plethora of their purposes. Undoubtedly unconsciously, Richards renders ineffable and invisible the connections between theories of discourse and the realm of politics, military force, institutional and cultural power, and public policy. Despite avowed and enacted democratic and humanistic commitments, he struggles with twentieth-century pluralism and his evolving conceptions of the force of purposes and intentions, and finally, near the end of his life, he begins to consider a more egalitarian model of communication.

Beyond (1974), Richards' final presentation of the process of communication, now very much limited to interpretation, is troubling in its argument for the canon and its concern with Platonic mysticism and elitism, and certainly he has not given up his fear of misunderstanding and his desire for control and order (163). Even so, in this late analysis of communication he suggests that meanings, "interpretations," are produced by the interactions of and reconciliations between a good reader's two "loyalties," loyalties to "inner and outer testimony" (26). Richards now acknowledges the necessity of play between "the textual and circumstantial (outer) data" and "our own (inner) uncertainties of experience." This acknowledgment, while made in passing, redefines all his earlier analyses of understanding and suggests an approach to interpretation only now beginning to be explored in literary rhetorics, only now in tandem with the development of hermeneutical rhetorics. A concern with the negotiation of meaning between the text as an outer other and our inner, uncertain experiences will transform the rhetorical tradition, but now, for the most part, the promise of play and space for interpretive difference continues to be evaded in literary rhetorics.

II

If Richards struggles to evade argumentation and negotiated meaning while simultaneously working for world literacy and political participation, Wayne Booth has produced work on rhetoric more reflective of discipline business as usual. Booth, many decades later and in many ways, replicates Richards' concerns with authorial intention, the radical possibilities of rhetoric, multiple sources of meaning, the dangers and beauties of public discourse, and the copious interpretive activity solicited by aesthetic texts. The difficult articulation of these concerns tends to characterize literary rhetorics: the decades have rolled on, but literary rhetoricians have not conceptualized a dynamic between the intentions of a rhetor and her audience.

My analysis of Richards and Booth, as well as my later exegesis of Fish's theory, suggests that literary rhetoricians' interpretive focus on the rereading and rereading of old, written, aesthetic texts creates an interpretive distance between writer and reader rarely felt by rhetoricians disciplined in speech communication departments where context or the rhetorical situation is both more apparent and less: more apparent in that the speaker tends to be addressing a local issue and specific audience and less apparent because analysis of the context tends to be transparent, facilely known. The consistent enactment of interpretive distance is a useful aspect of literary rhetorics; it helps rhetoricians develop formalist techniques, a complex understanding of interpretive practices, and concepts of resisting or misunderstanding audiences. Still, attempts to theorize the tension between interlocutors too often result in the dismissal of or deferred attention to argumentation, the negotiation of meaning and power, and *kairos* in favor of the formal structure of the text. These are Richards' weakness and Booth's, too.

Unlike Richards, Booth diminishes the tension and its resulting struggle; instead, he develops a linear, directive model for dealing with the negotiation of meaning and the dialectic of understanding/misunderstanding. He offers this model for productive dialogue apparently with sincere hope for functioning democratic practices, but as I will show, the effect is to legitimate existing power structures and institutions, and to subsume minority voices under those of the dominant in a zero-sum game.

Wayne Booth's most explicitly political text, the one concerned with situated, public discourse and its collapse into civil disobedience, is *Modern Dogma and the Rhetoric of Assent*. It begins with the drama of incommensurable discourses between bourgeois generations in the sixties. Examining student protests at the University of Chicago, Booth lays out political problems and questions that require public negotiations of justice, but that the community is unable to adjudicate, being split into two camps by five dogmas prevalent in modernism. Booth posits real splits between each group, professors and students, in how they conceptualized (1) methods for producing change, (2) the nature of the things changed (mind, soul, organism), (3) the world in which the things changed, (4) truth and its testing, and (5) the purpose of change. In Booth's analysis and demonstration, these dogmatic splits, this "rhetorical crisis" caused by modernism's pervasive skepticism and its binary of fact and value, can confuse the thinking of a philosopher as astute as Bertrand Russell, let alone that of a sixties' undergraduate who sees her only course of action as demonstration.

The rhetorical situation that initiates Booth's inquiry is significant, as are the questions that divided the population of the University of Chicago. How can demonstrating students and concerned faculty discuss issues as global as the Vietnam War and as local as the case of a popular woman teacher denied tenure? What is the purpose of a liberal arts education in a technological society? What is the relationship between the university and the state? Should students have a voice in tenuring proceedings? How about in the administration of a campus? Booth, however, never addresses these questions in any direct way though he does begin to answer the difficult question, What has happened to patterns of communication in the twentieth century such that two parties, students and faculty, at an elite educational institution, like the University of Chicago, cannot come to an understanding? Despite the local nature of his initial questions, Booth's solution is very general; he advocates a turn from modernism and a return to rhetoric, somewhat evolved from classical theory. That is, modernism has ruptured us, and somehow to address our problems and answer our questions, we must escape the modern situation, but how we escape and where we go is not so simple to articulate. While he doesn't, can't return us to the past, neither does Booth move us to a land of new rhetorics and voices.

To evade argument with its attending risks of alienation, separation, and loss and to pursue a conversational model of rhetoric, Booth ascribes meaning to authorial intention and then advocates that we become a docile audience who accepts "every belief" that passes two tests: (1) there are no "particular, concrete" reasons to doubt it, and (2) there is reason to think *"all men who understand the problem share your belief"* (40). Understanding then becomes the sharing of beliefs, not a surprising or novel position, though one problematized by twenty years of postmodern theorizing.[10]

Still, for Booth misguided misunderstanding is less the problem than the delinquent, dissenting reader. Richards assumes cultural, gender, and class differences that he desires to modify through education and widespread literacy; he assumes that all people desire to submit to the tradition, that all desire to maintain and improve the use of language. Booth, on the other hand, casts the difference in terms of assent and dissent—to whose (one) position?—belief and skepticism, and he is less sure of the intentions of the skeptics and dissenters. In response to their divergences, he seeks to stabilize meaning in the intentions of traditional authors. Richards struggles to articulate meaning's proper proportion of authorial purpose in relationship first to sense, feeling, and tone, and later in relationship to indicating, characterizing, realizing, valuing, influence, and controlling, and finally in relationship to context, text, and the interpreter's experience. Booth relies on authorial intention at the cost of reader's rights.

To understand the dangers of Booth's commitment to the transparency of authorial intention, it is important to understand the system he supports. That is, we must understand better what it means to give up doubt and dissent and to give assent to belief systems. Despite his initial engagement in political controversy, and his rejection of modernism and call for a fundamental cultural change in how we greet the other, Booth's rhetoric is surprisingly literary and tame. And though he plays with both approaches, he replicates the classical rhetoric of neither Aristotle nor Plato, but rather creates a subtle mixture that cloaks each's extremity and mutes each's potential to arbitrate the conflicting purposes of two differently empowered cultures, such as faculty and student. In contrast to the political situation that initiated *Modern Dogma,* Booth's rhetoric of assent

---

10. Argumentation theorists also have difficulty with this glib outline of what are grounds for assent. See Raymie E. McKerrow's "The Centrality of Justification."

works to evade both conflict and engagement with public discourse and power dynamics.

While Booth states investment in the Aristotelian concepts of the practical life, probable knowledge, and multiple means of proof (ethos and pathos as well as logos), he does not conceptualize rhetoric as "the faculty of observing in any given case the available means of persuasion" (Aristotle, *Rhetoric* I.1.1355b1-2), potentially a very broad activity that includes simple acts of presenting/presencing and even acknowledges the existence of nonartistic proofs such as torture. Rather Booth defines rhetoric as "a whole philosophy of how men succeed or fail in discovering together, in discourse, new levels of truth (or at least agreement) that neither side suspected before," or with different emphasis, "the whole art of discovering and sharing warrantable assertion" (*Modern Dogma* 10-11). While both definitions, offered in the same paragraph, seem to emphasize togetherness and sharing, the definitions themselves, like Aristotelian and Platonic theory, are in conflict. Like Richards in *The Philosophy of Rhetoric*, Booth conceives of rhetoric as a branch of philosophy, and with that connection, he sees seeking "new levels of truth" as rhetoric's highest goal, with agreement as the fallback position; furthermore, rhetoric, in the first definition, is epistemic in that divided camps of participants discover surprising (unsuspected) knowledge. The echoes of Plato reverberate here: hear truth, discovering together, new knowledge, higher level, dialogue. The second definition, however, is reminiscent of Aristotle in that it emphasizes art (*techne*) and the final outcome of a common position based on probable ("warrantable") evidence. Still, it leaves behind Aristotle's acknowledgment of persuasion's power and the concept of "means" that implies larger cultural purposes and strategic choices. And unlike Aristotle or Plato who acknowledge the dangerous, dirty aspects of rhetoric, in taking the good reasons' turn, Booth presents rhetoric as the benign activity of finding common grounds or new truth. He assumes that marginal positions will be given ground and that new truths will not harm us, the powerful or the marginal, the professor or the student, the rich or the poor. Just say yes.

Ironically the promised common ground, when Booth reveals it, transcends ordinary language and the agora to find a more ethereal home in the aesthetic. When, in the last two lectures, he turns to examples for his argument, he turns to Jane Austen, Johann Sebastian Bach, Leo Tolstoy, and John Lennon. While Lennon is not a figure of high culture, *none* of his examples are explicitly political. The aesthetic nature of his examples shows the subtlety with which he voices Aristotelian rhetoric and practical wisdom while advocating Platonic truth, dialectic, and transcendence. In the broad analysis, Booth utilizes his disciplinary fascination with art as the response to political crisis and civil disobedience. Even if it is not conscious or explicit, Booth's move to assent is ultimately a move to subsume diverging purposes, beliefs, and cultures within the dominant traditions of aesthetics, not politics (Aristotle, Locke, or Marx).

Booth begins with the premise that readers can know authorial intention and that the error or truth of their readings of intention can be determined (*Modern Dogma* 64-66). He even cavalierly ascribes this knowledge of other's intentions to Bertrand Russell despite Russell's years of struggle with problems of certainty. Later, in addressing modernist doubts about what we know, Booth writes, "I would like to suggest, in contrast, that of all the things I know, some intentions, both of myself and of other persons, are what I know most surely . . . [and] to admit that we make mistakes about some intentions no more rules intentions from the realms of knowledge than to say that we make mistakes about the physical world forbids knowledge about the physical world" (116). Using the first sentence of Jane Austen's *Pride and Prejudice,* he claims knowledge of her intended irony by his "strength of conviction," his community's agreement of the ironic interpretation, the interpretation's coherence with other knowledge (of irony, Austen), and finally, the "teachability or corrigibility" of her intention (University of Chicago students come to recognize Austen's ironic sentence under his tutelage) (116-21). The general acknowledgment of Austen's irony becomes the case supporting his premise that we can read across cultures, that we can understand political difference, that intentions are generally available to readers.

Booth's lecture was given at the University of Notre Dame in 1971 to a predominately white, bourgeois, academic, male audience, one that may have recognized each other's intentions with comfort, or at least, thought they did. In many ways, the comfort of those recognitions echoes Richards' discomfort with the diverse intentions and diverging interpretations of the "new millions." Just as Richards moves to canonical literary texts to examine the interaction of intentions, so moves Booth. He begins *Modern Dogma* with the deliberations about the very political student demonstrations of the sixties and the case of a woman professor denied tenure at a time when tenured female faculty were exceedingly few. However, rather than consider political issues, issues subject to rhetorical interventions, he ends his book with a discussion of interpreting aesthetic texts, the majority of which were old and canonical. Even his choice of privileged texts precludes problems; he neither presents an author whose intentions can be politicized in the situation and time of the sixties (for instance, Joseph

Heller on *Catch 22*) nor an author whose intention is often ambiguous (such as William Shakespeare). Furthermore, rather than asking the more difficult and controversial question of Austen's intended meaning about the effects and desirability of marriage, he picks a sentence well described and analyzed in literary history. Aesthetic texts can be quite revealing of deliberations and cultural clashes, but Booth's texts are not chosen for these revelations.

The critique of a rhetoric of assent and the docile reader is available in many places—though most consistently with feminist critics.[11] Not all of the academy's new participants have primary commitments to conversation and understanding; many would describe their primary work as the unraveling of orthodox culture and its replacement with one that acknowledges the insights possible through dissent and difference. In 1978, for instance, Judith Fetterley, without naming Booth, described the necessity of dissenting readings by feminist critics for their own identity, if not salvation. She writes, "The first act of the feminist critic must be to become a resisting rather than an assenting reader and, by this refusal to assent, to begin the process of exorcising the male mind that has been implanted in us" (*The Resisting Reader* xxii). A reader's conscious intent to maintain her purposes then may encourage her to refuse to share beliefs for the beneficial purpose of subverting authorial intention. Her "misunderstanding" and refusal to give "assent" can be strategic. Or in a further step, the dissenting reader may see difficulties, ambiguities, or polarities in the text's reality and go beyond the author's understanding to resolve them and create something new. Deliberative rhetorics historically must be able to talk about discursive relations that are coercive, subversive, conflictive, submissive, as well as those that are cooperative (Aristotle, Cicero).

The reader's actions posited by Fetterley may not be interpretation as defined in the literary rhetorics of Booth and Richards—in that the reader refuses the apparent or surface intent of an author, his text, their history—but if one defines interpretation within the perspective of reader-response theory, interpretive communities, or dialogue/dialectic, then clearly these actions can be interpretive, ethical, and valid. Booth's failure to appreciate the ethics of a dissenting reader is at odds with the elenctic tradition and, in fact, the rhetorical project of persuasion. Persuasion is premised on initial difference, and at a basic level, the rhetorical challenge is to engage the dissenting reader.

---

11. The critique of docility is a basic of feminist theory. For some arguments against assent that are particularly rhetorical, see bell hooks's *Yearning,* Nancy Fraser's *Unruly Practices,* and Judith Keegan Gardiner's collection, *Provoking Agents.*

Booth differs from Richards in that his desire is not just to place consensus in an education that promotes similar ideals, but also to guarantee consensus through creating docile, colonized readers. He also differs in his desire to understand and control *understanding*. Rather than focusing on *misunderstanding*, a study of what might go wrong, Booth promotes *understanding*, a term that implies the concept of the right approach, a goal. To achieve this goal, Booth, in 1979, theorized that one mind must incorporate another; understanding is not simply recognizing and respecting another's intentions and meanings, but requires the colonization of other minds. In 1923, Richards and Ogden equated communication with the identity of minds on the author's terms: "as a use of symbols in such a way that acts of reference occur in a hearer which are similar in all relevant respects to those which are symbolized by them in the speaker" (*Meaning* 205-6). In 1979, Booth defines understanding in a way that acknowledges interpreter activity, but still calls for matching or identity of experience, a position approaching that of Richards in the late 1920s. Booth writes, "*Understanding is the goal, process, and result whenever one mind succeeds in entering another mind or, what is the same thing, whenever one mind succeeds in incorporating any part of another mind*" (*Critical Understanding* 262). While he acknowledges that the mind is not separate from the brain, Booth asserts that his language of "entering" is not simply metaphorical (263). He posits that minds both exchange and are "made by symbols." The exchange of information, then, is understanding that "shades" into and "depends on an understanding of intention and motives" (263-64). While he acknowledges our ability to "read between the lines" and to disagree about meaning, Booth, as we already have seen, has great faith in our competence to infer intention and, thus, to understand. However, as he notes, "sharing of intentions usually includes . . . strong value judgements," including sharing of hatred (265). While acknowledging that understanding can be used for evil ends, Booth still suggests that understanding itself has universal value. After all, humanity depends on other minds, misunderstanding cannot be an end in itself, and human exchange depends on at least one of the parties seeking understanding.

Booth's desire that one mind "succeeds in entering another" is an aggression, a conceivably sexual aggression, resisted by many feminists. Even if some acknowledge the existing practice of this aggression, they see it as an activity foisted on oppressed groups by the dominant. That is, to survive in the patriarchy, women must understand men and their patterns of behavior while men can function successfully without being concerned with understanding women (see Spender).

Feminists concerned with political theory and jurisprudence have developed (several) responses to the privileging of understanding and identification; they see ruptures in understanding as differences in deeply held and significant beliefs that cannot and should not be easily discarded for a project of consensus.[12] The philosopher Iris Young, who seeks "a vision of social relations affirming group differences," models her ideal community on the city, attempting to envision "openness to unassimilated otherness" (*Justice* 227). She writes that "politics must be conceived as a relationship of strangers who do not understand one another in a subjective and immediate sense, relating across time and distance" (234). Misunderstanding, not knowing intentions, is the point at which political, rhetorical activity starts. Rather than being a particularly dangerous position, it is a prevalent one in human action and has positive aspects. As Young notes, if mutual understanding and identification is a group's primary goal, then other goals, such as diversity, may be jeopardized, and certain group members may become susceptible to "cultural imperialism" (235-36).

In contrast to feminists and other minority populations strategizing ways to be heard and to stay committed to alternative values, Booth, prizing the established reason of his culture, observes that "being reasonable in practical affairs is more like a process of systematic assent than systematic doubt" (*Modern Dogma* 104). One can read his claim that one *ought* to grant to the agreements of others unless one has specific and stronger reasons to disbelieve as supportive of marginal voices and alternative politics (that is, the dominant will grant space), but his codicil for disbelief—"specific and stronger reasons"—is not only tautological in that strong reason is the basis of most disagreement, but it also claims that the stronger party has more right to disagree.[13] The definition of strength is perhaps left open, but the openness of the definition, especially within the hierarchies of the university, offers weak patronage to the margins. In the end, his project of placing meaning in the transparent intentions of textual production diminishes the multiple intentional states implicit in the act of reading—or, for that matter, writing. Both, in the end, evade the problematic of ideology and hegemony under the mask of structuring productive communication.

---

12. Judith Butler and Joan W. Scott raise many of the issues related to postmodern feminism in the introduction to their collection *Feminists Theorize the Political*. See also Iris Marion Young's *Justice and the Politics of Difference*, Catherine A. MacKinnon's *Toward a Feminist Theory of State*, and Drucilla Cornell's *Transformations*.

13. This tautological problem is well developed in Robert C. Rowland's "Purpose, Argument Evaluation, and Crisis."

III

I am far from alone in my discomfort with Booth's claims for transparent knowledge of intentions and his denial of the effect of power, individual and institutional, on the negotiation of interpretations. Stanley Fish verbalizes very similar concerns from a slightly different perspective, basing his critique on Booth's *Rhetoric of Irony*. There, to develop a theory of how we recognize irony—a trope, with allusion, often used to argue for the necessity of recognizing authorial intention in interpretation—Booth works from a stable base of undisputed literal meaning to a rational, sequenced process of interpretation, specifically, the interpretation of stable ironies. Stable ironies, separated from unstable and unintended ironies (such as ironies of fate), are *"intended," "covert," "finite* in application," and do not invite the reader to undermine them through "further demolitions and reconstructions" (5-6). While acknowledging the possibility of failure within ironic communications, Booth evades the problem (or advantage) of open interpretation by taking a limited approach and conventionalist stand on a subject as fluid as irony.[14] Fish finds Booth's arguments for stability and his focus on stable ironies emblematic of two fears: (1) a fear that any individual reader might or might not find irony independently without explicit criteria, and (2) a fear that a text might be judged ironic based on persuasive argumentation (193-94). The fears are similar to Booth's fears in *Modern Dogma*, where he wishes to provide explicit criteria for understanding and to minimize the role of argumentation in the negotiation of meanings; here, too, he wishes to present and value an interpretive approach that is stable, if not static. Fish, in response, argues for comfort with debates about competing interpretations and asserts that interpretation is a historical, communal process of debate that establishes and overturns anchorages of meaning. Rather than controlling interpretation by securing it to authorial intention, Fish claims respect for the value of competing interpretations and places interpretive control within discourse communities and their ways of reading.

Like Booth, Fish likes intentions, though—unlike Booth—he does not conceive of them as the foundation of or a constraint on meaning, but rather as implicit in our recognition of meaningfulness and, consequently,

---

14. In *Limited, Inc.*, Jacques Derrida critiques John Austin for precisely this reliance on a standard example of successful communication rather than explorations of the misunderstandings inherent in language. It is unfortunate that he fails to hear Austin's ironic awareness of the instability of meanings and of the pragmatic, ad hoc ways we have of interpreting. See my later discussion of Austin in the Hinge/Acknowledging Prejudices interlude.

a factor in our interpretations. Like Richards, he sees intention as one factor among many. While he calls "the matter of intention, a vexed topic that usually brings out the worst in everyone" (*Doing* 116), he maintains that "to look at the text (in the sense of regarding it as meaningful) is already to have posited for it an intention (by assuming the intentional circumstances of its production)" (117-18). Even so, argues Fish, readers change their interpretations and, so, their interpretations of an author's intentions; neither irony nor interpretation is stable. Demonstrating his perspective by analyzing the historical progression of interpretations of Swift's poem "Verses on the Death of Dr. Swift," Fish argues that new ideas, contexts, and arguments arise, though they always are constrained by the interpretations, even opposing interpretations, already articulated in the community (186-93). Seemingly, readers' diverging interpretations of authorial intention are a source of new ideas, but what might constitute the "facts" of that intention is fashioned through debate.

In view of Fish's affection for intentions, it remains somewhat startling that—despite seeing the attribution of intentions as implicit in our interpretations, including interpretations of ourselves (*Free Speech* 183)—he argues that intentions themselves are not legitimate constraints on interpretation. He reasons that *"words are intelligible only within the assumption of some context of intentional production, some already-in-place predecision as to what kind of person, with what kind of purposes, in relation to what specific goals in a particular situation, is speaking or writing* (295, Fish's emphasis). This means that readers simultaneously produce and ascribe intentions in their interpretive processes. A reader, such as Booth, may find the ascription of authorial intention transparent, facile, but that is because the reader is using the ascription of authorial intention to support a particular interpretation (*her* interpretation for *her* purposes, *my* interpretation for *my* purposes). Alas, according to Fish, that ascribed authorial intention is as constructed as the larger interpretation it supports, and thus, a reader constructs both the interpretation and the intention with a consistency that reflects her own existing purposes and beliefs, purposes and beliefs that may have nothing to do with the author's.[15]

---

15. Fish's underlying skepticism haunts any descriptive power in his work. As a skeptic, he can not let go of the basic questions of how, if, and why we *know* the world and our neighbors, but despite efforts to describe the patterns of knowledge (including recognizing intentions), as a skeptic, he always answers that we can't. Skepticism does present a problem for doing criticism or theory as usual (though, as Hume pointed out, it has very little impact on doing life as usual). I find two approaches helpful for bracketing a skeptic's refusal to move from the problem of founding knowledge. One is Barbara Herrnstein Smith's approach to the clash of belief and skepticism. She

Fish's analysis of the relationship between intentions and a reader's meaning is supportable within the traditional texts of rhetoric, but that support is indirect because of the general omission of the term *intention* in rhetorical texts. Many rhetoricians assume an authorial purpose or intention, but they also acknowledge that intentions may be hidden from the audience or that the audience's construction of an author's intentions may diverge from the author's desired effect. Examples of these tensions abound, in both sophistic and foundational rhetorics. In his "Encomium of Helen," Gorgias analyzes four possible interpretations of Helen's trip to Troy. While Helen, a classical woman, is not presented as having intentions (that is, she is a victim of fate, force, love, or persuasion), Gorgias, at the end of his speech, opens his intentions to speculation, suggesting his programmatic intent was not so much to clear Helen as to entertain the audience and demonstrate his rhetorical prowess. Plato demonstrates a similar play in the *Phaedrus* when he presents three speeches of seduction or love, each of which are interpreted differently by Socrates, Phaedrus, and conceivably his readers. Interpretations of the speeches depend on the programmatic intentions that an interpreter grants Lysias, Socrates, and Plato, and the reader's interpretations of those intentions are likely to be more complex than the interpretations of Phaedrus, who seems stuck finding only transparent or active intentions. Even so, most first-time readers see Socrates' first speech as intended to be persuasive before he takes it back in shame and offers the second, longer, more articulate exploration: a classic bait-and-switch tactic. So, while Plato seems to have at least some identifiable intentions and Gorgias's intentions are less easily

---

sees their incommensurable logics as neither scandalous nor isolating, but rather "a contingent, experiential relation between historically and institutionally situated conceptual/discursive practices" (152). She writes that while often polarizing, sometimes the clash is transformative. With this lens, it seems that Fish's other-mind skepticism offers an important antithesis to Richards and Booth, one that transforms the question from how do we recognize an authorial intention to the more dynamic questions of can we recognize authorial intention and what is its relationship to a reader's intentions. The second approach—dependent on ordinary language philosophers (primarily Austin and Wittgenstein) and used by variety of theorists (such as Charles Altieri, Anthony Cascardi, Stanley Cavell, and Michael Fischer)—coincides more with my orientation. These theorists, while less enamored with skeptical accounts than Smith, accept that there is no constraint on linguistic free play or absolute knowledge of other minds, but go on to show that there need not be certain, divine, or natural foundations. Rather there are probabilistic criteria (based in our forms, culture, and natural world) from which we have half-truths, contingent beliefs, inferences, probabilities, and mutual attunement. Following Cavell, skepticism cannot tell us what is interesting; it does not tell us what it is we do, how we are able to proceed in our human finitude. The failure to tell us how we "go on" in part informs my critique of Fish in the next few pages.

agreed on, both are playing with the audience's concern for and problems with ascribing authorial intention.

It is possible to place Fish's work within the skeptical and sophistic traditions of rhetoric, a placement he desires and bids for (despite his fascination with poetry), but there remain (at least) two limitations to Fish's approach to intention and its connection to rhetoric. The first limitation is that—though Fish has developed the concept of change within an interpretive community since he wrote *Is There a Text in This Class?*—he still has difficulty acknowledging the usefulness of, let alone possibility of, theories of change. In contrast, 2,500 years of rhetoric, deliberative rhetoric particularly, has been theorizing how to effect change in an audience and create political actions. Fish has moved to describe the interpretive community as "an engine of change" (*Doing* 150, *Free Speech* 189)—clearly a mechanistic metaphor at odds with a diverse, sometimes cross-purposed group of actors. In his later model of community, its code is not a set of rules, but instead "an entirely flexible instrument for organizing contingent experience in a way that does not preclude but renders inevitable its own modification" (*Doing* 151). In effect, the new, improved interpretive community whose code is an "instrument" of "inevitable" change precludes agency and delimits cross-purposes as completely as did his earlier community. Furthermore, as someone who buys her groceries from members of the Amish community most Saturdays, I struggle with this statement as a broad or universal vision of inevitable change (whose code? whose clock?). While Fish would respond that different interpretive communities create, write, imagine different histories of continuity or change, there is some very empirical evidence for interpretive communities whose engine of change needs a mechanic. Fish even acknowledges "not everything changes at once" though he is less than specific about how institutional practices regulate change, denying even the possibility of "general account" or "a *theory* of change, complete with criteria and a predictive formula" (153). Rather, he asserts "anything" can cause change, and our understanding of change can only occur in the context of "a historical reconstruction of empirical conditions." Chaos, or rather chaos theory, now reigns; if earlier literary rhetoricians struggled to develop theories of control, form, and order, Fish categorically denies their possibility.

His project of describing interpretive processes within an interpretive community is very different than deliberative rhetoric's project of creating negotiated change within a discourse community or across discourse communities. While his connection of community change to its code is useful, Fish's refusal to theorize or to speculate on a "predictive formula" reduces the usefulness for a rhetor who desires an action or a change in a code. Fish lacks all interest in facilitating the rhetor's strategies and refuses a role in helping rhetors move from intentions to action to effect: application is not his province or production—although his willingness to look at contemporary texts, even legal texts, brings him close to these topics.

The second problem with his account of intention for rhetoric is in his definition of rhetoric as "proceeding on the basis of assumptions and distinctions that are open to challenge, even though there may be times when no one is challenging them" (297-98). This definition may simply be a better definition of human action; that is, it is so broad as to mean all human activity. As is, it is too broad and ambiguous a definition of rhetoric to assist us in understanding rhetorical practices.[16] In effect, he repeats a common move of literary skepticism in these postmodern, interpretive times: he emphasizes rhetoric's nonfoundational, dynamic, sophistic aspects at the cost of rhetoric's traditions of *paideia,* practice, production, situation, and tropology. Yes, the enterprise of interpretation proceeds on assumptions open to challenge; once one begins to talk about meaning, meaning becomes multiple and hierarchical, assumptions become explicit, intentions are ascribed, articulated interpretations are challenged, and the "engine of change" roars off. On the other hand, there are aspects of rhetoric committed to stability, control, form, order, and commonality. Stability may need to be promoted, and most education in rhetoric (and poetics), exhibitions of epideictic rhetoric, concerns with orality and literacy, and metaphors-we-live-by are aspects of the rhetorical tradition that build assumptions and promote their continued sharing. Even if interpretive communities are "engines of change," there are—within the production of discourse, in the output of any *discourse* communities— conservative, normative forces.

In the end, Fish leaves us puzzled over a very dynamic process of "inevitable" change that is "also orderly" (156). We have little sense of how the change looks in practice since, according to Fish, to interpret that practice would be to enact our assumptions and interpretations of continuity or discontinuity (157-58). While it may be unfair to expect a slippery Fish to be more practice oriented, his theorizing of intention and of discourse communities is weakened by his failure to examine political practices in detail, both practices of conservation and change (how are the

---

16. I cannot resist quoting Thomas Farrell here: "All knowledge is rhetorical in direct proportion to how trivial is one's initial conception of rhetoric" ("Parthenon" 82). One might read Fish as ruling out faiths and facts, and perhaps identity statements, but it is not clear that even these are not open to challenge.

Amish different than the *literati?*). Much like Booth, whenever he does turn to issues or examples of practice, he tends to turn to literary texts and his own interpretive community. His repeated move to a home community and its set of texts is problematic in that he engages only one community, a community where he is expert and comfortable. While expertise gives the rhetorician authority, if it places a rhetorician's authority and position already within the code that he analyzes, then expertise can be a limiting factor. Fish places himself in the sphere where he is guaranteed to have strong beliefs, the ability to defend them, little motive to negotiate them, and difficulty with any disengagement (I no longer even type *objectivity*). By his subject matter and data, he actively creates a world that replicates his theory.

IV

Despite their claims of desiring to engage political worlds, literary rhetoricians enact their associations with the interpretation of canonical literature, a privileged community, and the prevailing value system. In doing so, they evade the difficulties of negotiated meaning and pluralist politics; that is, they create a rhetoric that omits, denies, or diminishes deliberative and forensic rhetorics that depend on the recognition of competing intentions. Within this disciplinary manifestation, rhetoric—which is often conceived as the production of meaning and action and the negotiation of difference—is remade through the regulation of interpretation into a conservative force emphasizing language's formal features, metaphors, genres, codes, and institutional and conventional characteristics. Even Fish's commitment to change is undercut by his unwillingness to address theories of change or stasis, to consider radical difference, and to analyze empirical cases of negotiated meaning. Tragically, though literary rhetoric may be conceptually sophisticated and complex, it functions as one of contemporary rhetoric's most conservative branches. Belletristic methods do not foster understanding of cultural difference and diverging intentions.

For many very complex reasons, literary rhetoricians seek out literary texts which then function as idealized texts that transcend the struggles and practices of others and reinscribe the dominant traditions. Some classical rhetoricians, Socrates and Cicero, may have died for their production of meaning and actions, but contemporary literary rhetoricians avoid even the concept of risk and political action. Instead they work to ground meaning either in the intentions of the author or the interpretive community (often conceived of as their discipline), and thereby they evade the clutter of praxis.

The ethics of this avoidance are troubling. Richards may make important efforts in the area of literacy and pedagogy, but he cuts rhetoric away from those efforts. Booth simply promotes the status quo and continues literary practice, calling it rhetoric and thinning the tradition. And if Fish's rhetoric, with its explorations of community, possibility, and change, is richer, he denies much of the rhetorical tradition with his emphasis on sophistic and belletristic rhetorics. Each emphasizes different aspects of the tradition (and emphasis is a necessary move), but they all achieve the same effect, one of transcending politics, and that is symptomatic of a deeper trouble within rhetoric institutionalized in English departments.

While the poetic aspects of rhetoric clearly exist productively and the divide between poetics and rhetoric as discourse is always a wavering line, the desire to conflate the two needs examination. What is gained for rhetoric? What is lost? Clearly, in the discipline of English, rhetoric gains intellectual complexity and status, but is this at the cost of worldliness and conflict? Is this conflation with poetics simply an interesting historical moment within rhetoric's rebirth in the twentieth century, or is it symptomatic of deeper trouble in positing the importance of intentions, difference, and interpretation?

2

Intention, Invention, and Interpretation

Rhetoric at the End of the Twentieth Century

> *Rhetoric, that practically conscientious discourse of struggle and conflict, has been aestheticized. . . . The cult of textuality has had the effect of blinding many of us to and also insulating many of us from the places where real material grievances are stored and sometimes lost.*
> —Thomas B. Farrell, "Disappearance"

> *I did not translate them as an interpreter* but as an *orator.*
> —Cicero, *De optimo genere oratorum*

If many literary rhetoricians, by placing meaning either in authorial or audience intention, do not see the processes of deliberating and producing action, other rhetoricians increasingly neglect the complexities of deliberation by ignoring the issue of intention and replacing rhetoric—focused on intersubjective issues of power, manipulation, and persuasion—with textuality.[1] With this maneuver, intentions, especially as negotiated between a rhetor and an audience,

---

1. Dana L. Cloud provides a good background to and critique of rhetoric's increasing blindness to anything but the text.

become a only slim piece of the discussion, and rhetoric becomes a strategic approach to reading texts, not a praxis or *poesis*. This concern typifies many postmodern as well as hermeneutical approaches to rhetoric, but for purposes of understanding the place of a theory of intentionality within rhetoric, I examine the relationship between hermeneutics and rhetoric, in part because rhetorical criticism—a familiar rhetorical activity—provides a basis for hermeneutics in rhetoric, but as well because Gadamer's interpretive theory—with its emphasis on the interpreter—provides a start toward theorizing the place of audience intentions within deliberations.

Ultimately, hermeneutics is useful to rhetoric, but it is not the same project. Hermeneutics, concerned with texts and their relationship to historical consciousness, is not alien to rhetoric, nor is either activity autonomous. However, a too-ready collapse of one into the other destroys their differences, differences necessary to understand rhetoric as deliberative and to articulate the interactions of an author's and an audience's intentions. It is commonly acknowledged that rhetoric is easily transfigured, but as Thomas B. Farrell writes (of epistemic rhetoric in particular), "all knowledge is rhetorical in direct proportions to how trivial is one's initial conception of rhetoric" ("Parthenon" 82).[2] True, this is a rather snide comment, but it identifies the core problem of institutionalized rhetoric at the end of the twentieth century. That is, rhetoric represents too many things to too many scholars and winds up wearing too many caps. The winged cap of Hermes is one of them.

While rhetoric and hermeneutics have overlapped from the classical period onward (Eden, Copeland), they increasingly are allied in recent years (Gadamer, Mailloux, Gaonkar, Leff) with neither the purpose nor effect of the alliance adequately analyzed. This alliance, fueled by increased studies in rhetorical criticism and rhetorical hermeneutics and by the disciplinary move of rhetoric from departments of communication to departments of literature, suggests the evolution of a new rhetoric removed from the practice of textual production within public spheres. Some welcome this change, but others from humanist, feminist, and compositionist perspectives try to modify the discipline's turn. Dilip Gaonkar and Michael Leff represent two positions on the new New Rhetoric.

In "The Idea of Rhetoric in the Rhetoric of Science," Dilip Gaonkar begins to analyze the causes and effects of the interpretive turn, arguing that the universalization of the concept of rhetoric, its transformation into

---

2. In a not unrelated protest, E. D. Hirsch writes that hermeneutics is used as "a rather vague, magical talisman" (*Aims* 19).

"a hermeneutic metadiscourse" from a once "substantive discourse practice," is a response to the epistemic crisis caused by the demise of foundationalism and serves to deflect our attention from "finding what motivates and steers rhetoric" (267). Given our distance from traditional rhetoric and our fatigue (I might also add confusion) over the promiscuous use of the term *rhetoric*, Gaonkar would have rhetoric function globally as a supplement added to other discourses and interpretive apparatuses.[3] In what is a complex procedure, he does not attend to "what motivates and steers rhetoric," at least historically; instead he promotes the hermeneutical turn, resisting a return to the rhetorical tradition because of its emphasis on an outdated "ideology of human agency" (275).[4]

Michael Leff's humanist response critiques Gaonkar's approach as transferring agency from the rhetor to the audience and "from the forum, the law-court, and the pulpit" to "the study, the lecture hall, and the library" ("Idea" 298). That is, Leff sees Gaonkar's stance on agency, the basis of his claim of distance from the tradition, as falling into a pattern similar to the one that I demonstrated in Fish's stance on intentions; agency is shuffled from one human to another, from author to audience, with no real evolution or critique of our understanding of agency or intersubjectivity. Leff defines the interpretive turn in rhetoric as a turn from the public sphere to an aesthetized, academic realm. While Gaonkar and Leff draw attention to the relationship between interpretation and agency in rhetoric, significant problems for contemporary rhetoric, neither moves the present debates along. They demarcate the existing territories within the debates over agency, interpretation, and rhetoric's meaning, but suggest neither new practices nor routes for returning to an older, political rhetoric.

I

Leff, Gaonkar, and so many others acknowledge Hans-Georg Gadamer's hermeneutics as a model with positive implications for interpretive rheto-

---

3. In graduate school, we called this the "sexy marriage": rhetoric and philosophy, rhetoric and science, rhetoric and linguistics, rhetoric and poststructuralism. The list is endless if one has a promiscuous mind.

4. Gaonkar does not take up either the arguments against agency or the arguments for agency. At this point in critical discussions, agency is making a comeback, and I work with the assumption that agency is a real possibility. For arguments in response to Gaonkar's omissions, consider Charles Altieri's *Subjective Agency*, Judith Keegan Gardiner's *Provoking Agents*, and Paul Smith's *Discerning the Subject*.

rics, and so it would seem that Gadamer's hermeneutics, its ontological focus, and his definition of its relationship to rhetoric is the place to start analyzing interpretation and intention.[5] In fact, with rare exception, theorists see ontological hermeneutics as the hermeneutics of our time as it offers a way to avoid the problematic claim of knowing another's mind or intentions, a way to avoid the agency fight and yet continue to interpret our interpretations.[6] For rhetoricians, Gadamerian hermeneutics offers a way of theorizing an attentive audience, what might be called "the good men listening well," and this is an important offering because the behavior of the audience has become a significant concern as rhetoric acknowledges pluralism within societies. All to the good, but I find that while hermeneutics is a profound theory of one type of interpretation, it is of limited use in understanding acts of interpretation within rhetorical situations.

Earlier hermeneutical theories accepted authorial agency and intention as significant if not the grounds for interpretation and were concerned about how we develop knowledge claims about the meanings offered by another. With the work of the Romantic hermeneut Friedrich D. E. Schleiermacher, who first developed a generalized theory of interpretation, intention became a psychological term; prior to that it meant an author's choice of genre, in meaning not unlike Hancher's programmatic intentions.[7] Schleiermacher included intention under technical interpretation, as suggestive of an author's individuality (the speaker's life process). His hermeneutics combined technical interpretation with textual, or what he calls grammatical, interpretation to create understanding. Understanding is more than textual exegesis and explaining another's thoughts; Schleiermacher expects an interpreter to know the author. He writes, "We must not only explain the words and the subject matter but the spirit of the author as well" (212). He even wishes us to put ourselves "inside" the author (64). In Romantic hermeneutics, interpreters need to

---

5. Gadamer's hermeneutics appears repeatedly in rhetoric and communication. See, for instance, Michael Hyde and Craig R. Smith's "Hermeneutics and Rhetoric," Kuan-Hsing Chen's "Beyond *Truth and Method*," or Alan Scult's "The Relationship between Rhetoric and Hermeneutics Reconsidered." See also *Rhetoric and Hermeneutics in Our Time* edited by Walter Jost and Michael Hyde.

6. For an overview of the differences among hermeneutics, see Michael Ermarth's "The Transformation of Hermeneutics." For less than idolizing readings of ontological hermeneutics, see Charles Altieri's "Toward a Hermeneutics Responsive to Rhetorical Theory," Richard L. Corliss's "Schleiermacher's Hermeneutics and Its Critics," and E. D. Hirsch's *The Aims of Interpretation*.

7. Georgia Warnke's *Gadamer: Hermeneutics, Tradition, and Reason* develops some of the history of the term *intention* within hermeneutics (20-25).

understand the forces, public and private, conscious and unconscious, motivating an author. They need to dwell in the author's subjectivity, but by closely considering the text itself, they also need to join that understanding with their grammatical or semantic understanding of the text. If the claim to knowing the other's spirit is a troublesome and unreal task, there is here at least the acknowledgment of the other, a suspicion of any easy meaning within interpretation, and a demand for real negotiation with alterity. And really there is no way of knowing the other without a recognition of the other's differing life and a serious attempt to represent the other as an object of knowledge well worth knowing. This struggle connects the concerns of Romantic hermeneutics with those of rhetoric. We speak across difference and *somehow* must come to share an understanding and an action with someone different than us. We may never reach that understanding or action, but that is our goal.

Twentieth-century hermeneutics has a very different focus. Its projects are less useful in conceiving rhetoric as deliberative and aimed at future action, though more useful in understanding the processes of the interpreter. Schleiermacher asks how is it we are able to understand one another by means of language; he puzzles over our psychological distances and offers a means, perhaps inadequate, of engaging the spirit of an alien text, author, culture. Ontological hermeneuts, such as Heidegger and Gadamer, ask about human being-in-the-word and human being-in-the-world, the context of understanding a text, and the type of reality we have as humans. They focus on the interpreter's acts of knowing herself, the world, and the text. So while diminishing the author's place in meaning-making, they articulate the process of interpretation from the interpreter's stance.

In *Truth and Method*, Gadamer critiques earlier hermeneutical traditions and builds his hermeneutics on the tradition of biblical hermeneutics and Heidegger's analysis of understanding as the practice of engaging a world and as a power for seeing one's possibilities for being. Hermeneutics in its Heideggerian manifestation does not describe understanding as related to the epistemological knowledge of meanings or others; there is little Romantic, intersubjective, or rhetorical about this approach. Rather, for Heidegger, understanding is grasping the possibilities for one's own being in one's own situation; all understandings are positional, situational, and historical and so based in "a fore-having, a fore-sight and a fore-conception" (199).[8] The emphasis on ontology places the emphasis on the

---

8. See Richard E. Palmer's *Hermeneutics* for an extended discussion of the place of Heidegger in relationship to Gadamer.

interpreter, the interpreter's life history, the contingencies of his situation, and the projective nature of his understanding—a move away from the rhetor, her life, and the contingencies of her situation. From Heidegger, Gadamer primarily takes an awareness that the knower and the known "both have the *mode of being of historicity*" (261, Gadamer's emphasis). He writes, "Thus there is no understanding or interpretation in which the totality of this existential structure does not function, even if the intention of the knower is simply to read 'what is there' and to discover from his sources 'how it really was' " (262).

Gadamer's second major influence, biblical hermeneutics, is also removed from direct concerns with intersubjectivity and, unlike Heidegger's ontological hermeneutics, refuses any relativistic reading. In the biblical tradition of hermeneutics, meaning is considered greater than any one human author or interpreter, and Truth is greater than any one piece (verse) of the whole (Bible), greater even than the whole of the text. It certainly outweighs any individual's intentions. As Platonic rhetorics do for rhetoric, biblical hermeneutics creates a countertradition concerned with truth-content rather than the situatedness of texts, authors, and audiences. Gadamer's belief in truth is an odd antidote to Heideggerian historicism, especially within the same theory: this is symptomatic of Gadamer's broader (and more problematic) notion of universal, though communicative truths and universals over and above individual situations. While the dual influences within his hermeneutics offer a path between relativism and objectivism, they do so with a transcendent turn.

Gadamer combines biblical hermeneutics' concerns with truth and the ontological concerns of Heidegger to develop the concept of understanding as truth seeking, the primacy of history and tradition, and a theory of language as universal. Intention does not disappear, but it operates only in the problematic. We move to understand intentions only when the truth-content of a claim is in question; only when we are forced to wonder and struggle to understand do we become concerned with constructing authorial intention.[9] Even then, the intentions of the author and our differences with a speaker are secondary to the text, the almost always *written* text. For Gadamer, interpretation becomes a conscious art only when the *text itself* raises questions, when we do not understand its culture, "when there is no powerful tradition present to absorb one's own attitude into itself and when one is aware of confronting an alien tradition to which he has never belonged or one he no longer unquestioningly accepts" (*Philosophical* 46).

---

9. See Warnke's *Gadamer* or Gadamer's *Truth and Method,* 292, 296, 334-36.

When the fluidity of reading freezes and the interpreter becomes aware of a text's alterity, Gadamer sees the next step of the "hermeneutically trained" interpreter as the foregrounding of her "own foremeanings and prejudices" so that she is aware of many of her prejudices (*Truth* 269-70). Recognizing that an interpreter always approaches a text or an event with foremeanings and prejudgments and that these prejudices are never fully objectifiable, Gadamer argues that in intentionally making conscious—as far as possible, as many as possible—her prejudices, the interpreter is able to move outside a familiar tradition, even to make the other's arguments stronger (292). He sees the interpreter as, first, belonging to history, and the interpreter's self-awareness "is only a flickering in the closed circuits of historical life" (276). Accordingly, we participate in the continued development of tradition, but it creates us and our understanding through "the interplay of the movement of the tradition and the movement of the interpreter" (293). He writes, "Hermeneutics must start from the position that a person seeking to understand something has a bond to the subject matter that comes into language through the traditionary text and has, or acquires, a connection with the tradition from which the text speaks" (295). At an obvious level this means that, to understand, we must come to share some tradition with a text through interplay (a hard point to dismiss), but problems remain for interpretations within rhetorical situations: the tradition may be in raw and pointed conflict to the reader's beliefs, or there may be the possibility of dangerous actions, stemming from misinterpretation or corrupt traditions. One might try to imagine the traditionary starting point of the abortion debates or attempts to make peace in the Middle East: it is possible, and it might be the strategy that best facilitates dialogue and deliberation, but these rhetorical projects—immediate, conflictatory, experiential, life threatening, and involving too many parties—are less easily imagined than the textual exegesis.

In sum, Gadamer's model of interpretation—emphasizing understanding (not action), texts (not rhetors and audiences), writing (not speech), tradition and prejudice (not change, future effects, and intention)—is useful but misleading to rhetorical efforts to theorize audience. The interpreter focuses on the text and forgets that the rhetor has his own intentions and perhaps explicit designs on her. Only when there is an interpretive problem or a truth problem does the interpreter question the intention of the rhetor. Otherwise, she puts or should put her prejudgments at risk to appropriate or, in Gadamerian terms, to apply the text's meaning. The true radicalness of Gadamer's hermeneutics is that, for understanding, he requires the interpreter to place her prejudices at risk; she must test them, since understanding is not about receiving data but rather requires participation in meaning. Meaning, then, is a fusion between the horizons (perspectives) of the historically placed interpreter and the text.[10] The interpreter, to understand, must be conscious of the historical horizon of the text and her present horizon, and the horizons must meet (waver, multiply, clash, shift, overlap) for understanding. Both horizons shift, but in the end, the unity value of the philosophical tradition, truth, remains intact.

As Georgia Warnke teaches, consensus, for Gadamer, usually signifies the formal agreement over meaning; it is a formal agreement *within* the interpreter, not a decision to act nor a persuasive moment between disputants (*Gadamer* 107-8). The interpreter comes to understand the text or object and appropriates that understanding into her self-understanding, modifying her prejudices. Consensus here is not a consensus to act, a political consensus. Rather it is a consensus of understanding within the audience of one: Gadamerian consensus is a very small unity, one with subjective, not public implications.

Without a doubt, Gadamer's supplanting of authorial intention with language and text begins a more complex theorizing of interpretation than exhibited in the work of literary rhetoricians. Even in severely limiting consideration of authorial intention, Gadamer's larger project, his conceptualization of understanding/misunderstanding is more intricate than the work of early Richards, Booth, and Fish, all of whom see meaning as defined in a single site, either author or community. Gadamer acknowledges understanding as a dialectic process, for him, closely allied to dialogue and necessarily more than the apprehension of authorial intention. Understanding is positional, based in the interpreter's position, but not that alone for position is not static. He writes:

> Not occasionally but always, the meaning of a text goes beyond its author. That is why understanding is not merely reproductive but always a productive activity as well. Perhaps it not correct to refer to this productive element in understanding as "better understanding." . . . It is enough to say that we understand in a *different* way, *if we understand at all.* (*Truth* 296-97)

Understanding exceeds the text and the author; the historicity of the interpreter is necessarily part of meaning, and consequently, interpretation is a *productive* activity, not one of simple reception, but one of *creation or invention* controlled by tradition.

---

10. Hear the echo here of Schleiermacher's grammatical and technical techniques.

For Gadamer, understanding, while not repetition, is "an act of repeating." He quotes August Boeckh's definition of understanding as "the knowing of the known" (*Philosophical* 45). Understanding is not reproductive, but re-*productive* of the authorities and prejudices that we bring with us as well as of the texts we read. Like the process of translation, the process of understanding involves encountering difference and yet still requires both continuity with and an enriched return to the initial language and culture. Gadamer rejects psychological models of meshing minds, models that Booth and early Richards posit for understanding and that Schleiermacher posits for a part of understanding. Rather than attributing understanding to "base psychic transposition," Gadamer, through Heidegger, attributes it to a "mode of being" common to the knower and the known—"i.e., they both have the *mode of being of historicity*" (*Truth* 261). To interpret, there must be a degree of commonality, a sharing of tradition, and a careful listening, but the degree of sharing is unclear, underdefined: is it historicity, or is it the certainty that we are temporal and cultural creatures (our ontological nature or generalized being), or is it also that we must share a tradition of understanding and culture? If we always speak across difference and yet share, what are the ratios between difference and sharing? Can all of the ratios generate meaning or understanding? These are the questions raised in Gadamer's shift away from models of matching minds and determinate communities, a significant move forward in articulating processes of understanding. We are left, perhaps necessarily, with inadequate understanding of the trip across difference—especially in the context of tradition and historicity.

At times, Gadamer writes as if interpreters could create dramatically different and significant meanings in their struggles toward the new position of understanding, but his dependence on the terms *history, tradition, authority,* and *prejudice* suggests a conservatism that interrupts some of his most dynamic descriptions of meaning-making.[11] The struggle between the historical given and creativity, stability and instability, is the essential tension of Gadamer's hermeneutics. He can seem to have a rich, traveling, social sense of tradition when he writes, "Tradition is not simply a permanent precondition: rather, we produce it ourselves inasmuch as we understand, participate in the evolution of tradition, and hence further

---

11. This problem is critiqued by Habermas and others. See *The Hermeneutics Reader,* edited by Kurt Mueller-Vollmer, for two of the key texts in the Gadamer-Habermas debate. Warnke's *Gadamer* is a stunning defense against the charge of conservatism. While it is not necessary for this chapter to consider whether his theory is, at the core, too conservative to meet postmodern critiques of meaning, I find it a continuing concern that keeps me from wholeheartedly embracing Gadamerian hermeneutics.

determine it ourselves" (293). Tradition here can be read as dialogic and multiplying, conceivably including splinters and divergences (though there are no radical voices in Gadamer's texts). Elsewhere its possibilities seem more limited, as when he asks us to be open and listen to the tradition, "to accept some things that are against me" (361). Or perhaps, more tellingly:

> *A person who reflects himself out of a living relationship to tradition destroys the true meaning of this tradition.* . . . In seeking to understand tradition historical consciousness must not rely on the critical method with which it approaches its sources, as if this preserved it from mixing its own judgements and prejudices. It must, in fact, think within its own historicity. (*Truth* 360-61)

The move to listen always to tradition echoes the move to assent within Booth's rhetoric; both ask interpreters to undertake the assent and risk that is so dangerous to audiences without traditional power.

Interpreters can risk prejudice, but audiences have to be very careful about what they risk. The question of when to risk prejudices is key for an audience. Gadamer attempts to address the dangers of this risk in his redemption of the terms *prejudice* and *authority* (271-85). Against the single-mindedness of the Enlightenment's rejection of prejudice, against the Enlightenment's prejudice against prejudice, Gadamer affirms prejudice as the basis of all judgment, not just false judgment, and so he argues that *"the prejudices of the individual, far more than his judgements, constitute the historical reality of his being"* (276-77). There is no self-construction through reason; rather, hermeneutics must distinguish legitimate prejudice—productive of knowledge—from dogma, partiality, and overhastiness. The key question here becomes what are the grounds of legitimate prejudice; after all, if we are to risk our prejudices, we must know how to weigh them. Gadamer's primary source for legitimating prejudice is authority—though not that authority as manifested in Enlightenment conceptions of obedience, but rather one of acknowledgment and knowledge. He does not discuss institutional authority, but rather sees authority as based on "an act of acknowledgement and knowledge—the knowledge, namely, that the other is superior to oneself in judgement and insight and that for this reason his judgment takes precedence—i.e., it has priority over one's own" (279). Gadamer sees the value of authority in our acceptance of our ignorance and incompleteness, our act of conceding "superiority in knowledge and insight to the authority" (*Philosophical* 33). But here his argument becomes circular: one's acknowledgment of authority reflects one's prejudices, and one's prejudices are grounded in acknowledged authority. We can only guess when it is wise to risk our prejudices and that guess is formed by our prejudices.

Gadamer gives short consideration to this problem, perhaps because of the civility of his discursive world. As Altieri points out ("Hermeneutics" 90), Gadamer works with a conversational model of discourse when, in fact, the intimate domain of conversation is a poor metaphor for public discourse. In writing about hermeneutical conversation, Gadamer repudiates the instrumental, rhetorical qualities of language. He writes, "finding a common language [in hermeneutical conversation] is not, any more than in real conversation, preparing a tool for the purpose of reaching understanding but, rather, coincides with the very act of understanding and reaching agreement" (*Truth* 388). The conversation, bare of tools, is civilized, a tearoom activity. In describing our actions as interlocutors, Gadamer avows that hermeneutical consciousness requires openness where "partners do not talk at cross purposes" (267). In effect, we are always in the act of understanding, never in the acts of negotiation or of asserting our differences. Nor do the conversations end in action. Gadamer calls for a priority of the question, the endlessly open question, and sees "the art of the questioning in the art of questioning ever further—i.e., the art of thinking." Audiences who have purposes contrary to those of the text and audiences who have purposes beyond thinking, passions and commitments beyond reason, may never seek or reach understanding (though they may be moved to recognize, reciprocate, and act). People who shout, cry, lie, demand, manipulate, shake their fists, and scapegoat others will not make it in the hermeneutical tearoom.

In premising conversations with texts and privileging them over disagreements between interlocutors, Gadamerian hermeneutics has a second problem for a rhetorical model of audience. Gadamer evades the rhetorical condition of encountering complexly intending, partisan, and/ or sophistic authors whose texts are manipulating lies, mixed messages, and/or dangerous ideology.[12] Rather than the sunlit horizon of a text, in a rhetorical situation audiences may meet an author bent on conflict and destruction rather than cooperation or one who desires consensus for particular purposes, stated or not, that would damage the audience's lives.

---

12. I do not want to diverge into the old orality-literacy debate, but it is important to note that Gadamer writes, "In writing, language gains its true ideality, for in encountering a written tradition, understanding consciousness acquires its full sovereignty. Its being does not depend on anything" (*Truth* 391). Pretty Cartesian, eh? And removed from the material consequences of understanding.

For example, though it is a historically interesting text to understand, should I want to risk my prejudices by listening to Rush Limbaugh (or for that matter Hitler)? Can I get at his meanings, under his meanings without considering his intentions, political supports, and rhetorical strategies? What of my values do I risk in the drive to understand? Gadamer asserts, "Transposing ourselves consists neither in the empathy of one individual for another nor in subordinating another person to our own standards; rather, it always involves rising to a higher universality that overcomes not only our own particularity but also that of the other" (305). The move to a higher universality, with all of its Platonic echoes, depends on the premise that there can be a position that bridges the gap between Limbaugh's misogyny and my feminism, a position, or universality, as yet not expressed.

The problem of the text that (or rather the rhetor who) is dangerous to the audience suggests a third problem in Gadamerian hermeneutics, a too-casual positing of chameleon interpreters who ground their prejudices on acknowledged authorities, who are able to undertake the political risk of their religion, gender identity, and political alliances, who are oblivious, at least momentarily, to issues of power differentials, and who have no grounds for reasoned refusal of some horizons. There is real optimism and too much finesse in separating interpretation and evaluation into discreet categories and hoping that interpretation can be, even momentarily, even in the ideal, separated from evaluation. Even small alterity, small differences evoked by grammars and in semantic fields, solicits positioning. Furthermore, in the case of conflict, audience members may evaluate the situation and its potential for evolving to favor their interests; they may decide to hold on to the prejudices, purposes, and discourses with which they began in resistance to or aggression against dominant traditions.[13] As many feminists have argued, dominant traditions are co-

---

13. The refusal of persuasion need not be the fantasy of not needing the other nor a belief in the myth of autogenesis. Refusing persuasion—that is, refusing to be a potential convert—can engage the other (as in a game of hard-to-get), produce group solidarity ("with us" or "against us"), or preserve difference (a move of ideological ecology). Civil disobedience does all three.

Obviously the refusal to enter a dialogue is a dangerous strategy, one that can benefit the status quo. Even so, if an audience's purposes are important (part of a life-world), then that audience might well refuse to risk prejudices due to misgivings about being entangled in the traditions of an other. For while biases and prejudices are not intentions, when an audience risks beliefs and speaks in cultures and terms not their own, that audience will necessarily produce textual evidence for intentions that are different than those she had prior to risking them. If I try to engage, let alone present Limbaugh's perspective, I give up the discursive space of my biases and my claims on aspects of the world.

Refusing to enter spheres of persuasion need not be so adversarial and separatist as presented

optive (Fetterley, Guinier, hooks, Rooney). Gadamer, however, does not recognize the value of maintaining difference and defines the very being of language as understanding, writing that "language has its true being only in dialogue, in *coming to an understanding*" (446). The role of language in identity or the accomplishment of purpose is not recognized. He has not acknowledged the degree to which giving assent to alternative prejudices places the interpreter's identity at risk and asks her to enter a sphere of alien, conceivably pathological discourses. If the text's alterity is too extreme (and what defines extremity?), the rhetorical audience, even with conscious recognition of its prejudices, may not be able to risk them in a horizon not understood, and perhaps in wisdom should not.

Finally, Gadamer's focus on prejudice is also problematic in that he privileges how the tradition of our formed prejudices affects our interpretations. He does not recognize adequately our intentions and plans and desires for a fantasized future as also affecting our interpretations and actions. Intentions, plans, and desires are not separate from our historicity, but they are allied with critiquing methods that Gadamer shuns. While we come with fore-havings, fore-sights, and fore-conceptions, within the process of acting in and upon the world via our engagements with others, we also intend to change aspects of the world. In the intersubjective process of transforming the world, consensus and fusion have different denotations than they do within Gadamer. While an audience's prejudices are not her intentions, the speech acts of engaging a rhetor's text with its own biases necessarily reveal an intentional process of knowing and owning the world.

All four of these problems, problems highlighting the difference between interpreters and audiences, circle the same issue: audiences often have to make a choice—*conscious or unconscious*—between a logic of assimilation and one of separation. Audiences necessarily make choices about the future they want, the people they will be, and the world they will inhabit. Choosing a logic of separation means making commitments to particular traditions, refusing to change one's considered beliefs, and resisting authorities, history, traditions, and countertexts in the struggle to maintain an identity and affiliations and in the hope that interlocutors will risk their prejudices, recognize alternative commitments, compromise in seeking support and reciprocity on other issues, and comprehend the

---

above. As well, the refusal of persuasion can be a short-term strategy (walking away from the bargaining table). In the case of the short-term strategy, both sides will be driven to engage by common needs or institutional affiliation (management-labor negotiations, Montgomery bus boycott).

nature, value, and spirit of alternative traditions. To deny assimilation does not mean that one denies commonalities or the possibility of acting in concert (though it may). Rather, the choice of separation can mean that the logic of assimilation and the forces pursuing assimilation threaten prejudices, traditions, and being that cannot be risked without irretrievable loss. Separation may signal a demand upon opponents to do the majority of the rhetorical and political work, or it may simply be a move to conserve energy, community, and possibility.

Still, for purposes of understanding the negotiation of meaning in rhetorical situations, there are many useful aspects of Gadamer's hermeneutics. Unlike the theories discussed earlier, Gadamer's makes a significant advance by placing meaning not in the author's intentions nor in the community nor even in the individual interpreter. Instead, meaning is a fusion of the horizons of the text and the interpreter, a negotiation controlled by an interpreter but still a defined process of negotiation and compromise. The fusion is potentially shifting as horizons change with the interpreter's perspective. The true radicalness of Gadamer's hermeneutics, the reason it can inform a rhetorical theory of audience intention (despite his lack of concern with intention), is that it recognizes interpreters' positions and traditions and shows that *the achievement of understanding requires interpreters to put their prejudices at risk*. As interpreters or as an audience seeking formal consensus on meaning, at least occasionally, we must stop critiquing the other's texts and stop defending our perspective and stop strategizing relationships with others and submit our intents, prejudices, purposes, plans, beliefs, and motives to other authorities. This token of listening and caring is an ideal for a society with freedom of speech and a commitment to justice: to encounter others, we must be better than we are.

Even so, rhetoric, descriptive of persuasion, action, power, and effect, must offer—always—a hermeneutics of suspicion.[14] The problem here, common to all theories of discourse, is that Gadamerian hermeneutics relates only partially to practice, a problem to which I return in later chapters where I ask whether audiences do submit their intentions, prejudices, purposes, plans, beliefs, and motives to other horizons; whether interpretations and deliberations, in practice, are truth seeking, or whether this model is too limited for application; and under what conditions are those adjustments made if horizons do, in fact, fuse. Gadamer

---

14. What Gadamer is missing is a hermeneutics of suspicion. He seems to be aware of this since he begins to address a hermeneutics of suspicion in an essay by that name, but he becomes more interested in phenomenology and doesn't develop the concept.

wants us to risk, even overcome our prejudices and be self-reflexive: Can we? To what degree? For what purposes? Whose purposes?

II

Before demonstrating the differences between rhetoric and hermeneutics, between a drive to action and a contemplation of meaning, I would like to review two major discussions of the relationship, Gadamer's and Mailloux's. Many critics, from Schleiermacher on, have premised the connection. I argue, however, that the tension posited between rhetorical hermeneutics and hermeneutical rhetoric exists within the *interpretive* frame of hermeneutics, not within the *productive* frame of rhetoric; the relationship is only analyzed from a hermeneutical perspective, and this makes the relationship an unhealthy one for rhetoric.[15]

For Gadamer, hermeneutics is never persuasion, the negotiation of different discourses, pedagogy, or rhetoric. Hermeneutics, an art, and rhetoric, a faculty, are significantly different. He defines hermeneutics as "the art of clarifying and mediating by our own effort of interpretation what is said by persons we encounter in tradition" (*Philosophical* 98), and he defines rhetoric as a "task" for philosophers: "to master the faculty of speaking in such an effectively persuasive way that the arguments brought forward are always appropriate to the specific receptivity of the souls to which they are directed" (21). According to Gadamer, these *two separate studies,* as well as sociology, are interdependent because of the universality of linguisticality, but they work synergistically. Because of his hermeneutical orientation and his concern with philosophy rather than action, Gadamer has a limited sense of rhetoric.[16] His theory of rhetoric, tied too closely to his Platonic concerns with interpretive truth and souls, is not a great aid to understanding deliberation, intersubjectivity, intentionality, instrumental uses of discourse, and social and discursive power. These are not his projects; he is, by his own acknowledgment, promoting a model of interpretive truth with minimal address to many familiar rhetorical con-

---

15. This priority is evident in both Mailloux's essay and Leff's response to Mailloux ("Hermeneutical Rhetoric"). See also George Pullman's introductory essay to the special issue of *Studies in the Literary Imagination* on rhetoric and hermeneutics. The rhetoricians in both these volumes, with the exception of Altieri, eagerly blend rhetoric into hermeneutics.

16. Gadamer writes, "My real concern was and is philosophic: not what we do or what we ought to do, but what happens to us over and above our wanting and doing" (*Philosophical* xxviii).

cerns, dismissing both "all the shallow claims put forward by the contemporary teachers of rhetoric" and modern rhetoric's concern with "organizing a perfect and perfectly manipulated information" (21, 25). Like Richards, he fears persuasion.

Still, Gadamer sees rhetoric as helpful to hermeneutics. In addition to their interdependence through language, Gadamer seeks to ally hermeneutics with rhetoric because of its priority, vigor, and practical nature. He writes:

> Thus the rhetorical and hermeneutical aspects of human linguisticality interpenetrate each other at every point. There would be no speaker and no such thing as rhetoric if understanding were not the lifeblood of human relationships. There would be no hermeneutical task if there were no loss of agreement between the parties of a "conversation" and no need to seek understanding. The connection between hermeneutics and rhetoric ought to serve, then, to dispel the notion that hermeneutics is somehow restricted to the aesthetic-humanistic tradition alone and that hermeneutical philosophy has to do with a "life of the mind" which is somehow opposed to the world of "real" life and propagates itself only in and through the "cultural tradition." (*Metacritical Comments* 280; see also *Philosophical* 25)

Gadamer's quotes around "conversation," together with his Platonic sense of a philosophical, truth-serving rhetoric are telling. As written earlier, this model does not suit rhetoric in its forensic, deliberative manifestations. In forensic and deliberative rhetorics, the "loss of agreement between the parties of a 'conversation' " may have little to do with a loss of meaning and understanding and far more to do with diverging political and social purposes. In contradiction, what Gadamer wants from rhetoric is " 'real' life," to allow hermeneutical philosophy to escape the library and the parlor. He wants the conversation and understanding together with " 'real' life" without a wrestle in the Scramble, lie, and injury. But to even suggest that hermeneutics has " 'real' life" makes hermeneutics dependent on rhetoric, which must then precede and teach hermeneutics. Gadamer writes, "hermeneutics may be precisely defined as the art of bringing what is said or written to speech again. What kind of an art this is, then, we can learn from rhetoric" (*Reason* 119).[17]

17. See also *Philosophical Hermeneutics* (21-26) and "Rhetoric and Hermeneutics." In "Rhetoric and Hermeneutics," Gadamer links the development of hermeneutics during the

If ultimately Gadamer's differentiation of rhetoric and hermeneutics proves useful in suggesting the effeminate, limited nature of the institutionalized version of each and in asking how a definition of one limits the terms of the other, then Mailloux's rhetorical hermeneutics, so bare of differentiation as to make rhetorical hermeneutics simply a repetition of synonyms, emphasizes the difficulties of understanding deliberation within the collapse. Despite his rich, careful readings in *Rhetorical Power* of Starwar politics and nineteenth-century debates about *Huckleberry Finn,* Mailloux's theory is not particularly helpful in regaining a deliberative sense of rhetoric; his is a case where a rich practice based in political debates and startlingly sharp readings of controversial texts remains tied to the theories of literary criticism—despite his affiliations with rhetorical theory. In delineating and accentuating interpretive aspects of rhetoric, he deletes the rhetorical tradition of textual production, a move that is surprising in light of his definition of rhetoric as "the political effectivity of trope and argument in culture" ("Articulation" 379). Despite its seeming concern with rhetorical effect in politics and argumentation, this definition emphasizes the cultural effect of and audience response to a text and ignores the rhetor's activity of purposeful production. Mailloux's interest in studying historically based arguments ultimately evades the rhetorical tradition of teaching individuals "the available means of persuasion." If the rhetorical theorist is always the observer or interpreter of rhetorical exchanges, the observations are of text and cultural effect, how a text is interpreted, and not the traditional rhetorical observations of what the rhetor can do to *produce* a desired effect, a specific action. This small shift has significant implications.[18]

In "Articulation and Understanding," Mailloux outlines a collapsed relationship between rhetoric and hermeneutics by defining them as synony-

---

Reformation to the ancient, medieval, and humanistic traditions of rhetoric. In arguing for their connections, he fully acknowledges the loss of democratic practices during much of the period under discussion but fails to analyze how that effects his understanding of rhetoric or limits the connections between deliberative rhetorics and hermeneutics.

18. In conversation, Sue Wells made the excellent point that this has everything to do with the professional location of rhetorical work. Because traditional rhetorical observations can only be made in a social situation that offers, potentially, all speech roles to all speakers, there is little reason to be critical or analytic outside of production (and in a way, production is the best critique). But if the chance to produce a desired effect is asymmetrically distributed, then there is every reason for people to know how to analyze texts that they will never produce (e.g., the Pentagon papers). The question, for Wells, is how interpretive rhetoricians, such as Mailloux, do this in the absence of historicizing the *theory* (even if their interpretations are historically situated, their theoretical practices are not).

mous. I would like to look at his definition and analyze where he is too facile in allying the theories and practices of rhetoric and hermeneutics, or rather than too facile, where he is too concerned with interpretation and insufficiently concerned with production to define a rhetoric that allows for deliberation and action.

Mailloux begins the definitions by writing that the

> traditions of rhetoric and hermeneutics address very practical tasks. Hermeneutics deals with interpretation focused on texts, and rhetoric deals with figuration and persuasion directed at audiences. Interpretation can be defined as the establishment of textual meaning, while rhetoric (as figuration and persuasion) might be characterized more pointedly as the political effectivity of trope and argument in culture. ("Articulation" 379)

So far so good, his emphasis on trope as particularly significant to rhetoric is odd, but not outside of traditions (Ramus, belletristic, French). Mailloux continues:

> Interpretation involves the *translation* of one text into another, a Hermeslike mediation that is also a *transformation* of one linguistic event into *another*, later one. Rhetoric involves the *transformation* of one audience into *another*, which is also a psychogogic *translation* from one position to a different one. (379, emphasis added)

Here we have more trouble. I have emphasized "translation," "transformation," and "another" because the words are clearly shifting dramatically in meaning as their context shifts. As a matter of textual play this is pretty, but as a logical system it falters.

The first "translation" is the dictionary definition: "to interpret, to put into different words or different language" (*Webster's Unabridged Dictionary* 1972). This definition is supported by Mailloux's appeals to "Hermes" and "mediation." That is, if translation is not a simple worldly process, it is about messages and bridging or bringing meanings. The second "translation" corresponds not so much to words but rather to positionality; it corresponds to a dictionary definition coupled with *transfer* (bear across), such as "to convey to heaven," "to transfer (a bishop) from one see to another," "to move a saint's body or relic." By Mailloux's own word choice, the translation of the audience is physical and spiritual, and so involves a different realm of action than the discursive moves of interpretive translation.

The meaning of "transformation . . . into another" does not so dramatically change by the sentence context as does "translation," but rather what is transformed and by how much is the issue. The "linguistic event" is transformed into "another, later one," and probably a different one, but that is not a requirement of his statement. Given the pun (purposeful?) on transformative grammar and the strong tradition of "tradition" from which Mailloux is working, it is unclear as to how much the discourse can be transformed (and by whom); it is clear, however, that the text is passive. As required by the parallel structure, the audience transformation is also passive, according to Mailloux. That is, the audience, potentially many people, can be made into another group of people. This equation of persuasion with immediate psychological change is appealing (as are its implications for work with deans, legislators, and tenure committees), but any real discussion of transformations of audiences needs more nuance. Mailloux's premise of the passive audience reveals the degree of his commitment to avoiding issues of intentionality, agency, and deliberation, but obviously theories of passive audiences do not reveal much about deliberative processes and have been problematized by rhetoricians since Gorgias played at defending passive Helen.

The definition intermingling rhetoric and hermeneutics continues with fewer difficulties but still collapses the two activities and erases key differences:

> As practices, rhetoric and interpretation denote both productive and receptive activities. That is, interpretation refers to the presentations of a text in speech—as in oral performance—and the understanding or exegesis of a written text; similarly, rhetoric refers to the production of persuasive discourse and the analysis of a text's effects on an audience. (379)

The point here, that rhetoric and hermeneutics both engage processes of production and reception, is not controversial. The controversy lies in the degree to which production and reception characterize each and the degree to which any type of production or reception is similar in the context of rhetor and audience purposes. So, is "oral performance" (a recitation or production of *Hamlet*) really the same "interpretation" that Mailloux means by "hermeneutics," or is "oral performance" only a somewhat related concept that is particular to dramatic, presentational aspects of meaning-making? Even if we relate presentation (memory and delivery) to rhetoric, the tradition of rhetoric describes five parts (invention, arrangement, style, memory, delivery), and so the production that he associates with interpretation is a thin production, one scant of rhetorical invention, arrangement, and style though full of memory and delivery. Mailloux is accurate in describing rhetoricians as analyzing the effectiveness of their discourse, but is this the same reception that hermeneutics describes? Hermeneutics is a theory not about the effect on an audience, but about the truth-seeking approach of an educated interpreter. Furthermore, rhetoricians analyze and understand effects on audiences as well as the nature of the audiences themselves, focusing on them; among rhetoricians' purposes is always an instrumental one, a pointing to further persuasions, conceivably mutual, and to further productions. On the other hand, I can understand a text, especially a literary text, and have no purpose beyond pleasure or dalliance, no public task at least.

Our man Mailloux continues:

> *In some ways* rhetoric and interpretation are practical forms of the same extended human activity: rhetoric is based on interpretation; interpretation is communicated through rhetoric. (379, emphasis added)

This is a true, but trivial connection; linguistic behaviors are a large but finite, related set of actions. I argue that the ways in which rhetoric and hermeneutics differ as human activities are more revealing of language use and abuse. Mailloux then concludes this section of the essay, writing:

> Furthermore, as reflections on practice, hermeneutics and rhetorical theory are mutually-defining fields: hermeneutics is the rhetoric of establishing meaning and rhetoric is the hermeneutics of problematic linguistic situations. When we ask about the meaning of a text, we receive an interpretive argument; when we seek the means of persuasion, we interpret the situation. As theoretical practices, hermeneutics involves placing a text in a meaningful context, while rhetoric requires the contextualization of a text's effects. (379)

He has shifted here from the word "interpretation" to "hermeneutics," from "rhetoric" to "rhetorical theory." The earlier connections of practice, which I show are problematic, are now extended into theory and the fields' disciplinary manifestations. There is a large literature, dating back to Schleiermacher, which stakes a claim that all interpretation is the province of the theoretical field of hermeneutics. There is a large literature which stakes a claim that all texts, even all symbol systems, are rhetorical. Yet in moving to theory, Mailloux has diluted his argument of their connection: lots of interpretation happens without the "we" requesting an interpretive argument; lots of symbolizing gets done without the "we" interpreting the situation with any consciousness or efficacy. Hermeneutics may require argument; interpretation does not. Furthermore, saying that any use of argument is rhetorical is not the same as saying hermeneutics is uniquely or particularly related to rhetoric. With that line of thinking, any argument on any topic makes the topic itself into rhetoric. An argument about dinner does not make dinner into rhetoric; an argument about meaning does not make meaning into rhetoric.

Even if one concedes that hermeneutics is argument is rhetoric, rhetoric, not necessarily rhetorical theory, is always more than "the hermeneutics of problematic linguistic situations." Aspects of rhetoric and rhetorical theory are based in interpretations of "problematic linguistic situations," with rhetoric designated here as the production of an interpretation, and rhetorical theory designated here as the analysis of the ethics, consideration of approaches to the situation, and probable outcome from different approaches. Rhetoric, however, continues long after we interpret the situation: that is, there is a process that may begin in an interpretation, but it continues in the inventing, arrangement, styling, and delivering of a response. Furthermore, I suspect one can make too easy an argument for rhetorical situations as encompassing more than linguistic situations, starting with the example of the *Titanic* and working up to armed robberies and bad dates.

Finally, I am unsure as to what the last sentence of the above quote means: "As theoretical practices, hermeneutics involves placing a text in a meaningful context, while rhetoric requires the contextualization of a text's effects." The "placing a text in meaningful context" may be hermeneutics as a variation of Gadamer's fusion of horizons, that is, the text is meaningful and understandable within an interpreter's historical context. But I am less sure of what is entailed when rhetoric needs "the contextualization of a text's effects." I believe, because of Mailloux's affection for rhetorical hermeneutics and the parallelism of his argument, that this is an argument for historical readings of rhetoric, for historically based rhetorical criticism as the basis of rhetorical theory. But this is only one model of rhetoric. Aristotle did just fine without an explicitly historical approach; in fact, he set up a couple-thousand-year tradition using some second-rate psychology and the close analysis of texts (tropes, syllogism, and topics).

And rhetoric, as opposed to rhetorical theory, has to do with practices, not just readings of a text's effects.

Mailloux's collapsing of rhetoric and hermeneutics has implications for much of rhetorical theory, implications for its canon, methods, theories of agency, writing and speaking pedagogy, institutional housing, and so on. Unlike Gadamer, who posits rhetoric and hermeneutics as connected by their focus on language but separated by their distinctions, which may be inadequate but are still distinctions, Mailloux offers a more passive rhetoric than we should accept. He offers a rhetoric in which one does not speak, but is spoken.

III

It is my belief that we learn more about rhetoric and hermeneutics from the difficult task of differentiating them than from that of collapsing them. If we follow Gadamer in perceiving interpretation as a re-production with the emphasis on production, creation, and invention, and if we want to differentiate rhetoric from hermeneutics, it is potentially productive to start with the differences between rhetorical invention and hermeneutical invention. I suspect there are many productive places to explore their differences, but let's start at the rhetorical start (with the first of the five parts of rhetoric).

What are the processes of inventing a text within rhetoric and hermeneutics? Given the long history of each, rather than attempt a long discussion comparing and contrasting each of the traditions, I turn to a site in no way simpler but certainly more accessible, our everyday language. As Mailloux's difficulties demonstrated, connecting rhetoric and hermeneutics is a complex task; the concepts are broad, and the language slips. The differences in invention, so very hard to describe and argue for, are suggested within our grammar. We can get a sense of these differences by probing the limited use of *invent* in everyday language and how we paraphrase it in application. Who would announce, "I have invented an understanding"? Is it odder than to say, "I've invented an interpretation"? What would that mean? Is it as odd to say, "I've invented a speech" or "I've invented a poem" or "I've invented a solution" or "I've invented a computer that invents interpretations and speeches"? The last claim, scientific invention, is the ordinary claim within language, but not the ordinary action: while we may rarely claim to create a new mechanism, we constantly invent—in many ways—discursive forms. When we hear "I've invented a computer," we know that the speaker claims to have produced something that did not exist before, usually a machine, but not always so; it is unusual but understandable to say "late last night, in my laboratory, I invented a new polymer chemical" or "I'm going to patent the organism I invented." Newness and complexity are part and parcel with scientific invention; we know scientific invention by its requirement of "origins" and originality. Alternately, because inventing discourse or a response to discourse is not part of our ordinary language and doesn't have such a stake in originality, we are less sure what it means to invent discourse. Unlike scientific invention, it is a daily act, but we know it less well. Discursive "invention" is jargon, and like all jargon, it is useful at times and obfuscating at others.

Even so, one does have some idea of how to respond to the jargon with ordinary language. One might correct a foreigner who claimed to invent a speech or poem with the paraphrase "I made up a speech" or "I wrote a poem." One would understand here that the foreigner formulated words and ideas in some new order, maybe she even created a new word in her poem or found a striking metaphor. We might accept her claim to "invent" a new word ("I invented a word") because of the newness of the single word and its demonstrable origin in her poem, but her claim to have invented a metaphor would puzzle us more, in part because the words in a metaphor are not original, they existed within us, within our vocabulary, and we do not know how to assess her claim against the requirement of origin or novelty. At this point, we give up the requirement of origin or novelty to the event, recognizing that in her claim of inventing speeches or poems there is no necessary surprising novelty, only the novelty of every utterance in a differing context. We paraphrase for her that "the speech is made up" or "the poem is written." The words themselves have no demonstrable origin (the *Oxford English Dictionary* aside). In our corrections, there is no suggestion of how those words might relate to other words or texts or history, either the foreigner's words, history, or text or ours. Inventing a speech might easily in this sense include responding to another's speech with the invention of a counterexample, another story in support or opposition, or a discussion of its logical fallacy, but that would not make us place the foreigner's claim of invention in a different pile than if she began with her own facts, story, or logic.

The foreigner's inventing of these texts can be explained by rhetorical invention, whether by the type found in Aristotle's *Topica* or that found in a freshman handbook. The foreigner's claim doesn't suggest much about her theory of rhetorical invention. Hers might be a sophistic invention drawn from a moment caught in the flux between *dissoi logoi*. Or with equal plausibility, it might be an Aristotelian act of invention, where her ideas were shared with a community and simply recalled and arranged to effect the community's judgments. Or it might be an invention explained by any number of other theories; theories from Cicero to cognitive science to Barthes could be applied. The significant finding here: "to invent a speech" is to make it up in some way that does not explicitly duplicate other speeches, and inventing speeches is explainable in existing theories of rhetorical invention. We do not need to decide which theory to recognize it as rhetorical invention.

What is meant in the cases of "inventing understanding" or "inventing interpretations" is far less clear because they move us further away from what invention means in both ordinary language and traditional rhetorical jargon. In the case of interpretation, to correct the foreigner and say, "I made up an interpretation" or "I wrote an interpretation" is not to claim an original form for one's words, but rather to acknowledge one's words as responding to a *particular* text or set of texts. One might well ask the foreigner, "What did you interpret?" and she might reply, "I interpreted a line from *Hamlet*" or "I did a feminist reading of Shakespeare's tragedies." To say "I invented an interpretation" is, in effect, to claim a paraphrase or (and here's the rub) a reading of an extant text.

To claim a paraphrase is to claim hermeneutical invention, though a small and questionable one. Still, to paraphrase honestly is to put one's prejudices at risk. To claim a reading, however, is to claim an action that exists on a continuum between hermeneutics and rhetorical invention or at a site of their interactivity. If the foreigner has fused her horizon with that of the text, she has acted as a hermeneut. If the foreigner has responded to a particular text but is claiming to have formulated words and ideas in some new order unrecognized before (at least by her), she may be, as a resisting reader or a critic, moving out of the hermeneutical realm and into the rhetorical. Maybe she has found an extension of metaphor or a contradiction in the text that lets her voice a new insight persuasively, or maybe she has only extended the metaphor as the author intended, or maybe she has simply put her prejudices at risk and moved toward the text in a way she couldn't have before the hermeneutical moment.

In this intersection between our everyday language and professional jargon, hermeneutical invention is a mediation that produces something, but the emphasis is on mediation, not production. The foreigner's intentions are necessarily part of, but subordinate to those in the text. She works well from a dictionary and a grammar book, and according to most hermeneuts, she probably can go so far as exegesis or explanation without entertaining novelty and rhetoric.[19] The paraphrasing foreigner, taking care with her words, her syntax, and ultimately her meaning, tries not to elaborate the text, and in that failure to elaborate and risk her prejudices, she may not even have what philosophers would call understanding; she certainly buries her old prejudices and future intentions. The hermeneutically inventing foreigner risks her old prejudices to the horizon of the text: the meanings of the text and of the foreigner shift and fuse. The rhetorically inventing foreigner, suspicious of the text, full of her own intentions, reads with resistance and produces a meaning that allows her to take action. Rhetorical invention, too, is a mediation that produces something, but the emphasis is on production, not mediation. The foreigner's intentions are foregrounded as prejudices to be played out; what was a concern with the past, tradition, and prejudgments becomes a concern with intentions and future actions.

In *Inventions of Reading: Rhetoric and the Literary Imagination*, Clayton Koelb explicates this mode of reading, what he calls "rhetorical construction" and what others might characterize as "an aggressive form of interpretation imposing on innocent texts a reading that is 'invented' in the sense of being made up out of the critic's head with no thought given to what the texts themselves intend" (ix). Koelb connects rhetorical reading as invention to construction and use; the nature of textual production from the reading, though not the effect of the production, defines the act as rhetorical. Koelb sees the possibility of readings as infinite, but he sees rhetorical readings as defined within a rhetorical tradition of construction and use, deliberation and difference, and not in the tradition of resolution or fusion of positions (244). Reading is invention, but not all reading is rhetorical invention.

If we return to the street corner where we left the by-now-confused foreigner and her need to "invent an understanding," we leave discussions of rhetorical invention and enter the realm of hermeneutics, for inventing understanding is hermeneutical invention. In Gadamerian hermeneutics, the interpreter stops interrogating and manipulating the text and allows the text to interrogate his prejudices and intentions and finally to be applied in his present situation. For Gadamer, all interpretation is necessarily prejudiced, even the careful paraphrase, and there is no objective standard for an interpretation, not authorial intention, God's word, or scientific method, but neither *interpretation* nor *understanding* is a matter of free play or subjective opinion. Understanding that includes

---

19. Schleiermacher would place explanation under the art of presentation, though Gadamer would not. See Richard E. Palmer's *Hermeneutics*, 187.

interpretation also requires *application* or assimilation to our present, a fusion with our horizon. Understanding requires that the text become part of our being. He writes:

> Where there is understanding, there is not translation but speech. To understand a foreign language means that we do not need to translate it into our own. When we really master a language, then no translation is necessary—in fact, any translation seems impossible. Understanding how to speak is not yet of itself real understanding and does not involve an interpretive process. . . . Mastering the language is a necessary precondition for coming to an understanding in conversation. (*Truth* 384-85)

And dialogue with a text, given common sharing and open questioning, is the basis of Gadamer's hermeneutics, a basis which requires that interpreters put at risk their intentions.

The invention of discourse then has many modes, and the two strongest poles are defined (1) by the interpreter's intentions, privileged in rhetorical invention and diminished in hermeneutical invention and (2) by the interpreter's prejudices, risked in hermeneutical invention and accepted in rhetorical invention. A rhetorical theory of intention needs to recognize the meanings invented by an audience, an audience unlikely to be committed to ontological hermeneutics.

Rhetoric's increasing affiliation with textual reception, specifically Gadamer's hermeneutics, while increasing concern with discourse and text and presenting a nascent theory of audience intentions, potentially *diminishes* many aspects of textual production, aspects of rhetoric such as the interactions and negotiations of meaning and intentions between rhetor and audience, cultural processes of deliberation and the resulting productions, formal aspects of the text, the contingency and immediacy of the rhetorical situation, the instrumental and subversive qualities of discourse, and the power dynamics, ethical and unethical, in any rhetorical interaction. If rhetoric comes "from the forum, the law-court, and the pulpit," these aspects of rhetoric must be articulated.

3

Kenneth Burke on Form, Motive, and Purpose

> *Maybe the most fascinating thing about our relationship to Kenneth Burke is the clever way in which we have managed to consistently avoid him while seeming always to pay homage to his work.*
> —Frank Lentricchia,
> "Reading History with Kenneth Burke"

If literary rhetoricians evade the traumas of argumentation by placing intentions in either the rhetor or the audience, and if most tracts on the relationship between hermeneutics and rhetoric serve to emphasize hermeneutics and interpretation of texts, not deliberation and intersubjectivity, and to describe interpreters and not audiences (or critics), where can rhetoric turn for alternative discourses and models that address the complexity of competing intentions, institutional cultures, argumentative strategies, and the power differentials between communicators? There are two answers to this question. One, it is clear that no single source could examine all these aspects of interpretation and present a full-blown theory of intentionality, and in fact, many studies of practice will be necessary to develop models of intentionality and interpretation that are truly rhetorical. Two, despite the complexity of the undertaking, twentieth-century rhetoric itself already has models implicit in existing theories that with a bit of nuance and addition could be very helpful in augmenting the limited vocabulary we have for discussing competing intentions.

We've met the antagonists; Kenneth Burke is my prime protagonist. His theories of grammar, rhetoric, and symbol provide a vocabulary common to rhetoricians as well as a rhetorical orientation to interpretation. Burke, after all, begins with the premise that "all organisms are critics in the sense that they interpret the signs about them" (*Permanence* 6), and then approaches the act of interpretation from particularly rhetorical perspectives. Burke, no textualist, from *Counter-Statement* on, explores our desire to affect others and the power dynamics within those effects, and in doing so, he explicitly acknowledges rhetoric as political and social action. While he sometimes toys with the safe, tropological, patroller-of-WASP-boundaries rhetoric of Richards and even the head-nodding-masses rhetoric of Fish, and while, like Gadamer, he is conscious of the mystical and our situatedness, his interpretive procedures are suspicious of easy meaning, concerned with the risks inherent in meaning-making, and aware of the functions and powers of identification and alienation.

Burke's theories of interpretation both respect the multiplicity of possible meanings for the audience and the rhetor and acknowledge the social contracts, bargains, and betrayals within meaning. He is sensitive to the latent messages within texts and is well aware that authorial intentions are complex and not easily accessible, even to the author. According to Burkean hermeneutics, we flourish in self-deceptions and are fed by the resources of identifications and scapegoating. He, for instance, would understand that simply saying one is in favor of democracy and dialogue is not the same as supporting pluralistic processes and the multiple intentions of each subject. Burke writes:

> By charting clusters, we get our clues as to the important ingredients subsumed in "symbolic mergers." We reveal, beneath an author's "official front," the level at which a lie is impossible. If a man's virtuous characters are dull, and his wicked characters are done vigorously, his *art* has voted for the wicked ones, regardless of his "official front." If a man talks of *glory* but employs the imagery of *desolation,* his *true subject* is desolation. (*Attitudes* 233)

> The shepherd, *qua* shepherd, acts for the good of the sheep, to protect them from discomfort and harm. But he may be "identified" with a project which is raising sheep for market. (*Rhetoric* 27)

Burke reminds us that if a man speaks of multiple purposes and horizons but reifies tradition and authority, or if a man speaks of "new millions of participants" but fears misunderstanding, his commitment to diverging ideas is limited and his "true subject" may well be control and subjugation. Burke expects the audience to be vigilant and to have intentions of their own that should be used to expose lies and paradoxes in a rhetorical text and then used again to offer their own counterstatements with their own lies.

Given Burke's awareness of subtexts and the diverging purposes within and between author and audience, his own chaotic, ironic, and sometimes paradoxical writings have a unique significance in that he leaves us little able to answer the question of what is his explicit or latent message. He plays and gives us space to find ourselves in him. A chosen chaos cloaks his intentions, makes it difficult to put one's own prejudices at risk, and facilitates putting one's own intentions to the fore. To write on Burke is to play with the possibilities of his text and your text.

I

The first possibility in need of play is the possible meaning of rhetoric within Burke's corpus, since it is not a static concept, nor for that matter is it just one concept. For while Burke once made the parlor conversation a metaphor for human life, a conversational model of being not unlike Gadamer's, he usually offers a tougher, more purpose-driven process of communication. At his most Aristotelian, he defines rhetoric as *"the use of language as a symbolic means of inducing cooperation in beings that by nature respond to symbols"* (*Rhetoric* 43, Burke's emphasis). This definition, so unlike Gadamer's Platonic rhetoric and Mailloux's hermeneutical rhetoric, is highly instrumental in two aspects. One, he sees rhetoric as rooted not in society or history, but rather *"rooted in an essential function of language itself"* (43, Burke's emphasis). One of language's functions is to be "used" as a "means"; it is a tool to be picked up and employed by a purposeful being (consciously or unconsciously). The potential for "induced" cooperation is part and parcel of the symbolic actions of speaking and listening, writing and reading. The second aspect of rhetoric's instrumentality has to do with Burke's beings and their relationship to persuasion. Any language-user has an audience (at least herself), empowered and endangered by compulsions to respond to symbols, but the nature of the response is not a given. Multiple discourses, varying terminologies, different dramas, and ratios between terms all contribute to the response and create choices of response. Burke writes, "Persuasion involves choice, will; it is directed to a man only insofar as he is *free*. . . . Only insofar as men are potentially free, must the spellbinder seek to persuade them" (50).[1] Faced with the audience's ability to choose their purposes and actions, the effective rhetor, the rhetor who achieves cooperation, must recognize the variety of purposes and the forces favoring particular choices, and she must speak strategically.

This is Burke's traditional rhetoric, an almost disciplined rhetoric, but he also sees rhetoric as sophistic and from that perspective offers a street-talk, political-animal rhetoric. Despite the possibility of induced cooperation, rhetoric is "the region of the Scramble, of insult and injury, bickering, squabbling, malice, and the lie" and well as the region of "sacrificial, evangelical love," "sexual love," and "technologized," "desexualized" communication (or love) (19). That is, rhetoric is our intersubjectivity; for better and worse, it represents our gentle and brutal connections to others and offers us a way to make those connections peaceful.[2] Somehow Burke believes, despite all of rhetoric's distractions, perversions, and incarnations, that "[t]he *Rhetoric* must lead us through the Scramble, the Wrangle of the Market Place, the flurries and flare-ups of the Human Barnyard, the Give and Take, the wavering line of pressure and counterpressure, the Logomachy, the onus of ownership, the Wars of Nerves, the War" (23). Not the *Symbolic*, not the *Grammar*, but the *Rhetoric* is Burke's promise of a peaceable kingdom. The poetic and analytic are important, but the rhetoric creates our path through culture and the material.[3] Because it is "a

---

1. Burke sees "'the desire for freedom of motion' as a fundamental disposition of men (as might be expected of an organism that lives by locomotion)" (*Permanence* 226). One, however, would be very mistaken to see Burke as a proponent of bourgeois individualism, as Fredric Jameson does. I would characterize Burke's agent as so entangled in the drama as to be almost inextricable. It is revealing that Burke uses the term *agent*, implying agency, but does not go as far as the terms *actor* or *subject*, and consequently, one must ask, whose agent? The potential for choice and agency, in Burke, is created by delineating terministic forces in the forming of a choice. Lentricchia (*Criticism*) is very good on this.

Even in his last book, *The Rhetoric of Religion*, where Burke is more skeptical about the potential for choice and the existence of will, he is still concerned with the structures of will/determinism, order/disorder, and obedience/disobedience, fascinated by the grammatical problems that these terms present, and he still refuses to close out a space for choice (see, e.g., 183-96). I think Cary Nelson, by his own admission, "misreads" later Burke and posits an agent too written by the discourse, probably because he doesn't engage Burke's writing on the biological human and underappreciates the significance of paradox for Burke.

2. Burke is, after all, a man who lived through two world wars.

3. It is interesting that Lentricchia critiques Burke as being too poetic and insufficiently material in his approach to the concept of rhetoric. I share this concern, but among twentieth-

partisan weapon," a tool for both identification and division, Burkean rhetoric is our engagement with each other: the meanings of our utterances almost less consequential than the act of engagement and the negotiation of our purposes and effects.

For these reasons, Burke would not share Gadamer's disdain for a rhetoric concerned with "perfect and perfectly manipulated information" (*Philosophical* 21, 25), but rather would engage and analyze the perfect control, wonder at its sadomasochistic love, and figure out how to escape its malice and lies. He might lump it with "propaganda-indoctrination-authoritarianism," but he would know it as a force to be recognized, used, and opposed in democratic deliberations.[4] He wants it as part of the dialogue, part of "the employment of the possibilities of linguistic transformation" (*Grammar* 402). For Burke, even self-interested give-and-take can be a basic part of making both knowledge and the just society. He writes:

> I take democracy to be a device for institutionalizing the dialectic process by setting up a political structure that gives full opportunity for the use of competition to a cooperative end. . . . I should contend that the dialectic process *absolutely must* be unimpeded, if society is to perfect its understanding of reality by the necessary method of give and take. (*Philosophy* 328)

Burke's concept of dialectic, here explicitly linked to democratic processes and deliberations, is not limited to a dialectic of opposing concepts, but rather it includes a materialist dialectic, the symbolic and the real. The democratic process here leads to unity as an end, but unlike the troubling unity of liberal democracy, Burke's end is more the end of shared experience, a phenomenological end, and less the end of unified action. Exactly because hierarchy, manipulation, symbolic transformation, and scapegoating are such concerns, Burke would not posit consensus as other than linked to competition, and he would base the overcoming of difference in shared biology. Throughout the chapter, I develop Burke's dialectical relationship between bodily experience, "animality," and language, "sym-

---

century rhetorical theorists, Burke is among the most involved with deliberation and politics. See Greig E. Henderson for a developed argument for Burke as a cultural critic. Robert Wess provides an extended, "Marxoid" analysis of the evolution of Burke's approach to history, politics, and the material, from *Counter-Statement* to *The Rhetoric of Religion*.

4. Burke is fairly clear on this point in "Growth among the Ruins" in *The Philosophy of Literary Form*, especially 443–47.

bolicity," as the basic characteristic of humanity and the nature of our access to a reality.[5] For now, however, it is enough to acknowledge Burke's rhetoric for its valuing of suspicion within interpretation, instrumentality among the symbolics, and the competitive/cooperative tension within language.

II

Burke does not write at any length about authorial or audience intention, which is not to say that he has no interest in intentions.[6] He defines rhetoric and persuasion as based in the possibility of choosing, presuming purpose, and the interactivity between an audience, rhetor, text, and context (no simple textualist, Burke). His interest in intention, however, is largely played out in other terms: *form* or *structure*, *motive*, and *purpose*. The multiplicity of terms and the different perspectives they offer on instrumental language and human agency allow Burke to give intention a very complex analysis and position in rhetorical discourse. Rather than placing intention in the will of a single subject, he understands intentional states as deeply entangled in and limited by discourses and culture. Consequently, he can be read as approaching the concept from three perspectives. Structure or form suggests purposes within the structures and

---

5. The literature on Burke's concept of reality, our biogenesis, is growing in response to the general skepticism of our age. See Dale A. Bertelsen, Jane Blankenship, Frank Lentricchia (*Criticism*), Michael A. Overington, Samuel B. Southwell, and Robert Wess.

Burke's conception of reality—reality is found through our bodily experience but only seen through our terministic screens—is paradoxical and hard to find in any stable formation throughout his work. However, he did analyze the dialectical relationship between body and symbol, the only process by which we know the world, throughout his career. Even as late as 1978, he is clarifying the material base of symbols. In as clear a statement as one gets from Burke, he writes: "The realm of nonsymbolic motion needs no realm of symbolic action; but there could be no symbolic action unless grounded in the realm of motion, the realm of motion having preceded the emergence of our symbol-using ancestors; and doubtless the time will come when motions go on after all our breed will have vanished" ("Nonsymbolic)" 811).

6. He examines Pascal's letter on changing or purifying intentions to justify and explain actions done with different intent (*Rhetoric* 154-58). In "Poetics in Particular, Language in General" in *Language as Symbolic Action*, he connects critique with analysis of a poet's strategies that are informed by the poet's life. While he separates the work from the author's personality, Burke, very loosely, associates the critic's ability to the matching of poetry with the author's poetics or principles, informed by his or her life. This borders on an intentionalist stand, moving critique from text to author. However, Burke often addresses the need for a *textual* reading in the context of an author and a situation (e.g., in many of the ratios of the pentad).

genres of discourses and units of discourses, motive represents both the possible purposes assumed within a culture and the purposes inherent in being the human animal, and purpose, used within the dramatistic pentad, allies a more standard sense of individual intentions or purpose within the complexity of a specific situation. Intentions have a multiplicity of associations that, within Burkean rhetoric, are able to nuance a description of forces within speech acts.

Form or structure, especially in relationship to content and force, is basic to Burke's conception of rhetoric.[7] As early as the essay "Lexicon Rhetoricae" in *Counter-Statement,* he associates form with rhetoric, but his sense of the instrumental value, or at least causative aspect, of form extends to poetic discourses, too. Even poems are formed to function, to "'do something' for the poet and his readers" (*Philosophy* 89). Form allows Burke to avoid grounding meaning in individual authorial or interpreter intentions, and rather to acknowledge public discursive structures (including conventions) beyond individual creations or minds, "the situations behind the tactics of expression" (92). Burke sees discursive structures, including genres, metaphors, and reversals, as tapping into common situations to allow the reader and writer to overlap "with a difference" (90). When his readers and writers have meanings that overlap "with a difference," they do not have a fused horizon or a tradition shared, but rather because they are both agents, they share discursive structures which embody situations that are experienced, almost physiologically and anatomically, by both the writer and an audience. "A form is a way of experiencing" (*Counter-Statement* 143).

Given the experiential nature of Burke's concept of form, and given form's dependence on the symbolic, real time, and bodily experience, his definition of form as "an arousing and fulfillment of desires" has orgasmic overtones as do the five categories of form he offers us (124). His five categories are not standard genres but more like loose descriptions of argumentative forms (though his examples tend to the literary).[8] Syllogis-

---

7. William Rueckert may be the first to see Burke as a precursor to structuralism, and Burke can be associated with structuralism for his concerns with form as a universal. However, he is better understood as describing the structural aspects of language and utilizing them for what they can teach us about form and trope. He acknowledges the trap of structure and form and then balances against that trap the choices innate in discursive ambiguity.

8. Burke's initial literary concerns and connections are surprisingly persistent in his work. In *Kenneth Burke in Greenwich Village,* Jack Selzer provides an overview of Burke's aesthetic concerns and modernist connections prior to the writing of *Counter-Statement.* Robert Wess provides an account of how Burke's early literary concerns become subsumed by concerns with history and culture.

tic progression is the logical progression of argument. Qualitative progression is where the presence of one quality prepares us for another, often oppositional. Repetitive form is "the restatement of a theme by new details" (125). Conventional form is "form as form." Unlike the pleasures of syllogistic, qualitative, and repetitive forms, which are made in the process of producing or re-producing a text, conventional form exists prior to and outside the text; we expect a sonnet to have fourteen lines and Plato's writings to be dialogues (unless it's a letter). Burke doesn't write about the pleasures of breaking conventions explicitly, but the concept of qualitative progression allows us to describe the gratification of progressing from convention to novelty. Finally, minor or incidental forms, "such as metaphor, paradox, disclosure, reversal, contractions, expansion, bathos, apostrophe, series, chiasmus" (127), are the internal events that both work independently and add to the larger work.

Burke's concept of form and its emphasis on physical sharing or "overlap" is useful because it both extends and renders fuzzy the significance of Hancher's three concepts of authorial intention: programmatic, active, and final. The author's programmatic intention is the intention or plan to make some form or another, the author's active intention is the intention to be taken to mean something, and the author's final intention is the intention to cause an effect. The programmatic intention, when seen through a Burkean lens, is expanded beyond deciding to write a tragedy or to pick a familiar metaphor. Because Burke often is concerned with more than authorial intention and the evaluation and interpretation of literary texts, his concept of form has a different place in meaning and the negotiation of meaning. While the author may still pick the form and have a programmatic intention, the form itself is *experiential* and joins with the rhetor and audience in "an overlap with a difference." As Burke writes, "form would be the psychology of the *audience*" (31); within its public, shared aspects, form induces cooperation, identification, and alienation. And given the physical and psychological potential within form, a Burkean conception of form engages active and final intentions. Since form exists as a shared situation and experience and so innately has potential for a common meaning and effect, any form the author intends implies an intent to mean and an intent to effect, not just within the author, but within the form and so within the audience who shares the form. Form is not a separate, objective pattern, nor is it a subjective attitude or interpretation. Rather, one can conceive of a form as an act that sets processes in motion; consequently, it makes a demonstrable, observable relationship among the discourse, the speaker, and the audience.

This relationship based on form (which leaks and bleeds conceptually) suggests that the categories of interpretation and evaluation, though familiar in discussions of intention within literary criticism, are less clearly divided within the practical frame of a rhetorical theory of intention. Obviously any interpretation (even the best of Gadamerian risking) struggles with and blurs lines between interpretation and evaluation, but within rhetorical practice, as I show in later chapters, interpretation and evaluation largely coincide. The formal relationship among text, author, and audience sets in motion patterns of responses (experiences) that differ for negatives, narratives, and metaphors.

The physical sense of form as a shared situation and experience is a major aspect of a second important Burkean concept, motive. He writes "situation is but another word for *motives*" (*Philosophy* 20). However, there are many other words clustered with motive (tradition, culture, discourse, constitution, substance, conduct), for motive is one of those uniquely Burkean concepts. In everyday, non-Burkean parlance, motives are based in existing psychological states that explain actions; that is, unlike intentions, which are focused somewhat more on specific future outcomes (plans), they are more internal and descriptive of an individual's current or past mental state. And so, one would say, "I intend to make money; my motivation is greed (or love or power)." From the perspective of ordinary language philosophy, G. E. M. Anscombe writes, "A man's intention is *what* he aims at or chooses; his motive is what determines the aim or choice" (*Intention* 18). Burke's motive, however, is a step removed from ordinary language. He uses motive as a technical term that, on first read, seems less than concerned with communication and individual action, but on examination, provides both a sense of communication as well as a critique of simple conceptions of the subject and individualistic motivations. Motive is in no way a denunciation of the possibility of individual action (Burke repeatedly presumes both the problem and possibility of freedom), but rather motive is the *placement of individual action within the "associational clusters" of meaning available within the culture.* He writes, "To discover in oneself the motives accepted by one's group is much the same thing as to use the language of one's group" (*Permanence* 20–21). For Burke, motives are interwoven within texts, cultures, and agents.[9] This makes motive a synthetic term that joins many concepts, a collection term unlike the divisive or analytic terms of the "drama" that

---

9. See, for example, his discussion of Coleridge's multiple and interwoven poetic motives (*Philosophy* 18–25, 92–101) or his discussion of motives in Kantian ethics (*Language* 441–44).

separate concepts and present the narrower concept of purpose in several forms.[10]

To get at the complexity and contradiction with which Burke understands the agency implied *within* the concepts of act and motive, at least how he understands it in his middle period, I will quote him at some length and briefly sidestep the relationship of motive to intention. I also will use this quotation to demonstrate Burke's paradox of action and its use in understanding his dialectic. Burke, in this section of *A Grammar of Motives,* is discerning the cultural basis (perhaps dictate) of any individual act without deleting the act itself as a choice and action. He writes:

> We may discern a dramatistic pun, involving a merger of active and passive in the expression, "the motivation of an act." Strictly speaking, the act of an agent would be the movement not of one *moved* but of a *mover* (a mover of the self or of something else by the self). For an act is by definition active, whereas to be moved (or motivated) is by definition passive. Thus, if we quizzically scrutinize the expression, "the motivating of an act," we note that it implicitly contains the paradox of substance . . . to consider an *act* in terms of its *grounds* is to consider it in terms of what it is not, namely, in terms of motives that, in acting upon the active, would make it a passive. We could state the paradox another way by saying that the concept of activation implies a kind of passive-behind-the-passive; for an agent who is "motivated by his passions" would be "moved by his being-movedness," or "acted upon by his state of being acted upon." (*Grammar* 40)

This quote illuminates one of the postmodern dilemmas regarding intention and agency. Given the paradox of being socially constructed (being motivated) and constructing society (acting), what is the space remaining for action, especially individual or subjective action? *Language gives us paradoxes and so dilemmas and choices,* but, as Burke reminds us, we don't have to make the choices inherent in the limits of language. We can live with the paradoxes and make our choices judiciously. "Act" may have no single explanation:[11] Burke approaches the complexity from a variety

---

10. In "A Note on Burke on 'Motive,'" William Benoit provides a discussion of motive and its various interpretations.

11. J. L. Austin makes exactly this claim in "A Plea For Excuses" (*Philosophical Papers*). Austin warns us that "'doing an action,' as used in philosophy, is a highly abstract expression . . . a stand-in used in the place of any (or almost any?) verb with a personal subject" (178). He warns us

of perspectives, using the resources of a variety of terms and applications, showing—not defining—the interpenetration of the human and material world.

In describing the paradox, Burke writes, "Strictly speaking, the act of an agent would be the movement not of one *moved,* but of a *mover* (a mover of the self or of something else by the self). For an act is by definition active, whereas to be moved (or motivated) is by definition passive" (40). Samuel B. Southwell interprets Burke as seeing the paradox of action implicitly contained in the paradox of substance and as saying that act is not to be explained: "the real import of what Burke is saying here is that the act is not to be explained" (Kenneth Burke 33). Not surprisingly, Burke is less clear and more complex than that. He does acknowledge the relationship between the paradox of substance and the paradox of action, but he draws out the action paradox one step further. Acknowledging the grammatical tautology, Burke writes, "But to consider an *act* in terms of its *grounds* is to consider it in terms of what it is not, namely, in terms of motives that, in acting upon the active, would make it a passive" (*Grammar* 40).

To show the depth of the grammatical problem, Burke moves away from the grammatical opposition between active and passive to discuss three Greek words, *poiema, pathema,* and *mathema* (the act, the sufferance or state, and the thing learned) (41). Burke shows that the meanings of these three terms can be collapsed into the active and passive due to the indwelling semantics of active and passive. The Greek words are richly interdependent and interact so that "the things undergone," *ta pathemata,* include "both the sort of things a person actively encountered and the sort of things that simply befell him." *Pathema* includes "not only suffering, but state of mind, condition—and knowledge is a state." Having demonstrated the interdependence of act and state and the reappearance of the binary, even when triangulated, Burke moves to a dichotomy and begins an analysis of the actus/status pair, relating it to the dynamic act-scene ratio and interpreting "status as *potentiality* and actus as its *actualization*" (43): the implication is that being moved requires potential and knowledge, not *passivity* (state) but *passion* (act). The scene sets up the potential action; the action sets up the potential scene.

Burke's materialist example helps to clarify the indwelling nature of the

---

against "the myth of the verb" and our tendency to essential features where there are essentially none. We should not think "all 'actions' are, as actions (meaning what?), equal, composing a quarrel with striking a match, winning a war with sneezing" (179). As an example of difference among rhetorical actions, I might ask, Is scapegoating the same as unifying against a common enemy? Or, Is unifying against a common enemy like unifying for a common cause?

two terms and the potential for their reversal. Under classical Marxism, workers share motives because they share the scene of "factory situation" and "wage slavery." The capitalist god denies them freedom. Dramatistically, the work of the factory is motion, not act; work can become "actus only when the workers' status is understood in terms of social organization" (45). On the other hand, "the ownership of factories is a *state*," but it is not passive, rather it is an act of expropriation and governance. There is a deep grammatical problem here, one that makes it impossible for a state to "wither away," for according to Burke, "no continuity of social act is possible without a corresponding social status" (46). He is not doubting the material conditions of capitalism but is making any action-based analysis of that materiality unstable.

Less material examples also reveal the tension within the action/motion pair. I call you a name (I act), I name you (move you), and so I name my relationship to you (move me). As Burke puts it, "an epithet assigns substance doubly, for in stating the character of the object it at the same time contains an implicit program of action with regard to the object, thus serving as motive" (57). My act of naming makes you, but it also makes me. It creates an experience, a sensible reality, and perhaps effects a material reality, a "citable reality," an "observable reality."

Burke does not see the paradoxes/puns of substance and action as obstacles to our thinking, but rather finds the paradox itself both a resource and a characteristic of language (51-52). And language is our only way to grasp these concepts and our own experience. Rather than expecting substance to be substance, action to be action, reality to be reality, he sees that our "linguistic behavior here reflects real paradoxes in the nature of the world itself—antimonies that could be resolved only if men were able—to create an entire universe" (56).

Motive then is Burke's term for being socially constructed and constructing society. It is the term that Burke uses to signify the complex tension between an agent making the world and being made by the world. In addition to its paradoxical relationship to subject action, motive is also associated with cultural conflict, decisions, expectations, judgments, and policies (all terms suggestive of deliberations). Agents can have different motives, but the range of motives arising within any situation is limited and dictated by social constructions. According to Burke, we tend to use the term *motive* "to indicate a complex stimulus-situation wherein certain stimuli calling for one kind of response are linked with certain stimuli calling for another kind of response" (love or duty?) (*Permanence* 30). In stable cultures, Burke asserts, motives are defined and taught as well as assumed; consequently, participants tend to know each others' motives, and the situations in need of new description are limited in number and familiar in quality. In stable cultures, motives are highly predictable; we know why people act and can say, "like father like son." During unstable periods, though, the interpretation of motives becomes "liquid," and motives become difficult to name. There are more than ambiguities and ambivalences between what we say we do and what we do, there are visible conflicts. In an unstable culture, an interpreter does not understand the motives of the younger generation or the radical (not-so-radical) activist and struggles to name them. Rather than a "highly socialized, or universalized character" of stimulus-situations, there is an increasing sense of "individualization" and a turn to searching for introspective motives, a move Burke links with "total emptiness" (33). One might see this in terms of a break between public motives (traditions and institutionalizations) and subjective purposes, and while Burke does not speculate on this, it seems that unstable cultures create a discursive space for individual rhetors to name the conflict and the peace. The linguistic paradoxes in unstable cultures increase, and so do the choices.

Instead of introspecting for noble motives or describing specific instabilities (that is, looking at the situations of heroes), Burke turns to the *linguistic* nature of motives, writing that "we discern situational patterns by means of the particular vocabulary of the cultural group into which we are born" (35). Since old and new motives are made in language and language is "a communicative medium" (36), motive is a product (by-product?) of communication. Motive, in this context, is itself "a term for interpretation, and being such it will naturally take its place within the framework of our *Weltanschauung* as a whole" (25). Motives define and are defined by our worldview.

To further complicate the situation (motive?) or simply approach it from a different tack, sociologist Michael Overington points out that Burke has a "tripartite understanding of motives" (95). Since the only way that we know the world and can explain things is through language (situated, cultured language), Burke's problem, according to Overington, is that of recognizing and describing motives that are hidden in our assumptions and everyday language. Overington writes that Burke sees motives as evident and knowable in three ways, in "language *of* explanation, explanation *in* language, language *as* explanation" (95). Here, inherently, human action and language together are situational and cultural, and hence, human action is embedded in cultural explanations.[12] It is when we have

---

12. I return to the placing of motive in explanation in a discussion of narrative desire in the last section of Chapter 5.

to stop and explain our situation that our motives become foregrounded. Even more significantly, the ability we have for explanation and much of our ability to act are implicit in the culture and situation; motive, language, explanation, situation, and culture are so intertwined as to resist (not forbid) interpretations and inquiries and acts and purposes—beyond what the particular language and culture enact. Motive then is a term that indicates the cultural aspects of intention; the concept of motive suggests a framework or deep structure for our ownership of the world. It frames what can be explained, decided, expected, and justified and so consequently what can be deliberated on. The motivational patterns within different discourses can conceivably make deliberation impossible, but by multiplying discourses and perspectives, in dialectics, paradoxes, and deconstructions, Burke sees discourses as creating their own transformations (a developed theory of Fish's "engine of change"), which will bring us new explanations of the culture that forms us as we form it.

In addition to positing multiple perspectives, Burke further evades the potential problem of incommensurable motives by positing two types of motives, cultural and universal, the second of which, universal situations and motives, makes humanity always able to communicate, at least about some experiences. As early as *Counter-Statement*, Burke was concerned with the way in which people could coexist and have commonality in a world that they knew only through the mediation of symbols, ambiguous symbols. He argues for physical commonalities among all peoples: our physical situation and our dancing, breathing bodies allow an "overlap with a difference" between interlocutors:

> In so far as the neurological structure remains a constant, there will be a corresponding constancy in the devices by which sociality is maintained. (*Permanence* 162)

> Situations do overlap, if only because men now have the same neural and muscular structure as men who have left their records from past ages. (*Philosophy* 3)

Our common circuitry overlaps, and so whether the catalyst for experiencing fear is the soiled glove or the thundering cannon (*Counter-Statement* 150), we all are capable of recognizing the concept of fear. Still, the "overlap" is "with a difference." Burke describes the impossibility of sharing an experience as the same mode of experience, writing "the same universal experience could invariably accompany the same mode of experience only if all men's modes of experience were identical" (150). Fear may be universal, but its causes and modes of experience and expression vary. Still, because of our common circuitry and experience, if motivated, we can communicate across cultures and across motives.

Burke's regard for reality and situation acknowledges rhetorical issues and the scenes where deliberation and adjudication sometimes have deadly consequences. The concept of universal motive provides a connection to physical life and serves to mark our experiential means of knowing and desiring. Cultural motive recognizes the perspectival nature of our knowing and desiring. Like Altieri's definition of intention as dynamic processes concerned with claiming the world, the concept of universal motive is a good demarcator of how different Burke's project is than that of hermeneutics. He wants more than textual meanings; seemingly he wants a meaning based in the commonality of human actions with their life-based causes and world consequence. Cultural motive, on the other hand, is somewhat like Gadamer's hermeneutics in being linked to the concepts of history, tradition, prejudice, and authority; it is a theory of perspectival knowledge, though a paradoxical one.[13]

In setting up a tension between universal motives and cultural motives, Burke sets up a dialectic between commonality and difference that serves to articulate not just the discursive forces of the two, but the conflicts among significantly differing discourses. He suggests that an audience listens not for true meaning or interpretation, but for pragmatic and material reasons, driven by desires for identifications and scapegoats, consensus and freedom, and bound to cultural and biological motives that define those desires and intentions. Furthermore, his sense of the tension within "motivation to act," the activity of motivation and the passivity of action, acknowledges the tension within an agent's ability to choose and within the possibility of her freedom.

For Burke, motive, the concept associated with our unstated plans for future benefit and harm, stands under all we do. It is a key concept in understanding his interpretive rhetoric as more than simply phenomenological. If one has formalist leanings, one can simply focus on the effects of the form or the perspectives within a certain drama and miss the larger cultural consciousness within his corpus. Motive allows us to understand Burke as historical and cultural, as "Marxoid." Motive also places interpretation within a rhetorical tradition by expanding the idea of interpretation not just into critique, but into situations demanding action. Despite its

---

13. Burke read Heidegger and shared similarities of project thattenuously link his work to that of Gadamer, Heidegger's student. See Samuel B. Southwell's *Kenneth Burke and Martin Heidegger*. For Burke's ontological concerns beyond Heideggerian ones, see James W. Chesbro.

additions, however, the concept of motive is incomplete for understanding an agent's purposes, especially as negotiated in site. The breadth of the concept of motive, while allowing it to guide Burke's extensive inquiries, makes it too telescopic for a more specific, microscopic inquiry into intention and interpretive rhetorics, especially when the inquiry focuses on events, times, and places. The concept of cultural motive draws attention to the culture of the text, its discursive origins, the possibilities of many purposes, and the freedom of action of a rhetor or audience; however, the choices made by individuals, choices that Burke sees as basic to rhetoric, become secondary when seen through the concept of motive.

Form and motive help in the explication of a rhetorical theory of intentions. The drama, however, is the essential third piece that allows us to acknowledge subjective intentions and to approach them with the respect and suspicion necessary in the potentially dangerous act of communication, and it is the piece that allows the control of and an end to the infinitely regressing act of interpreting intentions. By acknowledging the multiple perspectives possible within any symbolic encounter, the drama allows for the critique of a clash of ideologies. It also provides a technical approach for examining the place of intention and its negotiation within a specific communication. Burke recognizes purpose as an aspect of any act, and while he does not develop the concept of intention, he is very concerned with the why, the purpose, of acts. After all, he begins *A Grammar of Motives* by asking, "What is involved, when we say what people are doing and why they are doing it?" (xv). As a method for approaching these questions and analyzing our positions inside language and culture, he posits five terms: act, scene, agent, agency, purpose. These terms, according to Burke, help us find what is enigmatic about motives and let us see the inconsistencies within, among, and between motives. The five terms—implicit in any statement about motive, in any statement about what people do and their purpose in doing it—reveal the strategic ambiguities that allow us to understand and critique the systems and discourses that define and maintain motives. He goes so far as to call the terms "transcendental . . . in being categories which human thought necessarily exemplifies" (317). The narrative form of the drama parallels human understanding of experience, and so the five terms are "forms of *talk about* experience" that might temper our "absurd ambitions," "political or financial," by giving us a better way to understand linguistic action.

While purpose is the term that most concerns intention, it impinges on the other terms as the why of human action, and so it moves with the other terms (in ways more subtle than a ratio would reveal). Burke defines purpose as *why* an agent performs an act; it is defined within a scene by an act and an agent as they are defined by it (which works to make purpose more legible and public). With its ambiguities, purpose dwells within the other terms, especially act, agent, and agency. And while purpose has the disadvantage of being the term "most susceptible of dissolution" into other terms, it is useful exactly in its connection to the other terms of the drama; it can be applied to any agent acting within the scene: a speaker, an opponent, a judge, or an interpreting by-stander. Intention as conceived in Burkean purpose is not as much a specific that defines the (Romantic) intention of consciousness as it is an engagement in the whole drama by every agent (and a part of every part of the whole). In its engagement in the whole, Burkean purpose is also a methodologically useful site for a critical rhetoric capable of shifting perspectives within an interpretive situation: it facilitates reflexive play within critique. With its connection to the other terms of the drama, purpose loses intention's affiliation with consciousness and mental state and develops the affiliation with plan, end, and action. Within its interactions and ratios, purpose challenges the false dichotomies between group and individual, internal and external. Burkean purposes work synergistically with motives to describe human intention without unifying the subject.

This dramatistic approach to intention is valuable for considering intentionality within deliberation, but alas, Burke's relationship to purpose is even more difficult than the above description suggests. Purpose is listed repeatedly as the last term and is explored by Burke less explicitly than act, scene, and agent. This is no reason to assume it is less significant: rather, if anything, more significant. I read Burke as concerned about the ways in which purposes are taken over by and, in turn, take over our discourses and emphasize our delusions of control and paranoid fears of others. Purpose, despite the health of its placement in the drama, can be isolated and can become a faulty term used for "absurd ambitions." Burke is particularly wary of overly focusing on purpose or agency, writing that overstressing purpose results in "an overly pointed consideration of all policies in terms of means and ends alone" and a resulting diminishment, if not extinguishing, of scene, act, and agent (*Grammar* 309). He fears that if purpose is made an absolute, then it leads to mechanistic thinking, and that results in a "dissolution" of purpose itself (288-89). Purpose, says Burke, is a term in need of moderation, a part of meaning, but only the whole pathologically.

Burke sees that analysis of purpose is dangerously domineering, and he critiques two dangers in analyzing purpose. His first position is that if a named purpose is seen as the point of speaking, then only *cause-and-effect* models of human communication need be applied to any rhetorical situation. We see this in the models of intention discussed in Chapter 1, where meaning existed in either the rhetor or community and either the rhetor or the community caused meaning. Positing a purpose as a "final cause" simplifies the complexity of any speech act to the point that the purpose itself is too simple to have significance or to reveal the dynamics of human interactions; in the extreme, a behaviorist sense of purpose will dominate the drama's term and overpower the related concepts of form and motive. Surrounded by postmodern theory, we have less anxiety about purpose and causal thinking than Burke did in the forties. Since now it is increasingly a commonplace to accept that people speak for and interpret with a great diversity of overlapping purposes, many of them unknowable, unconscious, or ineffable, many of them implicit in the culture, Burke's anxieties about purpose and mechanistic thinking—while modest and necessary in a more positivistic age—seem excessive in a postmodern polyglot where the loss of theories of purpose and agency is more the common anxiety.

His second, more articulated and relevant position concerns the subtle dangers of purpose conceived as interior and separate from the drama. Rather than being conceived as the *cause* of communication, purpose also can be conceived as mystical and internal to the point of exceeding even an individual's obsession, that is, to the point of creating a "totality" or "metaphysical fascination" (287). Using the entry on mysticism in Baldwin's *Dictionary of Philosophy and Psychology,* Burke writes that "references to 'the divine essence,' 'the creative source,' and 'the Being of beings' indicate why we would equate Mysticism with the featuring of our term, Purpose" (*Grammar* 287). Using Baldwin's clauses, Burke stresses mysticism's unification of the individual "with some *cosmic or universal purpose*" (288). According to Burke, mysticism arises in unstable societies, in skeptical or confused times, as a way of responding to weak public structures for explaining "the ends of life." In mystical explanations based in purified purposes, however, there are two paradoxes. First, a commitment to pure purpose removes the individual from the everyday sphere of action and renders purpose unworldly and removed from the individual agent, act, scene, and agency. Second, when the mystic joins or fuses with pure purpose, the purpose becomes a compulsion; any sense of purpose as freely chosen disappears as the individual disappears into the All, the Creator, that signifies absolute or cosmic purpose. Here purpose tends to the unworldly and unchosen, and in so tending, narrows the "motivational circumference" (291). Purpose, in this extreme, is transcendent and compulsive (essential): it becomes nonrhetorical and removed from public methods of adjudication.

To make this somewhat concrete, I offer two examples. Consider Sophocles' *Antigone* where Creon's commitment to the state and Antigone's compulsion toward the gods and death ultimately absorb their individual qualities and erase any nuancing within their value systems. They lose the ability to make choices or negotiate their positions; deliberation is impossible. Their purposes overcome any larger motivational system within Sophocles' discourse. If I extend Burke's paradox of purpose to the purposes embedded in the discourse of a community, the paradox of conceiving individual purpose is also a paradox of social purpose. While describing purpose or intention within a community is more aligned, in Burkean terms, with describing motive, Fish's model of the interpretive community helps to extend our understanding of how purpose or intention considered solely can result in a choiceless compulsion removed from meaning-making and negotiation. In the case of Fish's community, one's purposes are a social construct, a compulsion. He poses a community's codes as forming an "engine of change," but in the details of explanation, the engine becomes a black box that controls interpretation as mechanistically as any traditional appeal to authorial intention (*Doing* 150-53). Engine of change or black box, both function as metaphors for a *mechanized mysticism*. In focusing overly on the codes or the purposes (which are not synonymous) within discourse communities, one enters a mystical realm far removed from the everyday.

There is, in both examples, a sense that purpose itself is subtly dangerous and sets up the tragedy—Antigone's, Creon's, or ours—in the irreconcilable differences. Burke repeatedly warns of both purpose's tendency to be conceived purely and the unworldly nature of purpose conceived purely. He develops this insight in ways helpful to understanding intention in rhetoric by placing purpose in relationship to agency and agent.

Unlike the other terms, each in a separate chapter, Burke places agency and purpose together for their nexus in a means-ends relationship. Agency he connects to pragmatism, emphasizing the means, method, and mediatory aspects of agency and pragmatism. Agency is then connected to planning and usefulness. Purpose, in contrast, is connected to desire and end outcome or action. In a strikingly Burkean metaphor, Burke compares the relationship between agency and purpose to the perverse relationship between the maternal or useful woman and the erotic or desired woman (*Grammar* 284). Due to the incest taboo and not the nature of women, a man must choose between the two, disassociate the two. In the maternal-erotic dilemma, the erotic tends to transcend the maternal (though only to be "solved" when the erotic woman becomes the wife and in this new relationship becomes useful to the family). The drive to dichotomize exists just because the maternal is erotic, use and desire are implicated in each other.

Burke makes much of our pathological drive to differentiate and purify agency and purpose, analyzing several examples. I would extend his theme and add an example. Our conceptions of rhetoric struggle with the same impulse to dichotomy: as an instrumental discourse, rhetoric is engaged in means (agency) and ends (purpose). Rhetoric—historically "the faculty of discovering, in any given case, the available *means* of persuasion"—is obviously more than either a means or the end of persuasion. The instrumentality or utility of rhetoric needs to be balanced with the desired outcome. This, in part, is what Aristotle does in balancing the sophistic end of persuasion with the criteria of available (artistic) means (Garver, *Aristotle's Rhetoric* 220–21), fully articulating a means-ends relationship.

In addition to linking purpose to agency, Burke links purpose to agent, and this also helps him to demonstrate purpose's paradoxical momentum away from the everyday. With the second connection, he links purpose *in its extreme* to communion and the transcendent self. Earlier in *Grammar of Motives,* he had linked the concept of agent to idealism because of their mutual lack of concern with objects and their explanation of the cosmos "in the realization of reason, self-consciousness, or spirit" (171). The agent here is not a human agent/author, rather she exists as a paradox between "a super-self or a non-self" (300). To mix a witch's brew of purpose, communion, and a transcendent self or agent, Burke allies the pair mysticism-purpose with idealism-agent through the concept of union and our so-human desire to transcend disunity, the same desire for consensus that inspires most rhetorics. In the realm of the mystical and the ideal, at the limit of language (trapped still in the collectivity of language), humanity comes together: the agent or self becomes a super-person, "an individual 'collectively redeemed' by being apprehended through a medium itself essentially collective" (300).

When agent and purpose are conceived pathologically as an ideal and mystical unity rather than the realistic or dramatistic notion of people in situations, we find an imaginary, the fantasy of purpose behind the plague (God or the CIA behind AIDS), the fantasy of purpose behind the penny on the sidewalk, the fantasy of purpose behind the words on the page. The mystic, in finding purpose everywhere, must find purposes for the bad and good before and within her. The obsession with the purpose-agent ratio takes a sinister turn in that "all scapegoats are purposive, in aiming at self-purification by the unburdening of one's sins ritualistically, with the goat as charismatic, as the chosen vessel of iniquity, whereby one can have the experience of punishing in an alienated form the evil which one would otherwise be forced to recognize within" (301). The transcendent self is necessarily other than common humanity and necessarily defines that otherness. While the ideal agent and mystical purpose imagine unity, unity cannot quite separate from the disunity. When one attends to purposes intently, solely, Burke warns that one risks the loss of, if nothing else, a frame for negotiation with another agent. Implicit is the understanding that discussions of intention are dangerous when they are conceived solely as discussions of purposes, for to discuss purpose solely is to enter the hermeneutics of suspicion.

In the context of a discussion about the purposeful agent and her relationship to scapegoating and mysticism, it is useful to remember that Burke also has a concept of agent nuanced differently than the transcendent self that arises from an overt and sustained obsession with purpose. Despite his moments of transcendence, Burke does not eradicate the agent with specific purposes—though his agent (hearing, reading, speaking, writing) is more multidimensional than the agent portrayed in any of the intentionalist or textualist theories hitherto discussed. While agent is only one of five perspectives in Burke's description of what people are doing and why, agent is an acknowledged part of his structure. Most simply, one might say that the author is not dead, but rather sharing the stage with act, scene, agency, purpose, and other agents/authors. In the consideration of the variety of ratios and the effect of various circumferences drawn around a scene, Burke argues that "men are capable of but *partial* acts, acts that but partially represent themselves and but partially conform to their scenes" (83). Implicit in the partial act is partial purpose and the partial agent. The untranscendental agent is placed in language, culture, and the world: her purposes and actions are limited by forces without and within; her intentions are diffused in forms, motives, and purposes and in the possibilities of experience. Burke, despite his acknowledgment of mysticism and idealism in our thinking, desires reality. Unlike theorists who see language as floating, as endless possibility, Burke limits language, placing it within structures of culture and experience. To do this, he describes interlocking relationships between the experienced, the desired, and the socially created.

III

From Burke, I want to explicate one more concept that will help to discuss the negotiation of intentions. Burke develops the vocabularies of his drama and dialectical logic in the service of ambiguity.[14] In developing his vocabularies, Burke is seeking "*not terms that avoid ambiguity, but terms that clearly reveal the strategic spots at which ambiguities necessarily arise*" (*Grammar* xviii). Unlike many interpretive rhetoricians who are fascinated by the conservative forces within language, Burke sees ambiguity as a resource for innovation and transformation. Unlike the rhetoricians and hermeneutical philosophers discussed earlier—who seek the limited meanings of the original rhetor, the interpretive control by a community, or a fused horizon—Burke embraces the uses of ambiguity, accepts human variations on meaning, and argues for ambiguity's effectiveness and, of course, necessity in our thinking. Ambiguity and divergence are potential sources of new insight and possibility, characteristics to be welcomed in deliberative rhetorics that value future action and change.

It would be hard to overestimate the significance of ambiguity or even ambivalence within Burke's thinking; consequently, I return to his paradoxes. In his development of the "antinomies of definition," Burke discusses the paradox of substance. Substance, a word key to philosophy and to Burke's critique of philosophy, becomes a prime example of the value and necessity of ambiguity to even our most analytic utterances. As Burke demonstrates, the word *substance* is used to signify what something is, the essential or main part, but substance, in its roots, means "to stand under," that is, something apart from the what, the main. Burke notes, "though used to designate something *within* the thing, *intrinsic* to it, the word etymologically refers to something *outside* the thing, *extrinsic* to it" (*Grammar* 23). In the act of defining arises "an alchemic moment," when a thing is placed in terms of what it is not. Through "an *inevitable* paradox of definition," the context determines the thing; the class or family determines the thing. And in the paradox lies the potential for transformations of discourse, individuals, cultures, and situations, for Burke slowly extends the concept of paradox from dictionary activities of definition, writing "from such ambiguity is derived that irony of historical development

---

14. Burke offers us two vocabularies and asks us to use this "double vocabulary—to translate back and forth between logical and temporal vocabularies" for the purpose of studying the possibility of linguistic transformation (*Grammar* 430). The relationship between and the implications of the two approaches are well discussed in John D. O'Banion's *Reorienting Rhetoric.*

whereby the very strength in the affirming of a given term may the better enable men to make a world that departs from it" (54). That is, the instability of even an apparent god-term defined allows us to develop alternatives, conceptualize multiple contexts or families, and eventually leave the old intrinsic for a new extrinsic. Burke's analysis places ambiguity as the source of divergence from the cultural norm and permits the play within discourse to be a means of exploration and education rather than a dangerous tendency to solipsistic confusion needing the constant, corrective goad of cultural conditioning.

Ambiguity, seen as a resource, also suggests that misunderstanding is possible between interlocutors without anyone being in error. It encourages the pursuit of multiple positions about one text among and within multiple readers (or writers, for that matter). In doing so, the valuing of ambiguity discourages a movement to closure or horizon as a goal or desirable end and rather requires us first to acknowledge the alternative and the other. Given pluralistic practices within our democracy, there are inevitably different interpretations and forces (including multiple and fragmented traditions) forming those interpretations. Burke would see these interpretations and forces as the precious sites of linguistic transformation, not cacophony.

Since ambiguity is a given in language as are multiple interpretations, then multiple, nondiscursive forces, such as institutional structure, context, and prevailing motives, potentially influence the valuing of any individual interpretation. Burke, who is concerned with the material and its effects, characterizes our vocabularies as "reflections," "selections," and "deflections" of reality (*Grammar* 59). Interpretive ambiguities, according to Burke, beget the Barnyard and the Scramble where we create and struggle against unity, unity achieved both by tribal identification and through noncontradictory conceptual systems (reason). Interpretive ambiguities lead to alternative interpretations that unfold our differences and destabilize societies and traditions.

While an initial difference may not be adequate for an opposition, according to Burke, our patterns of thinking and living are capable of moving initial differences to opposites:

> Polar otherness unites things that are *opposite to* one another; synecdochic otherness unites things that are simply different from one another. The beloved's house is not *opposite to* the beloved, but merely *different from* the beloved. Under dialectic pressures, however, (as in political alignments) any difference may come to be felt as an antithesis. (*Philosophy* 78)

Our drive to oppose, to push difference to opposition is what makes serious deliberation so difficult; the discursive forces of antithesis certainly are equal to those of synthesis. On the other hand, the ambiguities of discourse can work to keep deliberation ongoing. Burke defines humanity as the symbol-using animal; our compulsion to symbolize (to reflect, select, deflect again and again) is stronger than the forces of antithesis or synthesis. In working to clarify ambiguity, resolve paradoxes, and understand the assumptions of political alignments, we continue to talk and to rethink our words about words. The human impulse to rhetoric "must lead us through the Scramble, the Wrangle of the Market Place, the flurries and flare-ups of the Human Barnyard, the Give and Take, the wavering line of pressure and counterpressure, the Logomachy, the onus of ownership, the Wars of Nerves, the War" (*Rhetoric* 23).

Hinge/Acknowledging Prejudices

Hinges are small pieces of hardware, holding and turning two bigger pieces by their strength of material and design. The pivot, the turn, depends on their strength. Having critiqued earlier rhetorical theories of intention and suggested an alternative theory, embedded in Burkean rhetoric, I turn to enlarging the theory through close analysis of forms in context. With the turn, however, many of my assumptions, formed prior to this project and throughout this project, become evident and open to question. The metal gets tested.

In the next three chapters I examine specific expressions and negotiations of purposes as they are formed in tropes and genres and informed by cultural motive; in part, I seek to lay out the relationship between intentional action and human ability to invent and interpret it, but most significantly, I develop an analysis of intention as rhetorical by seeing its play between interlocutors. I have chosen to examine particular disciplinary situations; that is, I look at how a few philosophers read Wittgenstein's negations, narratives, and metaphors. One might think that the move to a disciplined discourse evades the difficulties of multiculturalism, diversity, and power differentials and believe that I should be analyzing a more "political" site (such as the Fourth World Conference on Women where 130 nations came to consensus on a "Platform for Action"). However, it is because the political difficulties of multiculturalism, diversity, and power differentials inhabit even disciplined discourses that I turn to philosophy. In finding the forces of multiculturalism, diversity, and power differentials in philosophical discourses, I destigmatize them, show that failed understanding and the struggle to engage difference are normal, and document further that the political cannot be evaded by bracketing it in the institutions of politics.

The move to study philosophers reading Wittgenstein is complicated in that my analysis of intentions as public also is informed by the ordinary language tradition to which Wittgenstein's writings are central, if not originary. To minimize the blurring between the theoretical assumptions and the analysand, I will foreground my prejudices (I may even risk them) and lay out two: one about our ways of recognizing other people's intentions and a second about the implications of theorizing rather than describing.

A premise: as language is shared, public, and performative, we have *some knowledge* of the experiences, feelings, beliefs, and intentions of others. It is an uncertain knowledge in that we do not always and unquestionably *know* and we never *introspect* their experiences, feelings, beliefs, and intentions. Rather, we have evidence and experiences that allow us to proceed effectively, though not perfectly. Our mental states, ideological positions, and prejudices (and those of our interlocutors) are knowable through intentional speech acts.

Burke offers us three concepts—form, cultural motive, and purpose—as ways of discussing and recognizing the public aspects of our interlocutors' intentions. While all three terms are somewhat indefinite, he leaves us least sure about the nature of recognizing a particular purpose; implicit in Burke's discussion of purpose is a warning that purpose can only be understood (versus obsessed over) in the context of the larger drama because the narrative, with its situated and temporal nature, allows us access to purposes by their enactment revealed in signs and symptoms. Even before we start, we know that the criteria of recognizing purpose will never be a list of claims or a tally of conventions. Instead we will have to understand each other's purposes in some looser, antireductionist way.

Ordinary language philosophy responds to the arguments of skepticism, idealism, and mysticism with the premise that understanding is participation in a language, not an inner process.[1] A key argument has been provided by J. L. Austin's discussion of recognizing a goldfinch (or bittern).[2] In

---

1. My move to ordinary language philosophy, especially J. L. Austin, after a discussion of Burke is not as migratory as it might first seem. In reviewing *How to Do Things with Words* as a book concerned with language as a mode of action, Burke is very explicit on the connections between his dramatism and Austin on speech acts, performatives, and illocution ("Words as Deeds"). He does differentiate their perspectives on performance, characterizing Austin's as "conformative" (scripting) and his as "constitutive" (constructing), but in the end analysis, their commonalities in an action-based understanding of language and between their terms *attitude* and *illocutionary force* make their respective theories strikingly compatible. This is all the more delightful given the contrast between Burke's orientation (Marxoid, Freudoid, pragmatist, American) and Austin's (analytic, ordinary language, Oxbridge).

2. This is especially true in discussions connecting the literary with the philosophical; Austin's example is explicated by Charles Altieri (*Act and Quality*), Anthony Cascardi (*The Bounds of Reason*), and Stanley Cavell (*Claim of Reason*) among others.

"Other Minds" he argues that the criteria for recognizing the mental states of others are within the occasions and based in our experiences with those occasions: he writes that " 'being angry' is in many respects like 'having mumps.' It is a description of a whole pattern of events, including occasion, symptoms, feeling and manifestation, and possibly other factors besides" (*Philosophical* 109). The basic "organisms" of anger and mumps may evade us, but interpreters seek and find clues for recognizing each.[3] To understand human investigation and knowledge formation, Austin begins with our *grammatical* ability to make analogies between objects and mental states: When we say, "How do you know he is angry?" and "How do you know it's a bittern?" we are making grammatical analogies between anger and birds (77-79). When the bird-watcher answers, the replies are such as, "I was brought up in the fens," "I heard it," "Because the keeper reported it," and "Because it is booming." These replies, the basis of our everyday knowledge, describe either *experiences* of certain kinds or *acumen* of a certain kind and amount. These responses are not a list of the criteria of identity but rather "tell us about a practice or a usage, about how we deal in the world" (Cascardi 25). Austin notes that when a person says she knows, she may be asked to prove it. Proof in the bird examples means "stating what are the features of the current case which are enough to constitute it one which is correctly describable in the way we have described it" (*Philosophical* 85-86). We may not always know for sure it is a bittern (Is it real or stuffed? Is it the *right* boom? Is the keeper reliable?); events in the future may require us to rethink the claim (I find out bitterns are extinct): knowledge is fallible. Sense-statements ("I know what you're feeling," "He knows his own mind," "I see your intentions are evil") use the same syntactic patterns as statements about knowing material objects and so equate sensa and material objects in ways that make us uncomfortable with the degree of fallibility in knowing other minds and may make us think that we are introspecting. In everyday life, however, what we do and can do—given another's actions—is review our *experiences* and *acumen*, showing that the features of the current case are "enough to constitute it one which is correctly describable in the way we have described it" (85-86). Our replies about knowing other minds, the basis of our knowl-

---

3. Austin's examples here are revealing. Mumps and bitterns (and by extension anger) have a fixed identity (if only in their DNA), but not an essence. Austin's examples suggest that he is responding to both other mind and external world skepticism with the same argument, one based in experience. On the other hand, in his later philosophy Wittgenstein's examples tend to be about social constructions, imaginary discourses, and playful illustrations, what he calls "intermediate cases" (remark 122). This, in turn, suggests a far less biological underpinning of his philosophy than is sometimes premised. See my discussion of "form of life" in Chapter 6.

edge, are like replies about birds in that they are also descriptions of experiences of certain kinds or acumen of a certain kind and amount that tell us about linguistic usage and human practices. While replies based on experiences with other minds may be more significant to our lives, these replies are no more introspections or absolute knowledge than are those of the bird-watcher.

Recognizing other people's intentions, according to Austin, is about our everyday experiences, practices, usages, and conventions. Although he writes about recognizing the state of being angry, his general criteria for recognizing that particular mental state can extend to the state of having a particular purpose. To describe having a purpose also would be "a description of a whole pattern of events, including occasion, symptoms, feeling and manifestation, and possibly other factors besides" (109). We learn to recognize forms, motives, and purposes with the same conceptual abilities that allow us to recognize emotions.

The pattern of events surrounding a mental state is intricate and contingent enough that it is *shown, not stated;* if I claim, "I'm angry" or "I have evil intentions" while smiling, an interlocutor might be puzzled, think I'm clowning, or worry about my sanity. Experiences, practices, usages, and conventions do not equip us for some interpretive moments: we can be surprised, but we learn. We live unself-consciously within the pattern or the drama, assuming understanding and familiarity until our understandings falter, until we have to pause and question either the validity of our interpretation or of the author's meaning. Both types of pause make us anxious or suspicious, and in our uncertainty, we look again for signs and symptoms of the author's intentions.

In addition to accepting a sign-and-symptom approach to recognizing intentions, I also presume interlocutors to have means of adjusting their approaches if they fail to recognize each other's intentions. Even when faced with misunderstanding, interlocutors find ways of proceeding, and I see their means as not limited to shifts in conventions or semantic fields, but rather also including shifts in the way a discourse is constructed, shifts in a broad range of proceedings, such as practices (more bodily and biological), inventions, and expectations. Wittgenstein's later writings describe interpretive proceedings in a way congenial to rhetorical deliberations on another's purposes, especially as manifested in the Burkean drama. Like Burke, Wittgenstein emphasizes that meaning is immanent in practice and performance; "our talk gets its meaning from the rest of our proceedings" (*On Certainty* 229). Wittgenstein, however, is more optimistic than Burke about the accessibility of purposes; while they are constituted by practices (intention without interiority), they are recognizable without the dangers of mysticism and scapegoating. The public aspects of authorial intention are difficult to comprehend, or even apprehend, when one is faced with translating the Bible or making sense of Heidegger's *Being and Time,* but Wittgenstein would have us consider the dynamics of everyday practices.

He asks, "What is the natural expression of an intention?" He answers, "Look at a cat when it stalks a bird; or a beast when it wants to escape" (*Investigations* remark 647). This example, which removes people and the complexities of culture and language, places intention in the action and the agent and the scene: the intention is not separable from the scene, not an action in and of itself nor a mental state, yet one knows the cat intends to catch a bird and the beast intends escape. It is the outer manifestation that is recognized (see also *Investigations* remarks 305, 337, 644-54; *Zettel* 51). How do we know that we recognize it?

In part, we recognize the cat's intention of stalking because of our *experiences* of certain kinds and *acumen* of a certain kind and amount; someone who knows cats and birds is likely to describe more signs and symptoms than someone who avoids cats or birds. There is a basic physicality to our recognition of intentions. In explaining philosophy's problematic fixation on "inner processes," Wittgenstein writes, "When one says 'Still, an inner process does take place here'—one wants to go on: 'After all, you *see* it' " (*Investigations* remark 305). We not only assume intentions and attribute intentions to others, but we recognize intentions through our senses' reception of physical signs. We see the smile, his eyes shift, the larger print, the subheading. We hear the voice get softer, the tone duller, the too-subtle nuance of argument. We smell the sweat, feel the quality of the stationery, the speaker's hand upon us. Logos, ethos, and pathos are performed. The performance is what is recognized, not a mystical, inner process. It is true that sensory experience may be misinterpreted. Perhaps the cat is stalking a mouse hidden in the grass, not a bird; perhaps the beast cares less about escape and instead wants to eat us. If one sees this, one must pause and rethink his understanding, but then one can "go on" to bell the cat or complain about mice or run from the beast (remarks 154-55, 323-25, 652).

As Wittgenstein writes in his analysis of understanding (a concept also subject to artificial purification), "we are trying to get hold of the mental process of understanding which seems hidden behind those coarser and therefore more readily visible accompaniments" (remark 153). Rather than pursue the invisible, Wittgenstein changes the question about mental states: "Try not to think of understanding as a 'mental process' at all.—For *that* is the expression which confuses you. But ask yourself: in what sort of case, in what kind of circumstances, do we say, 'Now I know how to go on,' when, that is, the formula *has* occurred to me?" (remark 154). In looking at what interpretations and what grammars allow us to continue, rhetoricians can recognize the public aspects of intentions, not simply as a list of claims, a catalog of experiences, or a tally of conventions, but as a proceeding with interpretations and deliberations. To know intentions need not mean—in fact, cannot mean—to introspect the other's mind, but rather it means that the interlocutor is able to "go on" in her practice, with her purposes (conceivably with adapted purposes). "Going on" has different formulations in different cases and circumstances:

> We do say, "Now I can go on, I mean I know the formula," as we say "I can walk, I mean I have time"; but also "I can walk, I mean I am strong enough"; or: "I can walk, as far as the state of my legs are concerned," that is, when we are contrasting *this* condition for walking with others. But here we must be on our guard against thinking that there is some *totality* of conditions corresponding to the nature of each case (e.g. for a person's walking) so that, as it were, he *could not but* walk if they were all fulfilled. (remark 183)

What allows one interpreter to continue may be very different from what allows another to continue, and the nature of that continuing varies (remark 203). Even so, a certain regularity indicates we have mastered a technique: "To understand a sentence means to understand a language. To understand a language means to be a master of a technique" (remark 199).

New words, strange syntax or topics, bizarre intentions, even foreign languages—in and of themselves—do not stop communication and "going on." If one is addressed and recognizes it as intentional, and not just noise, one may well try to find a path to understanding, not just for the most obvious of meanings, but also for perlocutionary effects, the ulterior purposes of the address. Conventions—publicly recognized, socially formed criteria for interpretation—are a significant part of what allows us to proceed, as are the more physical practices of communicating, such as smiling (common across cultures), running away, mimicking, or modeling earlier successes. In addition to these normalizing strategies, we also invent ways of "going on"; if there is confusion over customary proceedings, interlocutors invent, as one invents new games and words with children or draws diagrams and maps for foreigners. Rather than not continue, interlocutors may shift their expectations of what is acceptable in understanding or sincerity or common action or coherence between replies. Invention and expectation represent our strategies for jerry-rigging meanings, for what constitutes "going on" has different formulations in different cases, and they are not simply conventional or predictable.

Having outlined the ordinary language argument against other mind skepticism and for recognizing mental states, including intentions, I also must discuss a second assumption, the suspicion of theory that I share in some ways with Wittgenstein, but in doing so I want to emphasize our disciplinary difference and its relationship to our final positions. While I assume that the use of theorizing is limited in describing rhetorical situations, given their contingent nature, and that the urge to theorize must be circumscribed, the later Wittgenstein is against all philosophical theorizing, seeing theory as a trap that captures us. He writes:

> And we may not advance any kind of theory. There must not be anything hypothetical in our considerations. We must do away with all *explanations,* and description alone must take its place. (remark 109)

> A *picture* held us captive. And we could not get outside it, for it lay in our language and language seemed to repeat it to us inexorably. (remark 115)

Wittgenstein's argument responds to the metaphysical tendency of philosophy and his period's concerns with science, logic, and linguistic structures; he urges the examination of everyday use and the abandonment of the ideal. Wittgenstein refuses theory as metanarrative.

I, on the other hand, find theory a mode of intelligibility, but am constrained in my writing of grand narrative by the nature of my field. Rhetoric historically examines everyday use, assumes positionality, and minimally engages in metaphysics, and so it rarely pretends to offer grand narrative and the true solution, offering instead a packet of strategies for persuasion, tricks of available means, and road maps of the Human Barnyard and the Scramble. Hence, I remain cognizant that my observations and generalizations are contingent and situated, never neutral. Since one of the tasks of this book is to return rhetoric to a more situated and publicly engaged practice and to question the use of studying ideal interpreters rather than rowdy audiences, I necessarily resist making broad claims (though I offer explanations and generalizations).

Chapters 4, 5, and 6 study how three forms—negatives, narratives, and metaphors—manifested in particular documents, are read by a few philosophers. They trace how Wittgenstein's intentions are described by scholars with interpretive experience and acumen, many of whom even knew Wittgenstein. These forms—in different documents where the audiences have different experiences, acumen, and relationships to the author—foster distinct patterns of understanding. The problem of theorizing from these cases is not that theory will lead us astray, but rather it is the historical dilemma of rhetorical theory: the dynamics of one situation are never those of the next. Still, even given the flukes of contingency and a suspicion of metanarrative, generalizations are useful, there is no more neutrality in describing than in hypothesizing, and theorizing need not lead us astray, especially if one is willing to pop theories on and off like sunglasses (remark 103).

4

Just Say No

Intentions Ignored

Wittgenstein makes me feel it is worth while I should exist, because no one else could understand him or make the world understand him.
—Bertrand Russell to Lady Ottoline, 1913

Now I'm afraid you haven't really got hold of my main contention, to which the whole business of logical prop[osition]s is only a corollary. The main point is the theory of what can be expressed (gesagt) by prop[osition]s—i.e. by language—(and which comes to the same, what can be thought*) and what cannot be expressed by prop[osition]s, but only shown (gezeigt); which, I believe, is the cardinal problem of philosophy.*

I also sent my M.S. to Frege. He wrote me a week ago and I gather that he doesn't understand a word of it all. So my only hope is to see you *soon and explain all to you, for it is VERY hard not to be understood by a single soul!*
—Ludwig Wittgenstein to Bertrand Russell, 1919

Granted, six years separate this claim of understanding by Russell and Wittgenstein's denial that Russell understands, still, Wittgenstein is denying that Russell—his teacher, mentor, advocate, and intellectual confidant—understands his main contention, the answer to what he sees as "the cardinal problem of philosophy."

If these two philosophers who met daily to discuss the nuances of symbolic logic and, for some years at least, were devoted to each other's thinking, *if these two* so seriously fail in understanding, even after careful discussions, what chance is there for speakers across cultures to understand and to negotiate meaning? Are there aspects of this failure of understanding that can help us understand misunderstanding and understanding? What is the nature of the problem between Russell and Wittgenstein? Is it in the differences of their purposes? Is it in the differences of their cultural motives, discourses, and inquiries? Is it in their failure to recognize diverging motives and purposes, and if it is in their failure to recognize diverging motives and purposes, how are the divergences related to concepts of textual form, cultural motive, individual purpose, and risking of prejudices? Why were deliberations over meaning here so difficult?

In this and the next two chapters, I examine practices of interpretation and deliberations over meaning, focusing on particular textual forms and genres and the written responses to the forms and genres by interpreters within a disciplinary community. In looking at how specific aspects or forms of Ludwig Wittgenstein's texts are read by a few philosophers, I pretend to be able to control the infinite expanse of interpretive possibility by seeking a disciplined site, I attempt to bracket, for the moment, the obvious difficulties of significant difference, major power differentials, sophistry, and incommensurable discourses, and I necessarily risk the errors of limiting contextual discussions, reading closely, and hypothesizing where and why certain texts overlap.[1] I work to evade what is most interesting and problematic, but in bracketing these interests, I find that they return even in a limited motivational sphere (ever the return of the repressed). For while, like Fish, we want to believe that the norms of formal sameness within disciplines create a homogeneous or more homogenous epistemic community, and while it is true that the limited number of questions and similarity of education do tend to obscure practical and experiential differences among scholars and subspecialties, when push comes to shove, we must acknowledge disciplines are comprised of discrete individuals with different intentions, ideologies, styles, and positions of authority. Individuals who read as audiences, not as interpreters. All that I attempt to bracket returns because (even within disciplinary discourses and academic institutions) cultural diversity, power differentials, incommensurable discourses, and basic misunderstandings are normal.

---

1. Dominick LaCapra lays out several of these problems very clearly in reviewing *Wittgenstein's Vienna*.

To begin with Wittgenstein is not to begin in an easy place. His writing is provocative and ambiguous, outside the familiar forms and formalities of philosophy: he is, after all, what Richard Rorty calls "an edifying philosopher."[2] But his texts prove a practical site insofar as they are so influential, so widely consumed, so copiously discussed, and so clearly important. After all, it is perfectly reasonable to say that Wittgenstein was an imaginative source for at least two major schools of philosophy, logical positivism and ordinary language philosophy, and that his work is basic to the evolution of analytic philosophy. He is recognized as the co-author (with Frege) of the method of truth tables. He wrote and lectured on the impossibility of private languages, the problems of skepticism, the relationships between language and reality, language and culture, language and knowing, and language and ethics and aesthetics. His writings, their meanings, and their significance are interpreted and interpreted, debated and debated. His are not easy writings, but because of this, they are the site of deliberations over meaning and intended meaning. Ultimately I turn to his difficult texts because of the sharpness of his forms and the rich discussions interpreting *Tractatus Logico-Philosophicus* and *Philosophical Investigations.*

I

The *Tractatus* is such an odd piece that describing its generic form is difficult. Only about eighty pages long, it concerns logic and syntax for about the first seventy-seven pages; then surprisingly, the last three pages appear to be about ethics and aesthetics. It is a terse, cryptic, aphoristic argument in three parts, one about reality discredited by one about logic discredited by one about mysticism, ethics, and aesthetics. Even to summarize its formal argumentative structure is to invite conversation, deliberation, and disjunctures. I cannot avoid these controversies long, but before examining Russell's and Carnap's acts of interpretation, I need to lay out theories of forms that negate themselves.

The negative: there are many ways to think about this broad concept, which is in some ways the signifying of *all that something isn't.* Within that broad category, several aspects let us understand how form and style

---

2. Many call him the most significant philosopher of the twentieth century. See K. T. Fann's *Ludwig Wittgenstein,* E. D. Klemke's *Essays on Wittgenstein,* and G. J. Warnock's *English Philosophy Since 1900.* Others have limited his influence, but A. C. Grayling responds well to their circumscriptions in "Wittgenstein's Influence."

work within the *Tractatus* and suggest several things about what happens when the negatives in the *Tractatus* are interpreted. From at least the "Dissoi Logoi" onward, the negative is used to posit a way of contrasting what is known and accepted, the cultural givens, with what is unknown and unacceptable. The negative is not only the "thou shalt not" but also a means to unearth alternative ways of proceeding in the world. Within the broader category of the negative, negation that denotes a logical or grammatical negative is supplemented by negativity that connotes a more abstract and elusive sense of denial and alternatives. Some have conceived the negative—negation or negativity—as a utopian or revolutionary concept, a syntactic means of creating new possibility and surprising knowledges. "Just say no" seems to promise as much to radical forces as conservative, but I am wary of promises without evidence.

Burke finds negation in definition, in the *not*. Following Spinoza, he writes that "all definition is 'negation' which is another way of saying that, to define a thing in terms of its context, we must define it in terms of what it is not" (*Grammar* 25). In defining something, in giving it an identity, we also must know what it is not and where it is not. The language of definition requires us to shift from the word or concept that is positive and seemingly known, at least to the author of the definition, to other words and concepts that at best approximate it. The interaction between what is presented and what is not (a *forte-da* game) pushes the limits of what we can know and say. What we want to define, both the signified and signifier, is in part present, but to be presented and represented, it appears as other signifieds and signifiers. By definition, we find a concept by describing what it is not: to define, in effect, is to look at the limits of what we can know and say, but to stay within the limits. Within a Burkean system, negation represents the giving and taking away, but not the ineffable. In fact, for Burke it is "the essential distinction between the verbal and nonverbal" (*Language* 420). To say "no" is to use language; *no* and *not* exist only in language. Some might see erasure and coverage as nonverbal *no*s, but I believe Burke would protest that they are not syntactic and so not *no*s.

If *to define* is to look at *the limits* of what we can know and say, then we are sometimes in a slightly different sense of negation, *playing with what we want or might want* in the very process of defining the familiar. In negation, desire and language intertwine, especially when desire is informed by lack. Using Bergson, Burke describes the negative as a "function of *desire,* or *expectation* or *interest*" (*Grammar* 296); the negative here becomes future oriented and less textual. Burke, in describing this sense, tells us what we desire or expect is positive (the absence of what we desire leads us on, shapes our purposes), and what is unexpected and undesired is negative (damages our plans and purposes). This second aspect of Burke on the negative diverges from the interaction of that which is present (positive) and all that is not (negation). If we want the temperature to be thirty-two degrees and it is not, our expectation is negated, and so we may use *negato* and *no* "where intention or expectation is involved" (*Language* 421). Here he seems to suggest that our intents, desires, and purposes would play beyond our definitions. The mental states of expecting and intending when posited in the act of their negation seemingly will connect to conceptual negativity, an excess of what is culturally represented and present, and in this leading to negativity, negation suggests a possibility of reading the excess beyond the signified. But Burke does not go so far with the negative. His concept of negation is confined to reversal of the *no*, the control of "thou shalt not." He goes so far as to see the negation as demanding the seeking of the positive elsewhere (usually in an opposite), but he does not see the negative as particularly liberatory or revealing of cultural codes or themes. Still, when the interlocutor is sent elsewhere for meaning, negation moves toward negativity and the revealing of cultural codes.

In summary, negativity is not so clearly structural or explicitly verbal, but negation is, and negation is the controlling structure of the *Tractatus*, a text that plays with definition, the revelations of intratextual contradictions, and resulting negation. As well as the usual syntactic structures of definition, negation controls the larger structure of its argument. In effect, the *Tractatus* has three main arguments, one about naming and the representation of reality by propositions, one about logic and its representation of formal properties of the world, and one about the unsayable or mystical nature of ethics, aesthetics, and metaphysics.

Wittgenstein initially presents an uncritical realism; the world is made of *Sachverhalte* ("atomic facts" in C. K. Ogden's translation, "states of affairs" in the Pears and McGuinness, or perhaps "situations" as translated in Anscombe's *Introduction*), which are composed of simple objects that can be named, though by names in need of the context of a proposition for meaning (*Tractatus* 3.3). But then young Wittgenstein argues that while factual propositions, like pictures, present a view of the world, they do not present a view of what made the original view possible. They do not connect directly to reality, nor do they explain how our system of language works. And since factual language cannot critique itself (Negation One), he turns to logic and argues that logic shows a form already inherent in ordinary language, and so the world. But after more analysis he finds the truth of logic to be in its form, which is tautological. Logic—which is *not* a second or ideal language—may expose the structure of our speech, but it does *not* extend the limit of what can be said. Hence, logic says *nothing* new about the world or how our system of language works (Negation Two). Having reached this conclusion about the inadequacy of factual language and logic for critique, Wittgenstein ends his text with three pages of mysticism on the unsayable nature of aesthetics and ethics. He writes that since "value" lies "outside the world" (6.41), transcendental ethics and aesthetics cannot be talked about sensibly in philosophy (6.421), implying that what can be said meaningfully in philosophy is limited to the propositions of the natural world. The propositions of ethics and metaphysics are logically senseless since some of the signs in them are given no meaning, no hook onto or into the world (6.53). Since "the solution of the riddle of life in space and time lies *outside* space and time" (6.4312), Wittgenstein asserts that philosophy cannot describe the significant problems of life: feelings, ethics, the mystical (Negation Three). This is not much progress, but Wittgenstein warns in his preface that his work "shows how little has been done when these problems have been solved" (29). In effect, the *Tractatus* must be read as a repeatedly retracting piece, one that demands the reader reshape what has gone before and acknowledge shifting purposes within the text, retroactive maneuvers not unlike those required by the end of Gorgias's "Encomium" or the three speeches in Plato's *Phaedrus*. Within its argument, it sets up expectations in order to negate them.

Within the larger structure of argument based on three negations, Wittgenstein writes sentences that define within a pattern of negating definitions. For example, the *Tractatus* starts:

1   The world is everything that is the case.
1.1 The world is the totality of the facts, not of things.

He begins by defining the world, then immediately limits the world by stating what it is not. Any world we know is not made of things but of the facts that, he tells us later, determine the truth or falsity of our propositions. This pattern of syntactic giving and taking away continues.

What is interesting about the pattern of syntactic shifts is that it parallels patterns of nonsense. Now Wittgenstein tells us his book both concerns nonsense and is nonsense.[3] In his preface, he describes the book as con-

---

3. For this discussion of nonsense, I go to the Pears and McGuinness translation because it maintains Wittgenstein's distinction between *Sinnlos* (senseless) and *UnSinn* (nonsense). Elsewhere I use the more commonly known Ogden translation.

cerned with drawing "a limit to thought, or rather—not to thought, but to the expression of thoughts: for in order to be able to draw a limit to thought, we should have to find both sides of the limit of the thinkable (i.e., we should have to be able to think what cannot be thought)" (3). Then in a separate paragraph only one sentence long, he writes, "It will therefore only be in language that the limit can be drawn, and what lies on the other side of the limit will simply be nonsense" (3). In the main text, in his penultimate entry, Wittgenstein tells us the book's propositions themselves are nonsense.

> My propositions serve as elucidations in the following way: anyone who understands me eventually recognizes them as nonsensical, when he has used them—as steps—to climb up beyond them. (He must, so to speak, throw away the ladder after he has climbed it.)
> He must transcend these propositions, and then he will see the world aright. (6.54)

In the claim of nonsense, Wittgenstein suggests a relationship between his reader and the text, not one of fused horizons, but rather one where the audience's relationship to the text is highly transitory. The act of reading, described in 6.54, is not as interpretive as instrumental; it is about going on—going on and beyond nonsense.

Despite Wittgenstein's lifelong consideration of nonsense and its relationship to philosophy, his claim of nonsense is commonly ignored.[4] One of philosophy's prejudices (for that matter, any discipline's prejudice) is that its work is serious, relevant, rational, and intelligent. But Wittgenstein's lines are worth pursuing at face value. As well as I, or anyone, can discern authorial intention, the author, Wittgenstein, wants his work taken as nonsense. By his definition at the time of the *Tractatus,* nonsense means

---

4. While the claim of the *Tractatus* as nonsense is commonly ignored, Wittgenstein's interest in nonsense is not. See Cora Diamond's and George Pitcher's work on his definition of nonsense and its appearance in his work.

In a careful discussion of his definition of nonsense, Cora Diamond develops the argument that Wittgenstein's sense of nonsense was technically specific and not part of the more normal senses of nonsense (category error, falsity, inapposition, odd syntax, made-up words, or gibberish). For Frege and Wittgenstein, Diamond argues, nonsense was senseless, a meaning withdrawn from circulation, and never a playing with what a proposition *might mean* given the meaning of its terms.

But I think it is less clear what Wittgenstein meant. Wittgenstein does state that tautology and contradiction are senseless (4.461), but not nonsense because they are part of the (possible) symbolism of logic, and so true even if vacuous. And he does give examples of nonsense, the meanings of which are in circulation.

a clause or text that cannot be understood because it gives no sense or only trivial sense; it is language outside the *limit* of what can be said meaningfully. One of his clearer examples of nonsensical philosophical language is "the question whether the good is more or less identical than the beautiful" (4.003).[5] I take Wittgenstein at his word: his philosophy is nonsense (outside the limit of what can be said meaningfully). However his work has—underneath but significantly—an impulse to parody the steps of logic and to deconstruct the progress of philosophical thinking.[6] I compare the propositions of the *Tractatus* to a more normally defined sense of nonsense, a negative language that somehow presumes sense in its negation of the common world of (philosophical) sense and its offering of the world aright.

Susan Stewart, like Wittgenstein, regards nonsense as a means of seeing the world aright; she writes that "nonsense, with its embracing of play and paradox, is a critical activity" (50). To demonstrate the critical potential for nonsense to manipulate sense, language, context, and frames, she investigates five nonsense operations, five ways of making nonsense (for the humor handicapped). She offers a very sensible taxonomy of how to make nonsense, from playing with infinity to playing with boundaries. Her distinctions among the reversals and inversions of nonsense work as well to distinguish the types of syntactic negations in Wittgenstein's *Tractatus* and to connect those negations to nonsense. Despite Stewart's dependence on child's play and nonsense for her demonstration, her divisions of reversals and inversions help to define a variety of grammatical negatives beyond the *no*-negation and to illustrate the role of negativity in reframing, rerouting, and re-creating discourse. The exploration of the connections between the nonsense operation of reversal and inversion and Wittgenstein's syntax demonstrates the degree of negative within his propositions.

Nonsense inversions and reversals are reversals and inversions of cultural categories, the categories that define hierarchies that in turn define development and processes within the culture. Wittgenstein's inversions and reversals, it would seem, are concerned with reversing and inverting

---

5. He would say that most logical propositions, tautologies, are senseless or vacuous but true. Logical propositions that are exceptions would be found in Russell's theory of types (*Tractatus* 6.1232, 3.33). See Gordon Baker's *Wittgenstein, Frege, and the Vienna Circle* for a discussion (248).

6. LaCapra also describes some of the parodic aspects of the Tractatus. Since the later Wittgenstein sees some philosophical nonsense as revealing (see Pitcher), I am inclined to see the parodic aspects realized in Tractarian nonsense as a foreshadowing of the shift to nonsense as useful that pervades his later writing.

categories, hierarchies, and processes within the culture of philosophy. As he wrote on the system of symbolic logic, he was concerned with inverting what might be called the logical system of philosophy. He was setting up the ruptures that would allow him to argue for the removal of ethics and aesthetics from philosophical propositions, propositions he wanted to limit to empirical description, "the propositions of natural science."

Stewart's first class of reversal and inversion is "proper nots," p and not-p, which she characterizes as symmetrical inversion and I characterize as negation, an aspect of Burkean negation. One of Stewart's examples of proper nots is a customer shaving the barber. Here again is a Wittgensteinian negation: "The world is the totality of the facts, not of things" (*Tractatus* 1.1). One of the characteristics of a proper not is that its categories are organized by levels of abstraction. Stewart gives examples of proper nots: "not floor" and "ceiling," "not master" and "slave" (63). One would not couple "not floor" and "year" or "not master" and "justice." Wittgenstein's odd pairing causes one to puzzle over the "not." One would assume a similar level of abstraction, but how? How are facts and things related? Are they equally abstract, or is this a more extreme inversion of categories and culture? The proposition is a puzzle that sets up a problem of cultural pairing, especially within philosophy.

Stewart's second class, "taking things back," emphasizes reversibility, making equals of opposites without consequences. If the natural world is constant, the cultural world is not, though much of a culture's reversibility is fictive. One can more easily reverse the role of a king and his fool in nonsense than elsewhere, though reversible acts or pranks also count in this class (soapy windows can be washed). When Wittgenstein plays with the "taking things back," he moves between the natural world and the culture of philosophy in ways that trouble that division. For example, in the following reversal, he is writing of facts that are not created by our thoughts and beliefs. He is rather boldly and oddly reversing the natural world without consequence.

> Each item can be the case or not the case, and every thing else remains the same. (1.21)

In the next instance, he is reversing, without consequence, the concept of logical form (which he may or may not see as cultural).

> Two objects of the same logical form are—apart from their external properties—only differentiated from one another in that they are different. (2.0233)

Objects sharing logical form share both a sameness and a difference; the hierarchy between sameness and difference seems to have no consequence, nor does the logical form have consequence.

Stewart's "inverting classes" includes both changing categories and play with the boundaries of possibility, and so it involves more inversion or negation than a proper not; rather than the customer shaving the barber, the barber would shave a pig (67). Unlike reversibility, there are consequences in inverting classes. In Stewart's example:

> Flea jumped on an elephant's toe
> Elephant cried, with tears in his eyes,
> Why don't you pick on someone your size? (68)

Or as Wittgenstein writes:

> The right method of philosophy would be this. To say nothing except what can be said, i.e. the propositions of natural science, i.e. something that has nothing to do with philosophy. (6.53)

If philosophy's class of propositions is the same class as natural science's, then philosophy has no providence, a very painful consequence.

Stewart's class "reversible texts" denies direction and progress as well as hierarchy. Most of her examples are of limited use for our purposes (reversing sounds, palindromes), but she does include ironic reversals in this class. Her example is a poem whose stanzas can be read across for one meaning or vertically for another:

> I love my country-but the king   Above all men his praise I sing
> Destruction to his odious reign   That plague of princes, Thomas Paine
> The Royal banners are displayed   And may success his standard aid
> Defeat and ruin seize the cause   Of France, her liberty and laws. (70)

Ironic reversals or playful negatives that deny direction and progress are part and parcel of Tractarian argumentation. They are among Wittgenstein's most startling and memorable lines.

> In it there is no value—and if there were, it would be of no value. (6.41)

> Whereof one cannot speak, thereof one must be silent. (7)

Stewart's final category that is helpful to demonstrating the propositional negatives of the *Tractatus* is "discourse that denies itself." She characterizes this as a "metacommunication" that "implicitly carries a denial and a criticism" (72). The denial is a denial of "the status of representation"; that is, what is said is both "real and unreal," meaningful and unmeaningful. The self-criticism is that the text has been "set off," "framed" away from action; it is a lie and not-lie.

> Ladles and jellyspoons:
> I come before you
> To stand behind you
> And tell you something
> I know nothing about
> Last Thursday . . . (Stewart 72)

> This book will perhaps only be understood by those who have themselves already thought the thoughts which are expressed in it—or similar thoughts. (*Tractatus* 27)

> My propositions serve as elucidations in the following way: anyone who understands me finally recognizes them as nonsensical. . . . (6.54)

The form of the *Tractatus* repeats negations, inversions, and reversals, and Wittgenstein's claim to nonsense is broadened and solidified when connected to the operations of nonsense; but in addition to elucidating the *Tractatus,* this tangent into Stewart's work helps demonstrate that negation, the not-*p*, is an inadequate description of all that is the negative.[7] And it helps us explicate what it means to say that the negative is a complex set of speech strategies that breaks frames of meaning, defies hierarchies, and puts discourses in new contexts.

Nonsense disrupts any idea of society as coherent and so works to rearrange and divide our categories. As Stewart concludes her book, "in nonsense, purpose becomes a continual and pleasurable movement away from itself, a reflexive gesture that spirals away from any point of privileged signification or direction. Both 'author' and 'audience' are continually fractured and rearranged" (209). Purpose or intention in nonsensical

---

7. Kristeva returns to this point several times in *Revolution in Poetic Language.* See pages 109-13 for an analysis of the role of negativity in Hegelian dialectic; 117-26 for a discussion of her distinction between negativity and negation.

forms, says Stewart, become difficult to attribute, but the lack of attributable purpose is a potential resource for insight and for rearranging relationships between author, audience, text, and culture—what Wittgenstein might want from his ladder-climbing audience. With the play of nonsense, there is the play of possibility, the unexpected, and surprise for the author and audience. This type of negative is not unrelated to negation in Burke, the defining of concepts in terms of what they are not, but the playful negations of nonsense are closer to the claims of novelty in negativity. And if novelty is not a claim made within Wittgenstein's definition of nonsense (of no or trivial sense)—though I think novelty is part of his claim in finding the other side of the limit—his use of nonsense and forms related to nonsense is, at least, a demonstration: the demonstration of the place of the negative in exploring newness and possibility. Nonsense and the negative invite the rhetorical reading. They set up an expected common experience between the reader and writer, but through a turn or stop, a reversal or inversion within the "no," they deny that expectation.

II

The form of the *Tractatus* is self-negating. In the end, there is a ladder to leave it and the silence of what cannot be said; the promised non-sense is delivered with the expectation that the reader transcends it. Since Hegel, if not Socrates, negativity is read as a valuable means for the subject to resist and transcend cultural motives and the other's purposes, but Wittgenstein's negatives were not read for meanings outside mainstream philosophical motives. Did something go awry? Do we have real reason to believe that an author's negativity affects a reader in a unique way?

The difficulty is that theories of the reader often are based in theories of the interpreter, and so are inadequate for describing the rhetorical or resisting reader. For this project, Wolfgang Iser provides a good example of the appeal, but ultimate inadequacy, of reader-response theories in that he is highly concerned with the negative and has a theory that describes reader-text interaction, though for most rhetorical projects he is excessively concerned with ideal models and aesthetic readings. Iser argues that the indeterminate factors of literature create the links between text and reader and that while the text guides the reader, the indeterminate factors push the reader's response beyond a simple cause and effect. Iser sees negation as the syntactic formation of gaps and omissions that require the reader to move into a position beyond the familiar and, through this movement, to form a new concept that then lies in conflict with the norms (*Reading* 213). Iser describes the process of reading as the interaction of the reader's norms and textual signals. The textual signals he calls "primary negations," and the concepts formed through the interaction between textual signals and the reader's *gestalten* he calls "secondary negations" (220-21), though when one reads secondary negations are necessarily inseparable from primary negations (221, 223). In any case, negations are the features that revoke, modify, or neutralize knowledge. Iser's concept of negation is not specifically tied to textual features (such as Burke's "no" or Kristeva's negative statements and syntactic distortions); instead his negations are textual signals that conflict with social norms. Consequently his negations include the strategies of inversion and reversal, though for their cognitive effect rather than for their syntax.

As well as negation, Iser develops a concept of negativity that does not negate the formulations of the text but forms the unwritten base, part of textual indeterminacy. He claims that "what is stated must not exhaust the intention of the text" (*Prospecting* 14). Negativity is the textual action that is not stated; it is the hidden infrastructure of reading and constituting texts. He evades defining it but goes so far as to write that negativity "enables the written words to transcend their literal meaning, to assume a multiple referentiality, and so to undergo the expansion necessary to transplant them as a new experience into the mind of the reader" (*Reading* 226). Note the internal, mystical nature of this explication: we never have the author; we quickly lose language and enter the mind of the reader. The text, beyond any simple intention on the part of the author, is experienced by a reader or audience. In explaining the creation of new experience for the reader, Iser also discusses three features of negativity. One, it is formal in that it links the elements of the text, tracing what is not explicitly public and provided; yet despite its linking function, negativity is unformulated. Two, unlike negation, which denotes a lack of or error in knowledge and problematizes content, negativity calls on the reader to analyze what is concealed or beyond the lack, error, or "deformation"—in the case of Wittgenstein, what is ineffable. Negativity calls on the reader to find meaning "as the reverse side of what the text has depicted" (228). Negativity is a remedy then for the deformations of the negative in that it calls for a more complex understanding, not a solution to the lack or problem per se, but "a construction of the text on a question-and-answer basis" (228). Three, negativity is the aspect of textuality (here Iser is writing of fiction) that is an "invalidation of the manifested reality" (229). Since the text is not in opposition to reality but only an alternative to or cure for reality, it calls into question the world as it is. Iser writes, "If the reader is made to formulate the cause underlying the questioning of the world, it implies that he must transcend that world, in order to be able to observe it from outside" (230). According to Iser, art provides something never given in the world in allowing transcendence. Negativity is the critical space provided that mediates between presentation and reception and initiates "processes of imagination" (*Prospecting* 142).

In negation and negativity, Iser offers a vision of reading as liberatory and inventive; that is, the reader is liberated from the world by the processes of imagination. The model here shares with the *Tractatus* a faith in the reader's transcendence and ability to deal with the ineffable. Iser's description of reading and of the creativity, particularly individualistic and cognitive, of the reader is much more at variance with Gadamer's theory of interpretation. While in both models the reader is to be transformed and her norms reexamined (the process of reading requires a transformed reader), and while both models are textual and do not recognize authorial intentions, the invention within hermeneutics requires that the reader put her prejudices at risk and enter into the text's horizon as best she is able. Iser's interpretive theory potentially allows for the protection of prejudices as a means of understanding and critiquing. Iser's reader is a more rhetorical critic who revokes, modifies, and neutralizes her relationship to the world while the hermeneutic reader is transformed in the seeking of understanding. Unfortunately, at least in readings of the *Tractatus*, transformation is not predictably nor necessarily revolutionary or responsive to authorial intentions.

III

Given a background of the conceptual ruptures possibly affected by textual negatives, the theoretical tension between hermeneutics and reader-response theory, and the differences between how readers might work in Iser's theory and how a few philosophers read the negatives in the *Tractatus*, I turn to interpretation in context, examining the reception of Wittgenstein's use of the negative in the *Tractatus* and discussing the nature of negotiating its meanings first within logical atomism and then logical positivism. In doing so, I find patterns in the interpretation of Wittgenstein's self-negating discourse. Wittgenstein's associates, Bertrand Russell and members of the Vienna Circle, in fact refuse the reversals in his argument and the implications of most of his negatives (negations and negativities) and instead interpret his work to suit their own purposes (in the face of his protests). Rather than searching for authorial intention and meaning or acquiescing to authorial purposes and meaning, these readers use their intentions and the norms or motives of their philosophical culture both to formulate their interpretation of his work and to make decisions about its incorporation in further work. In this instance, an author's negating of earlier positions, inscription of new positions, and even the resulting event of being read and understood are not enough to undo the prevailing motives and discourses, to effect the prevailing frame of interpretation, or to influence the purposes of his readers—though it is enough to trigger discussions of his purposes. Even in the context of those discussions, Wittgenstein's purpose of undermining the significance of philosophy and logic was not enough to influence the reading of his text, and it remained subject to the prevailing paradigm or system of motives and the purposes of his audience. He was perceived as an advocate of both philosophy and logic, and his final negation was ignored. Resistance, negation, and negativity led only to reader responses where seemingly no one risked his prejudices to the text or to authorial intention, and the reversals in the argument only worked to facilitate the audience's prejudiced readings.

In its time, the *Tractatus* was read for its formal techniques, its picture theory of language, the method of truth tables, and to a lesser extent its dichotomy between the factual and logical, the cognitive and emotive. Its earlier readership, however, ignored or neglected the work's final arguments, disregarding its ethical argument and seeing no need to diminish logic because of its tautological nature. Readers failed to climb Wittgenstein's ladder though they may have climbed their own. Only in the last fifteen or twenty years have philosophers turned to the ethical argument, intending to make better sense of the first book of a man whose second book, *Philosophical Investigations,* has become so significant for contemporary thought.

Wittgenstein's philosophy was influenced by two identified systems of motives, one arising from Viennese concerns with the limits of language and critique,[8] the other arising from his connections with symbolic logic,

---

8. Vienna, part of the grim decline of the Austro-Hungarian empire, had many theorists concerned with ethics and the limits of the effable, and Wittgenstein was familiar with the work of Viennese theorists such as Karl Kraus, Fritz Mauthner, and Sigmund Freud as well as physicists Heinrich Hertz and Ludwig Boltzmann. Perhaps the most accessible examples of the Viennese concern with the limits of the effable are evident in Freud's psychoanalytic theory.

At the simplest level, Freud found the sexual repression of this period to be destructive, but to articulate his theories he had to traverse taboos, develop a new vocabulary, and convince others to accept their latent incestuous instincts. Inherent in Freudian theory is an explicit critique of the

most prominently Frege and Bertrand Russell.[9] In *Wittgenstein's Vienna,* Janik and Toulmin argue that the questions of Vienna motivated Wittgenstein to seek out Frege and Russell; in effect, they argue that he began his study of philosophy and went to Cambridge with the intention of solving a Viennese concern with the place of ethics in discourse. This view, generally accepted now, radically circumscribes the logical aspects of the *Tractatus.*[10]

Undoubtedly Wittgenstein's two motivational spheres, his two cultures, interacted and aided him in developing a unique, if ineffable position as much as the process of negation gave him a unique voice: the interactions of the monograph's two motivational systems and its unusual form, leaving aside content, make the *Tractatus* a hard read. Wittgenstein's subjective intentions, despite his surrounding assertions in letters to a variety of conversants, are not transparent either. What is clear is that whatever the source of his purposes and theories, his contemporaries, such as Russell or Carnap, essentially ignore his last few pages; either these pages do not achieve significant presence for them (Russell), or they read his exclusion of ethical discourse from meaning as an exclusion of the significance of ethics (Carnap). His negatives are read selectively, and most do not affect disciplinary practices in philosophy.

The book enters Anglo-American philosophy largely through the work of Bertrand Russell, who wrote the introduction to the *Tractatus* as part of his effort to get it published. The fact that the publication of the book was linked closely to Russell's writing of an introduction is evidence that his voice was the authority for its reading by editors as well as philosophers.[11] In fairness to Russell's lack of interpretive efforts regarding Tractarian ethics, aesthetics, and mysticism, we must remember that his disciplinary relationship with Wittgenstein revolved around logic, and when they first

---

human inability to speak our inner being without recourse to sublimation, condensation, and displacement; and so the limits of literal language are the starting points of psychoanalytic theory.

For more elaborated contextualist studies, see Janik and Toulmin's *Wittgenstein's Vienna,* Haller's *Questions on Wittgenstein,* and McGuinness's *Wittgenstein: A Life.*

9. See Gordon Baker's *Wittgenstein, Frege, and the Vienna Circle,* McGuinness's biography of Wittgenstein, Russell's autobiography, and Blackwell's "Early Wittgenstein and Middle Russell."

10. For fuller discussions of its significance, see LaCapra's "Reading Exemplars" and Bernstein's "Wittgenstein's Three Languages."

11. In fact, the *Tractatus* was only published through Russell's intervention (McGuinness, *Wittgenstein* 287-99). Russell's place as the authority who is acknowledged in a Gadamerian sense presents a problem for Gadamer's sense of authority as being a grounds for risking prejudices. If Russell, Wittgenstein's mentor, is so attached to his prejudices (as I will show), the Enlightenment may have a better case about the limits of authority than Gadamer concedes.

met to talk about the *Tractatus*, Russell reports that Wittgenstein "talked logic without ceasing for 4 hours" (McGuinness, *Wittgenstein* 290). Logic was their common ground, the basis of their shared motives and purposes. In the *Tractatus,* Wittgenstein makes corrections to Russell's too-Platonic theory of logic (Pears 21-31), but these corrections were all of interest to Russell, ideas that suited his motives and purposes. Russell's difficulties in responding to the text primarily involve Wittgenstein's minimizing of philosophy's value and his mysticism; at least, those are the two difficulties I address.[12]

The "goal" of early analytic philosophy has been described as the "construction and methodology of applying such a regulating ideal as a theory of logical form," and so, as an analytic philosopher, Russell's aim was "a logically perfect language as a regulating ideal" (Cocchiarella 1).[13] Russell believed philosophy could develop an important second language, logic, with which to critique ordinary language, making philosophy a vital human activity. Wittgenstein may have shared this belief at one point, but by the writing of the *Tractatus* he finds that "the only strictly correct method" of philosophy is "to say nothing" but what makes empirical sense, "i.e. the propositions of natural science," which have "nothing to do with philosophy" (6.53). To paraphrase crudely, philosophy is only good for killing off its own metaphysical discourse. In elucidating the *Tractatus,* Russell ignores this and other closing statements that negate the significance of the work's earlier atomism and logic. When Russell discusses the role of philosophy, he uses earlier propositions (4.112-16), which speak of philosophy as "the logical clarification of thoughts." Thus Russell uses the bivocalism within the negating form of Wittgenstein's text; he attends to its first offering of a position and ignores its later negation. His purposes are aided by the mere presence of other propositions that provide the means for him to ignore negations and restructure the argument. This is a case of interpretation in an either/or fashion rather a recognition of a developing argument within a whole text. Russell's fragmentation of the text is not unique; later commentators such as G. E. M. Anscombe and Max Black go so far as to advocate a fragmentary or thematic approach to the

---

12. Teresa Iglesias considers their differences from a slightly different, though related perspective. She describes Russell's philosophical concerns as logical and epistemological while Wittgenstein's are semantic. Russell is questioning what can be known about the world while Wittgenstein starts with the premise that language says something about the world, the question being what has to be the case for language to say something about the world.

13. Richard J. Bernstein ("Three Languages") and Max Black ("Problems") also make this observation and make arguments against Russell's interpretation.

difficult text.[14] The negating form apparently works against a coherent interpretation or at least facilitates selective interpretive engagement.

Since Russell underwrote the ideal of early analytic philosophy, the construction of a logically perfect language, it is no surprise that in his introduction to the *Tractatus* he writes, "In order to understand Mr. Wittgenstein's book, it is necessary to realize what is the problem with which he is concerned. . . . Mr. Wittgenstein is concerned with the conditions for a logically perfect language" (7, 8). Russell writes slight variations of this three times in the first two pages and then focuses virtually his entire introduction on logic, some fourteen out of sixteen pages. And while it's true that Wittgenstein *is* concerned with logic, there is no evidence he is seeking a perfect language. Wittgenstein writes in *his* preface that his book "deals" with how the formulation of philosophical problems "rests on the misunderstanding of the logic of our language" and that his "book will, therefore, draw a limit to . . . the expression of thought" (27). Not at all the same concern. Even though both philosophers are writing in the same book and within a few pages of each other, each describes the *Tractatus* as concerning a different issue—though, as we shall see, Russell is aware at some level of Wittgenstein's intentions, but Russell hears and uses the affirmatives, and ignores and muffles the negatives.

Authorial intentions and meaning in the process of a diverging inquiry are minimally subject to deliberation; thus if one is pursuing a different line of inquiry, one usually doesn't extend much energy to re-creating an author's purposes or a text's meaning, and one certainly doesn't risk one's prejudices. In the case of Russell reading Wittgenstein, he does not spend much energy even in respecting the deliberative conventions of the discipline. In the small space (little more than two pages) where Russell acknowledges Wittgenstein's call to silence and his wish to limit what can be said (according to Wittgenstein, the point of the book!), in that small space where Russell deliberates over Wittgenstein's meaning and intent, he does not follow the conventions of rigorous, disciplined argument, allegedly a method for testing prejudices. What he does do instead is very suggestive: Russell creates a drama, in the Burkean sense, and uses it to play out Wittgenstein's purpose so that he can "go on" with his own purposes; he creates a textual agent, Mr. Wittgenstein, and gives him specific speech acts in the scene of a scholarly dialogue. The dramatistic

---

14. This is LaCapra's observation (67). He also makes the useful observation that the stakes must be high when commentators work so hard to overcome (or repress) the difficulties of the argument (68-69).

move suggests the importance of recognizing another's intentions, especially purpose, within the context of actions.

Russell summarizes Wittgenstein's position on the expressive aspects of language and the limits of philosophy in a few sentences; he seems to have some sense, as much as can be judged, of Wittgenstein's intentions. If, however, he were reading as an interpreter rather than an audience or writing as a explicator rather than an inquirer, he would place his prejudices at risk or acknowledge an authentic potential for rightness within the *Tractatus*. One would expect Russell the interpreter to recognize the depth of their differences and then, perhaps, to respond with a developed argument that might persuade Wittgenstein or the reader of his introduction that the book ends inadequately. But he doesn't do this; he reads as an audience and writes as a rhetorician.

While he acknowledges that Wittgenstein's ending arguments are "powerful," Russell hesitates to accept them. He writes that since "Mr Wittgenstein manages to say a good deal about what cannot be said" (ethics), there is a suggestion to the "skeptical reader" that there must be some "loophole" or "exit" (22). With this proposition, Russell seemingly acknowledges that, at this point in the text, his reading has stopped and must find an "exit" (a scenic word) to "go on"; he primarily has questions about the validity of the argument, but he also has some concerns about authorial purpose. To understand the author's purpose, he does not theorize purpose or seek mental states but rather creates a narrative in which to engage a character partially known. While he has referred to Wittgenstein alternatively as "Wittgenstein" and "Mr Wittgenstein" to this point in the introduction, for the next two pages the textual agent is Mr Wittgenstein, an indication of some distance between this Wittgenstein persona (not his student speaking on logic) and the "skeptical reader" (Russell's "I"). Russell avoids the compulsions of purpose by appealing to a very specific agent whose purpose stopped his reading, and he seeks to "go on" by creating a drama in which to recognize conflicting purposes and at least attempt a negotiation.

Having stated his desire for an "exit," Russell then acknowledges that "Mr Wittgenstein" would respond to Russell's critique by saying "the mystical can be shown, although it cannot be said" (22), in effect, ethics can be conveyed or presented, not analyzed. Though Russell replies "it may be that this defense is adequate," he writes that it "leaves [him] with a certain sense of intellectual discomfort" (22). Once again, he can't "go on." So Russell continues to explore their differences and the validity of the arguments in a dialogic matter. He shifts his critique to the logical theory of generality and presents a counterstatement that premises an infinite hierarchy of critiquing languages, but he acknowledges that "Mr Wittgenstein would of course reply" that his theory would work for "the totality of such languages" (23). Russell presents a new hypothesis, a "retort" denying "any such totality," but follows it with the statement: "Such a hypothesis is very difficult, and I can see objections to it which at the moment I do not know how to answer" (23). Despite creating a drama that embeds Wittgenstein's and his own purposes and helps them to be made public, Russell can't go on; he has no refutation of Wittgenstein's critique of logic and no articulated grounds for his prejudice, but that doesn't change his rejection of mysticism nor his support for the early logic arguments. Instead he brackets the last piece of the book and clings to his admittedly flawed counterhypothesis, writing that "even if this very difficult hypothesis should prove tenable, it would leave untouched a very large part of Mr. Wittgenstein's theory, though possibly not the part upon which he himself would wish to lay most stress" (23). Russell desires to preserve the arguments Wittgenstein intends to have rejected and to reject the argument Wittgenstein intends to preserve. Although he has no clear counterstatement to Wittgenstein's mysticism, Russell excludes the importance of Wittgenstein's last three pages.

When Russell cannot go on in the text because he cannot construct a consistent, whole meaning nor a meaning to which he can consent, he is forced to examine authorial purpose; to do this, he creates a dialogue with a constructed Mr Wittgenstein. Of interest in this engagement is the form of Russell's argument, which here begins to echo Wittgenstein's series of offerings and negations. Russell, too, offers positions only to withdraw them. He offers a critique, acknowledges Wittgenstein's rebuttal, offers a second critique, acknowledges Wittgenstein's rebuttal, presents a new hypothesis, acknowledges his own objections, but then preserves his hypothesis and the first two parts of Wittgenstein's book. The deliberations seem admissible until the last page, the last hypothesis where the conclusion breaks free of any rational argument and Russell simply uses the text as an instrument to further his thinking. Russell, who could paraphrase the ending of the *Tractatus,* doesn't succeed in imagining the basis of its different motives or in applying different purposes, but he does engage the form, which Burke tells us is "a way of experiencing" (*Counter-Statement* 143). Seemingly, a part of Russell's efforts to understand Wittgenstein's purposes entails a formulaic engagement, a sharing of experience. Mimicking form as a means of engaging purpose is a subtle move suggestive of the difficulties of "going on" and the polymorphous routes one takes in that effort. And if Russell seems unfair in his dismissal of the *Tractatus*'s last pages without an adequate disciplinary response, he does engage the book's form.

Russell also is fair enough to admit that these sections causing "intellectual disquiet" are "possibly" the parts where Wittgenstein would "lay most stress" (23). This admission, in Russell's final paragraph, suggests that Russell achieves a fair sense of Wittgenstein's purpose and is mostly seeking a means of subsuming or reversing it so that he can continue comfortably in his purposes with his prejudices. Through his narrative of engagement with Mr Wittgenstein and his imitation of form, Russell has achieved at least some recognition of otherness. In that framework, one could interpret Russell's manipulation of the text as an act of mentoring, an effort to help a brilliant, though misdirected young man. Still, Wittgenstein's intentions are easily dismissed when the argument is based on a process of assertion and negation. In view of Russell's inability to speak to Tractarian mysticism, it becomes obvious that his purposes, motives, and disciplinary procedures of justification and argumentation do not engage transcendental concerns with ethics and aesthetics. Russell's interest in the book's publication coincided with his belief that it was breaking new ground in solving logical problems, much like his own work on infinity, and in articulating the tautological nature of mathematics, for which he had already acknowledged Wittgenstein in *Introduction to Mathematical Philosophy* (Ayer, *Wittgenstein* 3).

In summation, Russell reads the text freely, affirming what matches his purposes and neglecting what cannot be incorporated into his projects. He demonstrates no deep desire for consistency building, no "fit" and "best light"—the basic criteria for adjudicating meaning, at least the basic criteria offered within hermeneutics—but he shows instead a primary desire to go on in forming his theory of logic, as one might go on in listing even numbers. Russell's interpretation and failed deliberations over meaning give serious support to Stephen Toulmin's claim that incommensurability exists at the level of aims, an argument that can easily be expanded to include intentions.[15] Wittgenstein and Russell can speak about their mutual interest in logic, but where their aims (here their purposes,

---

15. See *Human Understanding*, 126. Toulmin's point, a response to the rigidity of Kuhn's paradigms, is that there can be discussion in "rational" terms within disciplines, even if the interlocutors do not share theoretical concepts, when they do share intellectual aims. Consequently, while one cannot translate Einstein's propositions into the discourse of Newtonian physics, there need not be any "rational discontinuity" in the historical transition between them.

While there need not be any rational discontinuity, the case of Russell and Wittgenstein suggests that there can easily be rational discontinuity when the aims of disciplinary members are not congruent.

though conceivably their motives, too) diverge, Russell is unable to apply the criteria of disciplinary discourse to the critique of Wittgenstein's theory. He speaks of "intellectual discomfort" and toys with a hypothesis that he knows is flawed, but ultimately he has nothing to say about the disciplinary value of mysticism and ignores Wittgenstein's perception of philosophy. A nomadic philosopher may bring new motives and purposes, a negating text may offer new options, but that does not mean the new discourse is interpreted, that the meaning is received. Toulmin's point about incommensurability is even better supported by their disciplinary and personal divergence once Wittgenstein abandons logic. Russell is appalled by the *Philosophical Investigations*. He is not just unable to understand its importance; he is angered by it and observes in *My Philosophical Development* that "Wittgenstein seemed to have grown tired of serious thinking" (quoted in Ayer 134). Only when their purposes overlap can they deliberate successfully; disciplinary membership and some shared motives are not, in themselves, sufficient.

While Toulmin's insight on incommensurability arising over aims is useful here, the highly observable nature of incommensurability is facilitated by self-negating and nonsensical forms. Stewart writes that, in nonsensical forms, purpose "becomes a continual and pleasurable movement away from any point of privileged signification or direction, a reflexive gesture that spirals away from any point of privileged signification or direction" (209). We see that pleasurable movement away from Wittgenstein's insight in Russell's reading of the text, a reading that defines Wittgenstein's claims in terms of what they are not. The reading, however, is liberatory only in the sense that Russell is free to privilege his purposes and directions, and his purposes and directions are already privileged within the discipline, especially within the culture of British philosophy.

Like Russell, members of the Vienna Circle also interpret the *Tractatus* with motives and purposes different than Wittgenstein's, and because of their divergences, they too have significant difficulty in conversations with Wittgenstein. In Vienna in 1922, a group of philosophers including Moritz Schlick, Otto Neurath, Rudolf Carnap, Kurt Godel, and Friedrich Waismann aimed to revolutionize philosophy by making it a rigorous science and eliminating all the discipline's pseudoproblems (such as metaphysics). But to make philosophy a science, the positivists need a language that meets scientific criteria of meaning, and so all philosophical propositions must be empirically verifiable. Janik and Toulmin nicely characterize the difference between Moore's and Russell's motives and those of members of the Vienna Circle; the Cambridge "radicals" aim to reform philosophy by language analysis, while the Viennese positivists desire to remake the entire discipline into one that is empirical, inductive (212). Evidence, say the positivists, must be evaluated in terms of our senses. They find the *Tractatus* useful to their line of thinking for its emphasis on the tautological nature of logic. This insight supports their views that knowledge is always empirical and that a priori systems, logical deductions, and pure reason—though they may be valuable—are unable to conjure new knowledge.[16]

Members of the Vienna Circle had read and been influenced by the *Tractatus* before Schlick arranged a meeting with Wittgenstein in 1927. In his autobiography, Carnap discusses in some detail the *Tractatus*'s strong influence on the Circle's thinking. He writes that it "was read aloud and discussed sentence by sentence" and that sometimes, even after "long reflections," they could not "find any clear interpretation" ("Intellectual Autobiography" 24). Given that clear interpretation is a constant problem with reading the book, it is fascinating that so many try for clarity. Schlick, committed to making sense of Wittgenstein's work, corresponded with Wittgenstein for at least two years, attempting to arrange a meeting. Even after they met several times, Wittgenstein, no longer a disciple of philosophy, hesitated to meet other members of the Circle though he finally agreed. Ironically, while at this time he expresses no interest in doing philosophy, Wittgenstein fails—perhaps from lack of trying—to escape the discipline's structure.

Initially there was a great chasm between the disciplinary motives of the Circle and the purposes of Wittgenstein. In this case, Wittgenstein, somewhat like Russell, is the one unable to interpret or address a discourse with differing intentions. Wittgenstein finds the differences so significant that he does not talk about disciplinary issues; perhaps since he had given up philosophizing, taught grade school, and designed a sister's house, he simply has no disciplinary motives or individual philosophical purposes at this time. In his editor's preface to *Ludwig Wittgenstein and the Vienna Circle*, McGuinness reports that in the late 1920s Wittgenstein did not even own a copy of the *Tractatus*, which might lead one to suspect that he simply was indifferent to his own philosophy. In any case, the communication difficulties were such that even though he expressed good will toward Schlick, Wittgenstein says of their first meeting, "Each of us must

---

16. The arguments and tensions between empiricism and three schools of necessary truth—Mill's inductivism; Kant's doctrine of synthetic, a priori truth; and Frege's and Russell's Platonism—are well laid out in the last half of Gordon Baker's *Wittgenstein, Frege, and the Vienna Circle*. He uses the tensions to demonstrate why members of the Vienna Circle had to turn to the tautology argument in the *Tractatus* to create an argument for empiricism.

have thought the other was crazy" (Waismann 15). And at later meetings, while Wittgenstein does remark on philosophy, he also reads poetry, conceivably attempting to *show* the nature of aesthetics and ethics.

Members of the Circle use the *Tractatus* to argue for their own projects, though they do acknowledge its ambiguity and discern some differences between their position and Wittgenstein's; the *Tractatus* challenges their prejudices. Carnap is a useful example here because of the disagreement that Wittgenstein has with him over the use of ideas from the *Tractatus*.[17] While Carnap consistently acknowledges Wittgenstein as a major influence, Wittgenstein remains unhappy with that influence, refusing to speak to Carnap after 1929 and saying, "I don't mind a small boy's stealing my apples, but I do mind his saying I gave them to him" (Ayer, *Freedom* 171). Responding to Wittgenstein's accusations of misappropriation, Carnap describes their intellectual intersections in detail both in *The Logical Syntax of Language* and his autobiography.

In Carnap's notes for the autobiography, he makes particularly clear the *Tractatus*'s positive influence on his understanding the "importance of the analysis of language for philosophy" and "the creation of philosophical pseudoproblems by the bad use of language" (quoted in Proust 502).[18] He records the mystical as their first point of difference. Like Russell, Carnap does not read the argument as a system, seeking to understand Wittgenstein's main contentions or respecting his ranked and ordered points of argument and conclusion, but rather he too takes the pieces of the first two arguments, the pieces that suit him. French philosopher Joelle Proust describes the use that the Circle, particularly Carnap, makes of the *Tractatus* as " 'ideological' rather than 'systemic' " (503).

Carnap only grasps their differences over the mystical when confronted with Wittgenstein in person. Initially he has no trouble with the interpretation because he simply reads it through the lens of his purposes; Wittgenstein's argument of the mystical does not interfere with his ability to proceed because it never really achieves presence. Carnap writes, "Earlier,

---

17. Other members of the Vienna Circle see ethics differently; not all relegate ethics to metaphysics. Schlick, for instance, aligns ethics with social science and characterizes it as a social science: normative and factual. But whichever way the Viennese philosophers choose to view ethics, Wittgenstein's transcendental ethics do not achieve presence in their readings of the *Tractatus*. They instead privilege logic, the paradigm. Like Russell, they want logic to be a powerful tool of analysis and so do not engage the negations inherent in Wittgenstein's *Tractatus*—though they are eager to talk with Wittgenstein.

18. My discussion of their differences over the mystical has been particularly helped by Joelle Proust's "Formal Logic as Transcendental in Wittgenstein and Carnap." While my focus is on the ethical, I could not have contextualized it without this article's clear discussion of formal logic.

when we were reading Wittgenstein's book in the Circle, I had erroneously believed that his attitude was similar to ours. I had not paid sufficient attention to the statements in his book about mysticism, because his feelings and thoughts in this area were too divergent from mine" ("Autobiography" 27). When Wittgenstein places value (ethics and aesthetics) outside the world, Carnap first interprets that as a dismissal of the significance of ethics or as an inclusion of ethics with metaphysics. This suits Carnap, who sees ethical statements as "value statements" with "no theoretical sense" ("Ethics" 206). It is only in the reality of an encounter with Wittgenstein, a less textual encounter, that Carnap is pushed to examine authorial intention. Carnap initially reads from his own feelings, thoughts, and intentions, and only "personal contact" forces him to rethink the text and understand Wittgenstein's love of "religion and metaphysics" despite their "weakness." Carnap's initial reading is not stopped by questions of validity or authorial meaning, so he never pursues a consideration of what Wittgenstein's purposes might be. Rather than a dramatic engagement, it is the actual engagement with the author that causes him to think about authorial purposes and rethink his reading, though not his purposes. Carnap cannot go on only when faced with Wittgenstein's elaboration of mysticism.

IV

The major implications of this chapter are not commonplaces such as the text is complex and multivocal; the author's intentions are multiple, hidden, ambiguous, and embedded in two (at least) motivational systems; the discipline's structures stabilize its discourse and limit possible interpretations. It is significant to my project of considering negotiations over meanings and actions that despite discussions over the meaning of the text, *authorial intentions, while considered, were not deemed necessary to understanding the text and the text was not read for consistent meaning,* even when authorial intentions were imagined and meaning acknowledged in writing, and even when they were discussed by the author and his audiences. Solving the *Tractatus* as a systemic puzzle or interpreting it from the perspective of a single audience's intention reduces the work to either an ethics or a logic, silence or philosophy, mysticism or positivism. The readers discussed chose to interpret it in an either/or frame. When Wittgenstein's purposes had to be considered because the audience could not go on without that recognition, his purposes were considered, but ignored. There is an overwhelming tendency to read the *Tractatus* rhetorically, and this has at least four implications, all of which limit the likelihood of understanding or productive deliberations.

First, consistent or coherent textual meaning is not achieved nor truly sought with much energy. Even within the limits of disciplinary structure and during ongoing conversations about the text, textual coherence, related to authorial intention or not, is not an active criteria for evaluating meaning. The text is read instrumentally, that is, for its use or function within other systems of thinking. The *Tractatus* is a mine, gold or coal, for other philosophers to excavate and not primarily a meaning to be appreciated, evaluated, or judged (unless the judgment is of use to another's system of philosophy). Despite the existence of theories of communicative ethics and contemporary consciousness of the relationship between justice and interpretation,[19] this description of how interpretations and intentions are negotiated and how meaning is ascribed suggests that some texts are not read as received meaning, but rather as supporting structures to audience intentions. This refusal of authorial intention, even when the author is alive and speaking, suggests there is a certain validity to the perspectives of communitarian reader-response criticism such as that of Fish or Mailloux over the more interactive text-reader models posited by Burke or Iser. If the argument is useful to the reader, there may be significant interactions and negotiations between the reader and the text. If the argument is alien, there may be only insignificant interactions and negotiations and an increase in the significance of community assumptions and motives. As I develop later, some forms and arguments demand more interactions, but certainly the negative structure of the *Tractatus* does not work to this effect.

Second, in Russell's and Carnap's readings prejudices are not put at risk in any serious way. Gadamerian hermeneutics clearly is optimistic and even radical for demanding that prejudices be put at risk, but in practice, even between two significantly allied thinkers, prejudices are hard to risk. Given Russell's claim that Wittgenstein seeks a logically perfect language, the possibility that risking even occurred is very doubtful. Many of an interpreter's, or rather an audience's, motives and intentions are not recognizable, may be ineffable, and so are impossible to put at risk. The standards of judging validity, authority, or intelligibility might differ between rhetor and audience, but even if they don't—as Russell demonstrates—prejudices are hard to acknowledge, let alone risk. Gadamer's

---

19. Warnke's *Justice and Interpretation* provides a good literature review of ethics and interpretation.

metaphor, the fusion of horizons, works better here to explain the situated and historically conscious nature of interpretation. While the horizons of the text and the interpreter are imperfectly fused in that both Russell and Carnap recognize the incompleteness of their understanding of the text (but are not overly troubled by it), there is a sense of movement or joining within the process of their interpretation, especially when they begin a process of dialogue with Wittgenstein, or "Mr Wittgenstein."

Third, this study of Wittgenstein and the reading of the *Tractatus* makes the form of negation and its relationship to the resisting subject and epistemic change less abstract, and in doing so, it undermines any simple correlation between the resisting subject and a revolutionary figure. Negativities, the patterns of assertion and retraction within the text, aid readers in resisting the text; given the opportunities of paradoxes and fractures in the text, audiences can hear assertions and ignore retractions as they wish. After all, resistance is also a conservative strategy. Hence there is a problem in any broad claim of negativity as the discursive ground for change or as a means to forming a novel position. Iser is too optimistic about the effects of textual negation and negativity in changing the reader. They can work to authorize the reader's purposes, especially in unstable cultures where numerous motives, ambivalences, and conflicts exist.

Furthermore, negation and negativity are not demonstrably the site of Wittgenstein's novel position. Instead of the cognitive strategy of negativity, it may well be that Wittgenstein's access to multiple discourses—Viennese and English, scientific and philosophical—facilitated his speaking in unique ways. Wittgenstein's process of creating a unique position may have been more synthetic and situational than negating. While multicultural identifications may have aided his thinking (Janik and Toulmin), they did not influence his reception; his readers did not understand cultural concerns that were not theirs. Even if his very negative textual maneuvers did place his writing in opposition to existing discourses and allow him to develop new perspectives, his unique positioning did not control the text's readings or the changes that the readings initiated in the discipline. Despite his use of a complex set of strategies for negating discourses, despite arguing the book "line by line" with Russell (*Autobiography* 331), despite writing Russell that his book was about "the theory of what can be expressed (*gesagt*) by props—i.e., by language (sic)—(and, which comes to the same, what can be *thought*) and what can not be expressed by props, but only shown (*gezeigt*); which, I believe, is the cardinal problem of philosophy" (350), despite writing Russell that he is dissatisfied with the introduction "both where you are critical of me and also where you are trying to simply elucidate my views" (McGuinness, *Wittgenstein* 291), despite all this effort and authorial presence, Wittgenstein is unable to achieve the Iserian ideal of creating an interaction between the textual signals and the reader that results in a change in the reader's norms.

Fourth, when readers cannot "go on" and must look for authorial purposes, they may be most helped by a constructed or given context, what Burke would call the drama. Context, a concept that articulates (multiple) cultural motives and subjective purposes, may be a pivotal force in rupturing the reader's norms. A reader's success in remodeling signifiers apparently has biographical and historical components. This narrative function exceeds the reader's search for validity and meaning. While Russell's successes in logic are a controlling aspect of his interpretation, Wittgenstein's placement in two cultures, his biographical and historical context, is often described as the force behind his unique productions. Given the difficulty of rupturing audience norms, constructing a drama or narrative concerning the act of interpretation—be it Russell's written engagement or Carnap's conversation with Wittgenstein—seems more significant in creating real engagement than the creative textual forces of negativity. The point at which readers stop and, to "go on," must invent a text (be it a drama or their side of a conversation) is the point at which they recognize purpose. It is the inability to go on and the need to create a new rhetorical engagement that most troubles norms in these two cases. As a rhetorician, I am uncomfortable with limiting claims of power for the text, but I do think that claims of the power of negativity to affect readers need to be examined in practice and contrasted with the reader's response as well as the power of metaphors, assertions, evidence, tradition, narrative, context, and reader intentions.

Together these four findings suggest that achieving understanding and recognizing authorial intention is difficult in a form that enacts fractures, and it is particularly striking that this difficulty exists even within the small differences of disciplinary arguments. When the text rearranges the author's purpose as it proceeds, the audience (and I would bet even the interpreter) easily assumes authority. Multiple discourses, power differentials, and cultural difference all add to the complexity of interpreting the *Tractatus,* but form itself—which according to Burke offers an overlap with a difference between the writer's and readers' situations—hinders a coherent understanding. By allowing for the separation and segregation of concepts and arguments, negative forms—"a way of experiencing"—accentuate the potential differences, and the overlap becomes more localized. Understanding may be augmented through extratextual engagement and active consideration of the overlap and the difference; still, given the difficulty of understanding meaning (let alone authorial intention) in the forms of nonsense and negation, the *Tractatus* is a model text for what will evade disciplined engagement and subsequent deliberation.

5

Wittgenstein's Stories

Desiring Less and Accruing More

> *A wish seems already to know what will or would satisfy it; a proposition, a thought, what makes it true—even when that thing is not there at all! Whence this determining of what is not yet there? This despotic demand? ("The hardness of the logical must.")*
> —Wittgenstein, *Philosophical Investigations*

Recognizing intentional action in forms is a *comparatively* easy way to demonstrate the public nature of intentions. Purposes, which premise choice and an agent, also are public, but since they are deeply embedded in cultural motives, evidenced in forms, and associated with other mental states such as belief and desire, their recognition is more problematic. The problem of associated mental states is, at one level, the dilemma of recognizing sophistry: How does an audience or interpreter know whether she intends to seduce you because she truly loves you or because she desires your body? If interlocutors have ways (practices, conventions, expectations, and inventions) of recognizing and acknowledging "what Ludwig intends," do they have comparable ways of recognizing what he desires, what he wishes, what he believes? Having less easily identifiable signs and symptoms, these mental states are less visible than intentional action. Even so, we readily speak of belief and desire, and much is claimed for their force in a subject's action. Philosopher Donald Davidson, for instance, posits a causal chain from beliefs and desires to intentions to actions and consequently sees the mental states of belief and desire as the basis for intentional actions. From a very different set of questions, narrative theorists, such as Teresa de Lauretis or Frederic Jameson, building on Freud and Lacan, often describe stories as mediations of desire, for events and phenomena are not in themselves stories. So we who desire stories and who tell stories arbitrate between the real and language, between what happened and what we know, between all that has happened and what we desire to have happen, between what happens and what is possible in language. Narrative theory, like analytic philosophy, sees desire as a causal force.[1]

Given the originary force that many attribute to desire, it seems difficult to discuss rhetorical intentions and justified action without some approach to construing the place of desire in rhetorical discourse. Can the publicity condition for rhetorical intentions be extended to desire? How are purpose and desire evident, and how does narrative form effect them? In this chapter, I intend to demonstrate how the interpretation of speech acts through the requirement of exteriority blurs access to and analysis of the mental state of desiring, but I also want to show how narrative form (like negativity) engages and sometimes constrains the negotiations of intentions, both authorial and audience. In looking at the force of narrative form and the difficulty of recognizing desire in rhetorical narratives, I examine the relationship between cultural motives and narrative conventions, and I begin to locate ways of understanding the acts of a rhetorical agent, a rather public persona.

Initially one might think that the mental states of desire and intention share more than they do; philosophers of mind such as John Searle consider the mental states of intention, belief, fear, hope, and desire all to have intentionality, to be "about" something (*Intentionality* 1). Intentionality is the broad classification that subsumes desire and intention. Also it is common for philosophers of mind to define a relationship between mental states, describing a model of intentionality based on a desire/belief state: an intentional action may arise from a desire to act and a belief in the effects of one's actions.[2] The model fashions desire into manifest action through

---

1. There are two problematic assumptions here: (1) everything in mental life has a cause and (2) everything in mental life has a meaning. While these assumptions may have some biochemical basis, they leave no room for symbolic error, play, coincidence, or lapse.

2. Many analytic philosophers describe intentions as arising from a desire to action and a belief in action (desire/belief models of intention). Donald Davidson is a major, early advocate of this position, and Michael E. Bratman is very clear on the executory role of intention in relationship to the background states of desire and belief. See the *Philosophia* exchange between Robert Audi and Alfred R. Mele for a quick review of this model. See Roy Lawrence's *Motive and Intention* for an argument against a direct link from desire/belief to intention (83-99). Michael Moore's work

its interaction with belief and the intermediate step of intending. In this view, while desire precedes intention and action and is not the sole force behind intention, both desire and intention seem forward looking (bathed in longing or loathing), both arise in our needs for control and change, and both can be signified consciously and unconsciously, but intention is the mental state that executes belief and desire. Intention presumes desire. Borrowing this model from analytic philosophy is not without problems; to believe it and use it fully would require discussions of causality and the relationship between mental states (inner) and speech acts (outer) as well as an account of how it is testable.[3] Still, it proves useful for acknowledging the interdependence among desire, belief, intention, and action and for noting that their relationship is a complex knot that should trouble any theory which attempts to attribute only a desire, belief, or intention to any action.

Despite their close relationship, the concepts are distinct enough to separate. In *contrast* to desires, intentions are linear and material in their concern for making actions and ends (both in the aspects of "intention to" and "intention in"); that is, intentions are understood both as preceding and as visible in action, key segments near the end of a causal chain. Legally, for example, acts are called intentional in so far as they are demonstrable in plan and idea prior to existing in action (Salmond 382-93).[4] Intentions are purposive, and ultimately they are about determining aspects of the world as mine through actions. Linearity, materiality, and determination here cloak the subtle evasions, ambivalences, and second thoughts inherent in intending and between intending and action, but when laid close against desires, intentions appear public, iterable, worldly, and intelligible. Though we recognize intentions through their public signs and symptoms, intentions are described as the foreknowledges and

---

on act, movement, and crime uses this model to clarify the relationship between intention and criminal action and in doing so elucidates a more situated and political approach for understanding the public nature of intentions.

3. In *Actions and Events,* Donald Davidson provides arguments in support of this position and responses to his critics. He makes important distinctions in the model, including the one that intending is not a form of wanting. Not only does belief play into the process, but priorities based on wanting/desiring (pro attitudes) and possibility are also part of the process of intending.

4. This view is problematic for contemporary critical projects in that it posits a recognizable mental state prior to public action, but it is the traditional model that appears in the courts. There are now more nuanced arguments being made about intention within legal theory, including arguments that are skeptical about the possibility of placing intention within the individual and using intention as a criteria of judging. Jane B. Baron's "Intention, Interpretation, and Stories" provides a good overview from the perspective of testate law.

foreplannings of actions. That is, there is a temporal or narrative quality in coming to intentional action.

Desire—whether in analytic philosophy where it is linked to preference, goal, want, and interest or in psychoanalytic criticism where it is linked to wish, libido, and alienation—is concerned with a *lack* that potentially motivates intentions and actions. Because desire does not necessarily lead to intention or action (without belief, hope, priority, or opportunity, agents may not make desire manifest, and given the insatiable nature of desire, it may never be possible to bring it all to action), desire is not necessarily connected to causality or action. It is quite easy to imagine desires unknown, unacknowledged, unmet, and so the worldliness of desire is differently located than the worldliness of intention. And for many theorists, it is the least knowable aspects of desire that intrigue; given their descriptions of what is submerged, one might think of them as the iceberg theorists of desire. In *Ecrits,* for instance, Jacques Lacan writes that "desire is a metonymy" (175), a part for the whole, "the metonymy of the want-to-be" (274), perhaps the phallus for the other (288-89). Desire is always partially represented, always also something else: something that can never emerge, but somehow results in the subject's subjection to the other. In iceberg theories, desire is always partial, part of a less obvious whole (hole). While the work of iceberg theorists, such as Freud, Lacan, Roland Barthes, Julia Kristeva, Rene Girard, and Luce Irigary, is profound and in many ways satisfying, as I show later in the chapter, metonymic theories of desire have limited use in characterizing specific rhetorical situations.[5]

To desire is to covet control, to imagine gain, and to wish for change. Within desire, even if it is insatiable and only ever partially expressed, lies potential action, and action is where what is knowable of desire is revealed. As the philosopher G. E. M. Anscombe writes, "the primitive sign of wanting is trying to get" (*Intention* 67). Consequently, while desire concerns itself and the tantalizing process of wanting across difference and wishing for a difference, it needs the supplement of belief, based in a culture, and the execution of intention, based in a rhetorical situation, to become manifest as action in the symbolic. Within the particularities of a

---

5. There is one exceptional counterinstance. Susan Wells, in *Sweet Reason,* does a phenomenal job of using Lacan to describe rhetorical situations. Part of her success in using psychoanalytic criticism on rhetorical texts is that she uses Jurgen Habermas in counterbalance. On the other hand, when she discusses desire within rhetorical situations, the term loses some of its psychoanalytic (iceberg) connotations. Consequently, while Wells argues that we need a Lacanian reading of desire to understand truth and agency, when she uses the term to discuss the public sphere, communication, and different discursive situations, desire seems a euphemism for want.

rhetorical situation and the frame of a specific culture, the natures of intention, belief, desire, and action work synergistically, not as isolated moments along a continuum leading to action.

I

While most rhetorical theorists would accept an argument about intentions within a narrative (placing them variously in or among the author, the text, the reader, or the community), far fewer would acknowledge desire in a narrative—perhaps because the textual boundaries that rhetoric shares with poetics and sophistry are seen as danger zones, and hence the discipline of rhetoric remains skittish about associations with fiction. Rhetoric reads narratives as rational forms through which we know and speak of experience in time.[6] Rhetoric's ambivalence about narrative functions that do not explicitly reason, persuade, justify, or prove is ironic in that rhetoric, like narrative, mediates between the real and the desired, and also exists and comes to fullness as a process of desiring, responding, and accruing. The closeness of the two's imaginaries seemingly limits rhetoric's association with narrative; rhetoricians repress rhetoric's wishful, irrational, temporal tendencies so that they can more rationally adjudicate in legislation and education.[7]

Rhetoric's cognitive approach to narrative is shared with other discourses. There is a large literature that describes disciplinary narratives as working as reasons and reasonings to cause change or to stabilize and consolidate a worldview that reflects a disciplinary belief. Hayden White,

---

6. Not all rhetoricians ignore narratives or limit them to rationalized discourse. In addition to my earlier notation of Susan Wells, Burke attempts to acknowledge the erotic and desiring aspects of narrative while controlling them. Dreading the loss of the temporal in the static, the synthetic in the analytic, the personal in the instrumental, Burke allows desire and the erotic within the drama, a *narratio*. He acknowledges them but controls desire, sadism, violence (scapegoating), and eros with the ends of action and the materiality of the whole drama. Even when contemporary rhetorical theory accepts narratives more wholly, it works to control the libidinal and irrational forces therein.

At the other extreme, in *Human Communication as Narration,* Walter Fisher addresses the persuasiveness of narrative from a particularly rationalistic point of view, one which provides criteria for assessing the reliability of narratives as a guide to the world. I find helpful Barbara Warnick's overview of his position and critique of his concept of narrative rationality as a tool for assessing texts.

7. Thomas B. Farrell's *Norms of Rhetorical Culture,* for example, is very much a part of this cognitive bias within rhetoric.

in analyzing the interrelation of historiography and narrative, writes that in narration, "our desire for the imaginary, the possible, must contest with the imperatives of the real, the actual" (4). White sees the desire for the imaginary limited to the possible; the imaginary of disciplinary narrative (as White describes it) does not desire the fantastic, but rather, like rhetoric, the *possible* changes within a situation. I would go so far as to hypothesize that in the disciplines, the imaginary is rarely the imaginary of more (the fantastic of more knowledge, more power, more territory), but instead what might be described as the imaginary of less, of a controllable, describable world. This describable world is made real, or at least more possible, by the creation of a series of narratives that are not necessarily thick in description, but rather numerous: a contemporary *copia*. Disciplinary desires, historical validity, and paleological pleasures may come into being as much in accrual as by recognized methods, validity claims, or data depth. Accrual is one suasory key of narrative.[8]

I have set out two assumptions about our desires in disciplinary stories. First, in the disciplines, the desire tends to be for a controllable, describable world. Disciplinary narratives, like other disciplinary activities, are often described as conserving or reflecting social values,[9] and in their attempts to conserve social values, disciplinary narratives are easily characterized as partial, as evading parts and characters in the story. This characterization may not be fair or particularly telling in that all stories are partial, but partiality pushes us to examine what is omitted in the disciplines. Second, this tendency to desire a describable world is not a requirement of disciplinary stories. While it is possible for a disciplinary story to open discourse and create multiple perspectives, most are told with the intention to limit discourse and to communicate a limited perspective

---

8. Jerome Bruner calls for more work on the strategies by which narratives are accrued "into larger scale cultures or traditions or 'world visions'" (19). He sees our canonical past as what "permits us to form our own narratives of deviation while maintaining complicity with the canon" (20). In *Sweet Reason*, Susan Wells's discussion of narrative and accrual in cosmology provides an excellent example of the value of closely reading disciplinary narratives and investigating their interdependence (53-96). In reading cosmology, she also makes a case for the place of desire in reading disciplinary narratives, using Lacanian theories of desire to connect dark matter with the unconscious "as a reservoir of both libido and death instinct" (81). It is a memorable, perceptive, and delightful reading, an asset to the critical, but I remain unsure of how Lacanian reading helps us in the realm of persuasion and the political. Wells, in fact, does not define her reading in that realm, but rather, in the chapter on reading science rhetorically, is concerned more with critical rhetoric.

9. Research on the limitations of disciplinary narratives abounds, most often exposing the degree to which disciplinary narratives "smooth" away conflicting data or evidence and force a single meaning on events. For example, see Emily Martin on medicine, Debra Journet on ecology, Misia Landau on anthropology, and Jack Selzer's collection on evolution.

reflecting the social formations of the discipline.[10] Disciplinary narratives tend to be conservative, normative meaning brokers, re-creating the dominant forces in society, controlling and adding to, but not revolutionizing knowledge.

These tendencies mean that disciplined writers have difficulty in creating knowledge that does more than echo or replicate their social contexts; regardless of the individual desire and purpose, cultural motives and forms restrict what can be said productively. Authorial intentions to narrate disciplinary phenomena and express novelty are balanced with cultural motives, beliefs, and an innate discursive limit within which the disciplinary motives are easily expressed and recognized. The forces of cultural motives and narrative forms do not minimize the importance of details and context building as a disciplinary activity or in any storytelling, but rather emphasize the conservative aspects of disciplinary knowledge production. Despite the innate demands and rewards for novel disciplinary narratives, it remains difficult for disciples to invoke innovative formations or to affect the metanarratives of their disciplines.

Wittgenstein, whose early relationship to disciplined philosophy was tenuous, was very dissatisfied with interpretations and discussions of the *Tractatus Logico-Philosophicus*.[11] Since it was published after he left Cambridge and philosophy's disciplinary structures, it is conceivable that he felt an imperative to protect and direct the interpretation of his later work, especially the *Philosophical Investigations*. Certainly, throughout his life, he had the somewhat contradictory fears of being misunderstood and of being plagiarized.[12] Consequently, while there is no way of knowing whether the "misunderstandings" of the *Tractatus* influenced his return to Cambridge and his formal involvement in philosophy, it is worth noting both the disciplinary community he carefully built for his later philosophy and how that community worked to support a particular, paradigmatic reading—or at least a limited number of readings—of his work.

After leaving Cambridge philosophy in the teens, fighting in the infan-

---

10. This distinction is not unlike Kuhn's distinction between the processes of revolutionary and normal science.

11. In his biography, Brian McGuinness details Wittgenstein's disappointment with Frege's and Russell's inability to adequately address the *Tractatus*. Ray Monk and Fredrich Waismann describe his difficulties in being understood by the Vienna Circle.

12. Ray Monk's biography notes Wittgenstein's frequent (constant?) frustration with others' inability to understand him (160-66, 275, 320, 335, 346, 358, 436, 461, 484, 503). Yet despite the failure of his teacher Bertrand Russell and even his own students to understand him, he accused Rudolf Carnap of stealing his ideas from Waismann's notes (324-25).

try, publishing the *Tractatus* (1922), and then teaching elementary school, Wittgenstein visited Cambridge in 1929 and began philosophy again. In submitting the *Tractatus* as his doctoral thesis, he became credentialed in the discipline. He participated in a series of philosophical conversations with members of the Vienna Circle and finally took up residence at Cambridge and became a Trinity College fellow. During his years as a Cambridge lecturer, fellow, and chair of philosophy, he attracted such outstanding students as G. E. M. Anscombe, Norman Malcolm, and G. H. von Wright, students who later had successful careers translating and editing his unpublished notebooks, interpreting his philosophy, and developing his insights (Ayer, *Wittgenstein* 10-13).[13] He identified students who were serious and singled them out for careful involvement in his work. For example, having decided that attendance at his 1933-34 lectures was too great (thirty or forty students), he selected five favorites, limited his lectures to them, and allowed them to transcribe his ideas as the *Blue Notebook,* which introduced the metaphor "language-game" to Cambridge philosophy (Monk 336-37). When later he withdrew from Cambridge, he recommended a disciple, von Wright, to his chair (521). In many ways, Wittgenstein's relationship with these scholars resembles the disciplinary relationship that Stephen Toulmin describes, one where the great thinker defines the disciple's questions (110). And his narratives define their narratives.

In the *Philosophical Investigations,* Wittgenstein tells tiny stories that work to disrupt philosophy's patterns of argument and narration and bid to change the broad motives of the discipline. Wittgenstein, I argue, exploits our desire for control, our disciplined desire for less, to develop a method of revealing plenty within the poverty of a narrative's limits. He tells stories differently, and his stories force a new way of reading on us. All of Wittgenstein's stories of human meaning-making are tiny (the knowing hero who climbs and discards the ladder, the shopkeeper struggling with drawers of meaning, the builders laboring with few words and few tools), but in their curt telling, they critique not our desire for more, but our desire for *simpler* meanings. More completely: even though Wittgenstein's apparent purpose is not to simplify our ideas about language, his stories present simple ideas about language; to describe all that is discourse, he fantasizes what a simpler, describable language would be and what a single

---

13. While Wittgenstein only prepared two books for publication, *Tractatus Logico-Philosophicus* and *Philosophical Investigations,* his disciples edited many books assembled piecemeal from his notes. For example, Anscombe edited or co-edited seven books and von Wright, nine.

speech act might mean. These simpler stories read together picture what both the describable and ineffable aspects of meaning might be, but they also ask us to consider them in relationship to our everyday language. Their very brevity invites, even requires, deliberation.

Written as a series of numbered paragraphs, *Philosophical Investigations* starts with a demonstration that one story calls forth a responding story, a trading of views, and an accrual of anecdotes. The telling of a tale and the authorial intentions—programmatic (form/genre), active (meaning), and final (perlocution), as they are recognized within the telling—solicit a response, often another narrative, from the audience, first as witnesses, then as interlocutors. Wittgenstein's first meditation starts with a Latin quote, Augustine's story of how he learned to speak through naming, a description of language not unlike Wittgenstein's early theory. The quote, as translated at the bottom of the page, starts: "When they (my elders) named some object, and accordingly moved towards something, I saw this and I grasped that the thing was called by the sound they uttered when they meant to point it out," and it ends "after I had trained my mouth to form these signs, I used them to express my own *desires*" (remark 1, emphasis added). In this narrative, the young Augustine sets out on the quest for language; aided by a troop of elders, he overcomes ignorance and achieves the expression of his *desires*. Not a surprising goal given Augustine's reputation for passion. In describing the fulfillment of his desires through the mediation of signs, Augustine tells a forensic tale, one that looks back and interprets for the purpose of making a judgment about the true nature of language acquisition. Augustine claims desires as the starting point, but they are manifested through a belief in the efficacy of language (founded in the elders' behavior), which leads to intentional utterance. Augustine's concern with desire suggests a tie between the recognition of desire and the need to analyze, rationalize, and justify the enactment of desire, a theme to which we will return.

Wittgenstein, writing in German to an English audience, by his very choosing of a story written in a dead language and one already too simple to satisfy mid-twentieth-century philosophers, problematizes Augustine's story of language acquisition as mimetic and based in naming the object of desire. Wittgenstein's choice of a Latin piece told by a canonical figure implicitly raises such questions as, What is translation? How does a translation reflect the original object, now long decayed? How does one acquire a second language? What desires can be achieved in the contemporary use of Latin? What are the relationships among writing, memory, orality, and desire? Whose memories are told? Who then repeats them? Repeats them to what ends? With what intention? With what desire?

But Wittgenstein does not voice these questions, and so I wonder if the questions are part of his intentions or mine, the purpose of his telling or the purpose of my reading of Augustine's story. I have to stop and consider his meaning and intention, and mine. Wittgenstein's short short story invites the rhetorical read and the invented response. Even though the questions are mine, I would argue that my response is an aspect of Wittgenstein's final intentions and that he wants me to finish reading with questions and a need to tell a countertale. I argue this because in the next paragraph he shifts to a critique of theories that describe naming as "a particular picture of the essence of human language," and he wonders about the possibility of a word's *single* meaning and its correlation to an object as well as Augustine's failure to differentiate between kinds of words. Wittgenstein does briefly, in about 150 words, address these issues in critical exposition, critiquing Augustine and instructing the reader. Then he quickly shifts again to narrative, this time playing on Augustine's memory of language acquisition, giving an image of what it might mean to communicate in the language of single words that Augustine describes. He retells Augustine's story as a mystery, one whose plot ends in a crisis of action and motivation.

> I send someone shopping. I give him a slip marked "five red apples." He takes the slip to the shopkeeper, who opens the drawer marked "apples"; then he looks up the word "red" in a table and finds a colour sample opposite it; then he says the series of cardinal numbers—I assume he knows them by heart—up to the word "five" and for each number he takes an apple of the same colour as the sample out of the drawer. (remark 1)

Note this story does not smooth out Augustine's narrative. It responds to Augustine's narrative with more context and specifics—specific desires, words, drawers, actions—but it doesn't explain any more about how the names function to achieve desired effects ("apples," "red"). The story echoes Augustine's with little development. The shopkeeper's story does not fit into a specific culture, either; instead, the narrative avoids what we know as real or true or even possible. The reader is left trying to fill out the story, wondering: How many drawers are in this store? How large is the color chart? How can the word *red,* the color swatch, and the apple line up? Is this a capitalist exchange? How do the shopkeeper's language abilities compare to the narrator's ability to write a list and send someone? Are they working in the same language? What kind of purpose or agency does the shopkeeper manifest? Does anyone in this narrative use language as I do? Could we talk? Who is the protagonist: the narrator who can cause action, the shopper who quests for apples, or the shopkeeper whose behavior Wittgenstein puzzles over, asking, "But how does he know where and how he is to look up the word *red* and what he is to do with the word *five?*"

That's right, lest the reader be too passive and go on with the reading too easily, lack in desire and purpose, and be too much the shopkeeper in responding to the text, one of Wittgenstein's narrators raises questions in an effort to change the reader's strategies and force the puzzle of language upon her: he desires and insists on the change from reader/interpreter to alert and suspicious audience. This second voice raises the question of how the shopkeeper knows how to proceed. The (apparent) primary narrator responds that "it is in this and similar ways that one operates with words," and another speaker (which one?) protests (remark 1). *The narrative is not offered as a single truth or judgment.* Rather it is offered *to damage* any single way of telling about or using language. The narrator, perhaps the primary narrator, says explanations may have to come "to an end somewhere" (remark 1), but that end, writes Wittgenstein in the next paragraph, may be primitive; philosophical narratives of how language works, he suggests, reflect a form of language more primitive or more early than ours. The apple story—with all of its implications of a past primitive paradise, the destructions innate within desiring, and the origin of knowledge—plays with the chronology of first speech, first knowledge, literacy, and the desire for and alleged advance to philosophical thinking by placing the action in another time-space dimension. Having started out with Augustine's ancient piece of philosophical writing which reflects high literacy, Wittgenstein demonstrates, through the alien shopkeeper's parody of functional literacy, the failure of philosophical narratives to explain satisfactorily even the most basic communication.

The shopkeeper story demonstrates the limits of the known world in contrast to the potentials of imagined worlds, but Wittgenstein also tells his stories to demonstrate the limits of our philosophical comprehension of language, and he shows, too, that one story calls forth a complementary story. The world is limited, but it can be expanded through accrual, though maybe only expanded in counterfactuals and definitions of the limitations of our explanations.

The tales then represent the struggle between fiction and the real, and in that gap, they imagine a way of proceeding into the unproven. Unlike Augustine, Wittgenstein is not justifying his desires, but acting to engage us in critiquing ours. We do not need to wander through the next narrative, the "epic" of the builders, because even the contrast of just these first two narratives shows how Wittgenstein uses our desire for a controlled, familiar meaning to engage us in the interpretation of his unfinished mysteries: we desire the gratification of clear meaning, but he provides the frustration of confusion or, perhaps, complexity. Augustine gives us possession of the clarity we desire; Wittgenstein steals it and deepens our desire to understand. After reading his tale that parodies the master narrative of the child learning at the feet of the elders, we are uncertain how to proceed, how to place his tale within any frame of cultural motives. In our struggles to make sense of calling for apples, we do not reveal anything as simple as the error or falseness within Augustine's tale, but rather the inadequacy of his theory, any theory of naming, single meanings, referentiality, and stored memories of single words.

Wittgenstein's narratives, unlike the normal disciplinary narratives of physical and social science, are puzzles for us to interpret, parodies that perform an earlier tale in a way that arouses us without fulfillment. And if we guess Wittgenstein's purpose is to change our reading strategies, we do not know what changes he wants. Nor do we always know where his voice is in the text, nor do we always recognize the parodies. What we know is that he intends us to think through again the best course of action: he invites deliberation.[14]

II

Wittgenstein's first interpreters and audiences were his disciples, scholars who had attended his lectures and believed in his method of philosophizing. Their responses to Wittgenstein's stories are often the rather usual responses to narratives, repetitions of telling and interpretive clarification, but as well, Wittgenstein's stories generate new stories (e.g., those of Norman Malcolm and G. E. M. Anscombe). In some way, Wittgenstein's stories call forth the desire to create proof by a second act of storytelling, mimetic, variant, or counterfactual. As Wittgenstein's response to Augustine's story teaches us one way stories accrue, the tales told by his disciples

---

14. In his short short stories, Wittgenstein intends an open, dialogic narrative; he uses strategies that are similar to the ones Bakhtin identifies in Socratic dialogues. Within Wittgenstein's stories, we confront different discourses on the same subject (syncrisis), and our responses are elicited (anacrisis). Of these two strategies Bakhtin writes, "Syncrisis and anacrisis dialogize thought, they carry it into the open, turn it into *rejoinder*, attach it to dialogic intercourse among people" (111). The open narrative dramatizes a desire for an interlocutor and, in that dramatization, demonstrates intentions. I am grateful to Jim Zappen for the Bakhtin reference.

show how echoing forms can preserve and distort intentions in the initial form.

Wittgenstein's open-ended and partial tales ask for deliberation and a future action. And one might hypothesize that his disciples would tell stories to similar effect. However, the accrual of retellings and countertellings slowly becomes a process of amassing anecdotes as evidence, and this works against the open form. The complexities of retelling transform the nature of deliberation intended by Wittgenstein, even if that intention seems respected by the disciple. Accruing stories do not necessarily engage the initiating author's intention, even when the second storyteller generally supports the first author's intention. Against Wittgenstein's open tales of deliberation, the accrual of disciplinary tales offers propositional, but not illocutionary support.[15]

In his piece "Thinking," Norman Malcolm, a philosopher closely aligned with Wittgenstein, seems committed to extending the narrative system.[16] He begins his essay—actually thirteen numbered sections, sections significantly longer than Wittgenstein's tend to be—with narratives that might be described colloquially as stories of speaking without thinking. Without introduction, he tells six narratives; among them are the tales of the man who insults an Italian when "speaking without thinking," the army sergeant who "rattles off" the drill while considering something else, and a counterinstance of the delirious patient who speaks incoherently rather than without thinking. In paragraph following his six tales, Malcolm immediately refers to paragraph 93 in Wittgenstein's *Zettel,* the source of Malcolm's deliberations. He reverses the historical order of Wittgenstein's presentation (Augustine's originary tale followed by new tales), but he retains the use of a foreign language by quoting Wittgenstein's German, though his intention here seems more for disciplinary authorization and identification than critique of discursive theory. As part of his disciplinary identification, Malcolm is very careful in interpreting paragraph 93; he provides the German and his own translation and describes his project in direct relationship to Wittgenstein's project: "I have been trying to illustrate Wittgenstein's point by describing cases in which the question whether a person was speaking without thinking *would* arise" (411). Rather than consider Wittgenstein's narratives about the difficulty of sepa-

---

15. The distinction in purpose and effect here may be not only in narrative style, but also in the Kuhnian distinction between revolutionary and normal disciplinary practices.

16. Malcolm, an American, spent two years (1938–40) studying with Wittgenstein in Cambridge. Wittgenstein brought a draft of the *Investigations* to Ithaca, New York, for a mutual reading and discussion in 1949.

rating speech and thought, Malcolm moves to develop the cases or tales that ground how one might judge a speech act unthinking. He consciously gives the history of his intention in acknowledging Wittgenstein's earlier statement and in tying his storytelling to Wittgenstein's exposition. In building a detailed context, he begins to interpret his narratives for the audience. This is where his divergence from Wittgenstein's desire begins: Malcolm desires disciplined readers or diligent interpreters who follow a tradition and will place his interpretation within the norms of the discipline.

The emphasis on historical development within Malcolm's investigation encourages the scholarly reader to return to Wittgenstein's *Zettel*. There, paragraph 93 is preceded by two small tales about the relationship between thinking and language; in the tales of the calculating prodigy and the attentive reader, neither can speak of a separation between his actions and thinking nor intelligibly describe what is going on *within* him. Having told and analyzed these two narratives, Wittgenstein goes on to consider the difficulty of distinguishing thinking from not thinking in another's conversation.

> If a normal human is holding a normal conversation under normal circumstances, and I were to be asked what distinguishes thinking from not thinking in such a case—I should not know what answer to give. And I could *certainly not* say that the difference lay in something that went on or failed to go on during the speaking. ("Thinking" 411)

Wittgenstein's insight into thinking and speaking is rather a lack of insight, a refusal to connect speech and thinking. Since Malcolm translates this, he knows this. Even so, Malcolm desires more clarity; in repeated quotations from the *Investigations* and *Zettel*, he demonstrates that Wittgenstein finds thinking "a concept that joins together many expressions of life" (*Zettel* 110). To underscore this, Malcolm returns to his narratives and shows that his instances give different senses of thinking without speaking, say, giving offense unintentionally or speaking from memory. In doing so, he demonstrates that the meaning of thinking without speaking remains unclear and situational and that it is a problem worthy of his address. In the process of telling at least seventeen short short stories over eight pages, Malcolm amplifies the difficulties of conceiving thinking as ongoing when one speaks and of considering thinking either as an internal or linguistic phenomenon. The cumulative effect of Malcolm's stories then supports his conclusion that "thinking is often *exhibited* in work, play, writing, conversation" and still "is not something that can only be inferred or postulated to explain those activities" ("Thinking" 418); that is, thinking has different ways of being expressed in our lives (facial expression, silence, internal images). The progression from Wittgenstein's inability to say whether thinking happens in speaking (an inability that suggests Wittgenstein finds this the wrong sort of question) to Malcolm's conclusion that "thinking is indeed often a mental activity; but equally often is not" (418) is not a particularly dramatic advance, though it was found to be worth publishing and therefore, presumably, worth reading.

So then one must ask, What is the advancement? Even if Malcolm's stories only serve to complement the two told more than a decade earlier in *Zettel,* they fulfill a disciplinary need or motive to expand Wittgenstein's initial narration. But they, in effect, do more. Malcolm's accrual of stories dilutes Wittgenstein's reticence and his refusal of coordination and subordination and, instead, creates a larger order of assertion and declamation.[17] Wittgenstein's desire to see the connection as elusive and his use of accrual as disjunctive is rewritten through a more unified accrual resulting in near completeness and fullness, an accrual that thins the original critique of philosophy's desire for a controllable and cohesive meaning. The connection between speaking and thinking may still (always) remain elusive, but Malcolm, in his stories, manages to demonstrate that while language and thinking do not exist in a one-to-one relationship, while language and thinking are discontinuous activities, perhaps telling the right stories can clarify their relationship.[18] Wittgenstein's stories are anecdotes or perhaps parables; Malcolm's groupings, in the repetition and accrual, come to work as evidence. They are interpreted and extended not as deliberations on what goes on or fails to go on during speaking, but rather as deliberations on the judgments we make about what is unthinking speech. The stories or cases are understood more forensically, concerned with judgment and hindsight. While his method of telling short

---

17. I am tempted in discussing Malcolm's relationship to Wittgenstein and his texts to develop Girard's concept of triangular desire or mimetic rivalry. That is, Malcolm desires the short short story because his model, Wittgenstein, does, but Malcolm's ambivalences about identifying with Wittgenstein as well as the cultural order's ritual forms and activities (the discipline's requirement of novelty) prevent Malcolm from desiring an object identical to that desired by Wittgenstein. This psychoanalytic theorizing, however, takes me away from describing a simpler process of narrative accrual, which is a newer explanation and, as the simpler one, would be considered better in many systems.

18. This may reflect a movement from the genre of meditation or demonstrative meditation (Wittgenstein) to the genre of pure demonstration (Malcolm). Foucault makes a distinction between meditation, which produces new utterances and modifies subjects, and pure demonstration, which rationalizes and neutralizes differences (Frow 35).

short stories and his concern with the relationship between speaking and thinking seems Wittgensteinian, he has moved the rhetoric from deliberative to forensic, and so the effect of his stories changes. The accumulation of stories or evidence encourages Malcolm to judge that "speaking without thinking" is always a special case and that there are "different *senses* to the phrase" (411-12). He can conclude his case: he achieves his intentions and fulfills his desires.

Malcolm, through paraphrase of and dependence on Wittgenstein's texts, superficially appears to echo Wittgenstein's intentions and to deliberate on the problems and questions raised by Wittgenstein, but his desire to echo Wittgenstein's forms, purposes, and motives miscarries. Despite his careful reading and response, the accrual of narrative works against authorial intentions, both Wittgenstein's and Malcolm's. In repeating Wittgenstein's form (his programmatic intention), a repetition that is solicited by the narrative form, Malcolm subverts both Wittgenstein's active intention of an open text giving a partial account and his final intention of creating a deliberating reader, and in so doing, Malcolm subverts his own intention of respect for the method and meaning in *Zettel* and the *Investigations*. His accruing narratives formally subvert the partial telling and mute the claim of not knowing. With different narrative genres, with different authorial intentions, narrative accrual might successfully function to forward deliberation to action, but in Malcolm's case narrative accrual works against authorial intentions, especially the programmatic ones of Wittgenstein's method and the active ones of Malcolm to echo Wittgenstein's method. On the other hand, narrative accrual works to limit proliferating meaning and so grants a degree of control to disciplinary motives and to Malcolm's purposes of clarification.

III

If Wittgenstein's and Malcolm's short short stories tend to be tiny descriptions of minimal actions and changes, disciplinary stories can be prescriptions with significant tensions and aggressions. If one reflects a moment, it should be no surprise that disciplinary stories can be forceful and concerned with punishment as disciplines are normative and critical. A major desire within a discipline is one for control, a control that might be seen as sadistic. To describe one possible view of control in disciplinary narratives, to keep the focus on the relationship between desire and intention, and to understand how one might discern the public nature of each, I turn to Laura Mulvey and Teresa de Lauretis, feminist film critics who are articulate on the cultural nature of desire (patriarchal) and concerned with visible, narrative enactment of meaning. Since Mulvey and de Lauretis examine the relationship among narrative, desire, and judgment from slightly different perspectives, they present two understandings of sadistic pleasure. Ultimately I argue that both Mulvey and de Lauretis posit more complexity than is needed (a slash with Occam's razor), but their theories provide a rich counterpoint to the rationalist approaches to narrative within rhetoric.

In developing a general (too general) theory of narrative, Teresa de Lauretis interrogates the forces at play in narration, specifically the forces of sadistic desire and control inherent in storytelling and hearing. In defining a space for an emerging feminist cinema, she argues that patriarchal narrative, meaning, and pleasure are structured from an Oedipal (masculine) view.[19] Her argument evolves from Laura Mulvey's statement that "sadism demands a story, depends on making something happen, forcing a change in another person, a battle of will and strength, victory/defeat, all occurring in a linear time with a beginning and an end" (de Lauretis 103). While de Lauretis's discussions of sadism and narrative center on sadism's *force,* "forcing a change in another person," and narrative's Oedipal structure of a (masculine) hero overcoming the (feminine) other/obstacle, Mulvey's discussions are more dependent on the *pleasure of judgment* in sadistic desire: "pleasure lies in ascertaining guilt (immediately associated with castration), asserting control and subjugating the guilty person through punishment or forgiveness" (21-22). Mulvey's sense of sadistic desire, through its explicit concern with punishment or forgiveness, is far more restricted than simply the forcing of a change or making something happen. Mulvey also is more articulate about the dialectic nature of sadism and (reasoned) judgment; sadism demands a justificatory story.[20] In Mulvey's view, making the shopkeeper open a drawer

---

19. Much of the discussion of desire in literary theory begins with Rene Girard's *Deceit, Desire, and the Novel* (1965) and diffuses broadly from there. See Jay Clayton's "Narrative and Theories of Desire" for a review of three positions on the relationship between narrative and desire (Peter Brooks, Leo Bersani, and Teresa de Lauretis). His argument that all three positions are ahistorical, including that of de Lauretis, is very persuasive, though he doesn't quite show us how to describe the relationship between narrative and desire historically. I do not succeed in this chapter in a historical analysis of desire in narrative, but I do believe that in broadening the concept I defuse some of the essentialism that other positions embrace.

20. There are discussions of sadism that link its violence to reason and see violence and reason as a dialectic pair. Georges Bataille, for instance, argues for the coextensive and dialectic nature of violence and reason. He asks us to acknowledge the normalcy of our excesses, to recognize that we cannot escape our capacities for both reason and violence. Through reading the Marquis de

is not sadistic because he is not judged or forgiven, neither is Wittgenstein's requirement that the reader shift from the role of interpreter to that of audience. On the other hand, due to de Lauretis's enlargement of sadism to include all change and beyond that to see all narrative as Oedipal, she tends to see sadism as coextensive with, if not constitutive of, narrative.

In this vein, de Lauretis considers the effects of narration, asking significant questions, such as, "Are we to infer that sadism is the causal agent, the deep structure, the generative force of narrative? Or at least coextensive with it?" (103). While de Lauretis overstates Mulvey's claim and reduces the contingent nature of narrative to the deep structure of plot (hero overcomes obstacle), her question is a variant of my question, What is the relationship between desiring and intending? In more specific terms, what is the relationship between (sadistic) desire and the public performance of narrative? While de Lauretis seeks a general theory of narrative that allows for feminist reading, for deviant or willful reading, I seek an understanding of whose intentions (forms, motives, purposes) speak in the readings and tellings. Her approach to desire is a structuralist-derived, psychoanalytic, and feminist exploration of the contradictions in imagining female desire and subjectivity. My approach is a rhetorical exploration of a set of narratives that reveal and justify sadistic desire within a discipline. In looking at the pleasures of judgment, I want to understand its relationship to desire in the hope that the public nature of judging and justification might tell us something about the relationship between desire and intention.

In December 1989 the American Philosophical Association (APA) held a symposium on Wittgenstein's thought. Published in *The Journal of Philosophy*, the two talks and a response occurred almost forty years, two generations, after Wittgenstein's death and represent a significant departure in method from Wittgenstein and Malcolm in that there are no numbered paragraphs and few short narrations for focal analysis. Instead three

---

Sade, Bataille argues that the expression of violence paradoxically becomes the reflection and rationalization of violence.

> Conscious understanding wishes to extend its range to include violence, for such an important part of man's make-up must not be neglected any longer. And on the other hand violence reaches beyond itself to lay hold of intelligence, so that its satisfactions, brought to the surface of consciousness, may become profounder, more intense and more compelling. But in being violent we take a step away from awareness, and similarly by striving to grasp the significance of our own violent impulses we move further way from the frenzied raptures violence instigates. (193)

This places violence so deeply at our core that its analysis becomes problematic—though, since we are human, we will strive "to grasp the significance" of our violence.

alternative narrative strategies dominate: (1) vestigial stories are used as evidence to support a position or thesis, (2) tales of characters or interlocutors show them struggling unsuccessfully to win the counterargument, and (3) repeated and demonstrable efforts are made to create a unified philosophy from Wittgenstein's fragments and short short stories. In each of the essays, there is a sadistic narrative concerned with the forgiving or punishing of guilty antagonists.

The first and longest (thirteen pages) paper, Crispin Wright's "Wittgenstein's Later Philosophy of Mind," uses three evidential short short stories, but its argument depends more on an extended narrative involving two characters. In a technical argument about the relationship between doubt about the possibility of a private language (*Investigations* 258) and the author's ideas about our knowledge of our own intentional states (an argument basically about the possibility of judging the consistency of words representing concepts in a private language), Wright creates two figures who appear repeatedly throughout the text: "the user of a private language," also described as "a linguist," and the "friend of privacy," apparently a philosopher who is arguing for the linguist's ability to explain the truth of thought expressed in private language. These characters are presented dramatically as a means of engaging their purposes and understanding what would justify their positions.

The essay works a bit like an elenctic dialogue; Wright lays out what is needed to support their positions, and through repeated questioning and refutation, he judges them—though it is with concern, tolerance, and forgiveness. For instance, he writes:

> But if the sort of second-order error which attends the possibility of conceptual recidivism and similar lapses is the worst the linguist has to reckon with—and I am supposing it is—does that put obstacles in the way of a successful argument against private language? Would it be more straight forward to design such an argument, if we had forced the linguist to face the possibility of simple misclassifications—false first-order beliefs?
>
> I do not think so. If the linguist makes such a second-order error, there will be a distinguished belief which, though he has unintentionally drifted away from the concepts necessary to grasp its content, he nevertheless takes himself to hold truly. (629)

As evident in the above quote, Wright premises some openness and ongoingness even to the last sentence and so claims space for future deliberations: "But, in any case, *if* the argument I have adumbrated succeeds in detail, no purely constitutive conception of the seems right/is right distinction can be *sustained"* (634, emphasis added). He seems willing to meet the "friend of privacy" again. Despite Wright's apparent tolerance of the views of others, he does maintain, explicate, and develop his perspective *against* the imaginary moves of his creations: "There are two salient *lines of defense* open to the friend of privacy" (624, emphasis added). But the lines of defense, supplied by Wright, always fail. In the end the friend is left with only one "possible recourse" (634), and so the linguist is left with only one hope, to which Wright responds, "I do not believe that there is really any hope in that direction" (634).

The characters enact Wright's paradoxical desire to engage others and yet control the argument and the discipline. Despite pages of apparent engagement and concern, in the end he leaves his antagonists devastated and without a real direction for retreat, not hurt or dead, but hanging on to slim recourse and hope, judged for their moves against him in the extended narrative of philosophical battle. His last sentence allows the possibility of appeal. They linger on, perhaps (if hope and recourse come to fruition), but they linger more from Wright's pleasure in forgiveness than through any power of their own.

In "Wittgenstein, Mind, and Scientism," the symposium's second paper, Warren Goldfarb is more uncomfortable with narrative. One could read the paper as having a long, embedded argumentative tale of Wittgenstein's argument (or attack) against the usefulness of a scientific knowledge of believing, thinking, understanding, and remembering as particular or definite mental states, but this is only the most general and abstract of narrations. It is more interesting that Goldfarb makes his opposition into a character—though one without much substance. He begins, on the first page, with "the *scientific* objection" based in neurophysiology (635), but by the fourth page the objection becomes a character: "the scientific objector has a retort" (638). The character appears suddenly and quickly disappears, apparently borrowed for one sentence only from Wittgenstein's *Investigations* (remark 158). Goldfarb continues on, instrumentally reading Wittgenstein throughout the paper. He diminishes the possibility of identifying a particular brain state (neurophysiological) that could reflect our criteria for ascribing belief, thinking, remembering, or understanding (642). Then, in the last sentence, the scientific objector returns as an "objector" who has envisaged "a tenuous claim" (642). The character is judged guilty of being less than founded in her thinking (quite an accusation for a *philosopher* to throw at a *scientific* objector). The punishment, in part, is that the interlocutor is given neither respect nor real textual presence: unlike Wright, who recognizes otherness and gives it some play throughout his essay, or Wittgenstein, whose multiple voices are found throughout his texts, Goldfarb works to remain in the analytic tradition, and the objector seems to appear only for the pleasure of being judged as an inadequate opponent.

The sessions' respondent, John McDowell, does not write an easily identified narrative with humanoid characters. Though his paper can be read as a chronicle of his differences with the symposium's two earlier writers, McDowell's genre is basically one of the analytic tradition; he weighs and judges their arguments and offers us no engagement with personae, real or fictive. McDowell, however, does end the session on Wittgenstein with a summative disciplinary metanarrative, tidy and controlled in one last sentence. The last narrative of the session: "A lesson of Wittgenstein's philosophy of mind is that we can dislodge philosophical misconceptions, and reclaim the inner world, populated by definite states and processes, for unphilosophical common sense" (644).

At the end of the symposium, the tale of the successful quest arises as transparent as it is sadistic, determined to force a change, a victory for "common sense," defeat and punishment for "philosophical misconceptions." Unlike Wittgenstein's edifying anecdotes, instances to be considered for the possibility and impossibility of coherence, McDowell's summation creates and fulfills his disciplinary desires for coherence and control and displaces Wittgenstein's intentions with the motives of an analytic discipline. Wittgenstein's programmatic intentions are illustrated by the paragraph and the short short story, jagged fragments pieced together to create a wary audience led by no hero or myth. How different is the form of McDowell's tale! Philosophers, instructed in a magical philosophy of mind, can dislodge and banish the dragon, Misconceptions, and reclaim the inner world (de Lauretis would say a synonym for womb) and its population (of states) for the common sense/man/wealth. Where, in Wittgenstein, is this inner world?[21] McDowell's metanarrative smooths out and normalizes the variation in Wittgenstein's initial collections, and the effect of the move to metanarrative even supplants the fragile coherence of accrual that Malcolm's case studies work toward. Rather than accruing gestures toward possible coherence and fullness, McDowell's narrative supercedes the earlier self-aware tales and is instead a disciplinary myth of accomplishment and enlightenment. He clearly offers, instead of deliberations, a *forensic* tale that judges the progress of the discipline

---

21. Wittgenstein certainly wants to reclaim the concepts of understanding, belief, intention, and so on. But he does not argue that there are particular states constitutive of understanding, remembering, and so on. Nor does he argue for the inner world.

and the appropriate lodging for misconception (banished away from the population of "definite states and processes").

It is not controversial nor particularly insightful to write that the narratives in the symposium demonstrate the desire to control other knowledges and, in turn, the need of sadistic desire to either justify or rationalize its actions of forgiveness and punishment (Mulvey). At the most structural level, the three stories together demonstrate a consistency in celebrating a mobile hero overcoming an antagonist or obstacle (de Lauretis). These psychoanalytic readings are predetermined by the method and do not tell us more than that there exists an enunciation of desire for knowledge and control and so a pleasure in judging opposition to knowledge and control. The sadistic desire we find correlates to our method. While the psychoanalysis of philosophers is intriguing, what would be more revealing, for rhetorical concerns with public matters, is an analysis or interpretation of the nature of desires in particular texts, the nature of the justification for each author's desire, and the justification's implications for the relationship between an author's purpose and its enactment before an audience.

IV

The stories of the symposium are different than the stories told by Wittgenstein and Malcolm in that the symposium's characters advocate different answers to a disciplinary question, some are judged deficient, and they are either punished or forgiven. The forensic nature is unmistakable and suggests that the narration of judging is part of the disciplinary tales. The readings suggest that conventions within disciplinary narratives have similarities to those of courtroom trials. Instead of describing desire as what is repressed or what is simply less visible in the field of consciousness, desire can be seen as discursive convention (disciplinary judgment). Rather than asking if judging arises from the sadistic desire (what iceberg theorists might label as castration anxiety or the will to oppress) and how that is recognized, or whether desire is transmuted as it becomes textual actions and requires justification particular to the culture, I ask, How is it productive to separate desire (lack) from judgment, intention, and the context of specific narratives?

Judging needs justification, and disciplined philosophers judge. Even Wittgenstein can be read as judging Augustine's philosophy—though in not stating clearly a verdict, justification, or penalty, he leaves the case open to further explanations and deliberations.[22] The APA philosophers, on the other hand, engage in traditional forensics: they judge and, like judges in a court, write justificatory discourse that "leaves traces of decision-making" (Jackson 26). Once there is a narrative, an intrusion of temporality, in their analytic essays, the intruding agent and his purpose—given the forensic and evidential nature of a discipline—require judging. Much as courtrooms serve as sites for decisions between competing accounts of prior events and judges as interpreters of laws, each of the three APA authors offers his own counterarguments, and then the author-as-adjudicator rules on the winning account, a ruling that reflects his particular purpose within the cultural motive as revealed in his explanation. It is true that, in the mock court of a philosophical essay, the other is written as a weak antagonist, but the feigned engagement with an other's purpose seemingly compels a courtroom drama.

With the turn to judgment and justification, the correction imagined and desired in the narratives tends to increase. *I am reversing the order:* making the pleasure of punishment or forgiveness come from the judgment and the decision making, not from the (sadistic) desire or a recognized lack. It may well be the act of judging that defines pleasure and allows us to attribute a sadistic desire. We can see this in the cases at hand. Malcolm's narratives balance future disciplinary action and a description of Wittgenstein in such a way as to set his project apart from the essays of the symposium: it omits sadism and narrative violence, at least in part, because it refrains from judging the other. The essays of the symposium, on the other hand, consistently end sadistically—for it is the very nature of judging to attribute guilt and to change aspects of the world.

Disciplinary narratives share more with legal narratives than they do with literary narratives because legal and disciplinary narratives both are written in cultures with institutions that authorize formal judgments.[23] As law professor Robert Cover explains, unlike literary interpretation of narrative, legal or judicial interpretation "takes place in a field of pain and

---

22. In a sense, Wittgenstein provides a new model of forensics, one in which concepts of guilt and innocence are rejected, alternative understandings are suggested and weighed, but the law is never fixed. Judgment, justification, and the law become secondary to descriptions of alternatives weighed by interlocutors.

I write this with the understanding that some see Wittgenstein as rejecting Augustine's philosophy. That is not clear to me. I read his presentation of the naming theories (stand-ins for the *Tractatus*) as being a critique of their incompleteness. They are one type of language-game.

23. Law professor Robin West's *Narrative, Authority, Law* is very clear on the debate in legal studies between the interpretists, who ally adjudication with literary interpretation, and the imperativists, who understand adjudication as the creation of law backed by force.

death" ("Violence" 1601). When a defendant is sentenced, his world is changed. The judge interprets the law and decrees punishment, which in our justice system mandates the actions of others "to restrain, hurt, render helpless, even kill the prisoner" (1609). As Cover argues, the social codes that inhibit these actions in other arenas are bypassed in the courts and prisons through the hierarchical judicial system, an institution which guarantees that no single individual authors the violent act. The institutions of philosophy also work to justify judging without amplifying the antisocial, sadistic, or aggressive aspects of the judging agent. Cover's point—that it takes the institutions of the courts and prisons to interpret legal narratives and to legitimate a real-world and real-time response of violence—also sets philosophical narratives apart from legal narratives. While philosophy and law both have formalized structures of judging, the institutions of philosophy are concerned with the judging of concepts, not lives. The concepts come from the disparities between speaking, living members of the community (unlike literary narratives), and the judgments on concepts do affect actual interlocutors. While the punishments and forgivings are fictional, the guilty positions are identifiable with colleagues, and consequently the institutions of philosophy and the academy need to authorize and legitimize fictional actions of punishment and forgiveness and control the degree of punishment to promote ongoing communication. In this interest, disciplines define critique as basic work, and one is to be pleased when one's work receives thoughtful, well-placed critique. In this interest, "misconceptions" can be banished, not intellectuals.

Cover's discussion of legal interpretation within the courts is an odd place to turn for an articulation of the relationship between sadistic desire and intention. Even so, he sheds light on the way in which different intentions, especially the intention of judging, legitimate different acts of reading and writing. In approaching rhetorical texts and looking for signs and symptoms of desire and intention, it is unclear whether we need to recognize sadistic or psychoanalytic desire as initiating judging and forgiveness. It is possible to read desire, embedded in cultural systems and made public in intentional action, as formed by its situation and surrounding discourses. Occam's razor may not be the ideal tool for deciding among interpretive methods, but it is certainly a valid tool. The publicity criteria of intention makes suspect claims of psychoanalytic desire or, at the very least, increases the evidence requirement. In disciplinary narratives it is unclear that "sadism," rather than judgment, "demands a story" (de Lauretis 103). Sadistic desire, which gives pleasure in "ascertaining another's guilt," requires judging and justification, but the act of judging itself also calls forth narrative and pleasure. Instead of sadistic desire demanding a story or leading to intention, instead, once judging opens the possibility of punishment, a justificatory drama—one in which both sides are given court—is expected by the audience.

Ultimately, the problem with positing desire as an identifiable force is that it is unrecognizable outside of a text and a context, and this makes it difficult to separate desire from intention and belief and the context of that speech act. To return to Wittgenstein's quote at the head of this chapter: "A wish seems already to know what will or would satisfy it; a proposition, a thought, what makes it true—even when that thing is not there at all! Whence this *determining* of what is not yet there? This despotic demand? ('The hardness of the logical must.')" (*Investigations* remark 437). Here Wittgenstein notes that the path from a wish, intangible, to a proposition (from the "demand" for what is not there to its enunciation) is hard to imagine; it seems that theory struggles against a too-crude ordinary language to engage the concepts of "wish, expectation, belief, suspicion, and so on" (remarks 436-44). But Wittgenstein responds to the pathology of seeking inner states: "It is in language that an expectation and its fulfillment make contact" (remark 445).[24] It is in discursive action and interaction that we recognize wishes and desires, but with those recognitions, we are entangled in purposes, motives, and forms. Again and always the crudity of ordinary language. Desire, even in essentialist poetics, is not knowable outside of forms that may subvert it, cultural motives that create and control it, and the purposes of an agent who may deny, displace, or project it.

---

24. After writing this chapter, I read Jacques Bouveresse's *Wittgenstein Reads Freud*, a wonderful discussion of Wittgenstein's critique of Freud and psychoanalytical philosophy. While the monograph attends to the evolution of Wittgenstein's responses to Freud, it is revealing of the tensions laid out here, "the confrontation between two types of rationality" (122). Bouveresse's philosophical approach is much more giving to psychoanalytic interpretation than I have been in my rhetorical analysis.

6

Metaphors as Enthymemes

The Evolution of Language-Games and Form of Life

> *It is easy to imagine a language consisting only of orders and reports in battle.—Or a language consisting only of questions and expressions for answering yes and no. And innumerable others—. And to imagine a language means to imagine a form of life.*
> —Wittgenstein, *Philosophical Investigations*

J. L. Austin writes, "if the poet says 'Go catch a falling star' or whatever it may be, he doesn't seriously issue an order" (*Philosophical* 241). Given a poetic context and the speed, heat, and rarity of falling stars, Austin seems sensible to consider the author's order as outside the usual form and seriousness.[1] On the other hand, when

---

1. J. L. Austin's humor and irony are often underappreciated by scholars familiar with *How to Do Things with Words* and unfamiliar with the collection *Philosophical Papers*. After all, this is the Austin who wrote *Sense and Sensibilia*. "Performative Utterances," the essay that the "falling star" quote comes from, begins, "You are more than entitled not to know what the word 'performative' means. It is a new word and an ugly word, and perhaps it does not mean anything very much. But at any rate there is one thing in its favour, it is not a profound word" (233). In the essay he develops the now-familiar notion that some utterances perform tasks, often legal tasks such as weddings ("I do") and warnings ("Passengers are warned . . ."), but as well tasks such as gambling ("I bet") or recognizing accomplishment ("I congratulate"). There, however, can be infelicities. One might not be sincere (intend the performance), things may be wrong in the overall performance, there may be a misunderstanding, or the act may not be seriously performed (as in the poetic command). In showing so many infelicities and in expanding the "falling star"

Wittgenstein, in the aphorism above, bids his reader to imagine languages limited in propositional possibility, given the philosophical context and a reader with a reasonably rich imagination, one is prone to believe that Wittgenstein intends something serious with these limited games of language and means something rather specific by the metaphor form of life. Readers have ways in which they make decisions about the author's intention in metaphors; there are signs and symptoms, though not hard rules, that guide the reading of a metaphor and the discussions about its author's intentions and its meanings. From the very quick example above, it would seem that disciplined metaphors work differently than poetic ones.

Metaphors, like negations and narratives, have claims made as to their transformative potential. Ever since Max Black in *Models and Metaphors* (or, if you prefer, I. A. Richards in *The Philosophy of Rhetoric*) defined metaphors as interactive and connected them to cognition, scholars have been asking how does a metaphor mean and have been using metaphoric generativity to argue for the epistemic nature of language. Metaphors are reified and even posited as revolutionary sources of change (Arbib and Hesse 156). In the plethora of books and articles, however, questions of the relationship between epistemic metaphors and their contexts are underdescribed; too frequently one or two examples, often propositional, are used to illustrate the semantic aspects of metaphors, and the pragmatics remain underexplored.

My position—that the importance of metaphors is situational and that their formation and extension are based in the motives of a specific community and the purposes of particular audience members—is not groundbreaking; my evidence is new, but not the thesis. Max Black himself warns that metaphors belong to pragmatics, not semantics (30), and Searle asserts that the meaning of a metaphor does not lie in the interaction between terms per se but in the effect on the audience, an effect based on working through shared communication strategies and shared values ("Metaphor" 123). For a metaphor to be meaningful, Searle argues that the audience must have (1) shared strategies for recognizing the utterance as not literal, (2) shared values for relating the metaphor's two terms, and (3) a shared means of limiting the "range of possible values" (120). One could easily describe Searle's vision of metaphor as enthymemic; that is, a meta-

---

example with "whatever it may be," Austin both emphasizes the contingencies of our utterances and interpretations and demonstrates that we almost always can recognize the meanings and intentions, felicitous and infelicitous, of utterances.

phor works because of the shared, but unstated assumptions of the audience, and as with any enthymeme, the metaphor persuades the audience by emphasizing their connectedness to the speaker. If their meaning then is either contingent or local, metaphors need to be understood not just for how they mean, but for why, where, when, and to whom they mean. In the interpretation of an individual metaphor, there is a struggle that needs to be recognized, a struggle between the creative force of two terms reverberating against each other and the socially formed assumptions held by the reader.

Disciplinary metaphors—because of their institutional tie to knowledge production, their circumscribed use, and their extensive documentation—frequently have been studied for their generative processes of problem setting and theory articulation. For instance, the urban planner Donald Schon argues that metaphors generate new concepts because they allow a disciplined speaker to "set a problem" (261). Problems, after all, are not given but instead are constructed by people "in their attempts to make sense of complex and troubling situations" (261); the appropriateness of solutions then depends on the nature of how the problem is defined. Schon, despite—or because of—his clear focus on metaphors as defining agendas, does not address how the metaphors themselves come into existence or how they come to guide the disciplined audiences who solve the problems. But in advancing the problem-setting nature of metaphors, he suggests that metaphors have a unique and potentially deliberative place in disciplined thinking. Since metaphors define problems, they potentially determine the motives and assumptions informing a decision or course of action.

In addition to setting problems, certain metaphors are described as evolving into conceits and directing disciplinary discourses. Richard Boyd, among others,[2] demonstrates that some metaphors evolve to articulate theories in science, and he suggests that theory constitutive metaphors work by both catachresis (filling a gap in terms) and interaction. Rather than cutting the world into pieces—as do many linguistic categories (such as nouns)—these metaphors, according to Boyd, allow "epistemic access" to parts of the world that do not neatly work as pieces. In his words, metaphors can function as a "nondefinitional form of reference fixing" and thus can introduce "terms referring to kinds whose real essences consist of complex relational properties, rather than features of internal constitution" (358). They can allow a researcher to access and frame greater

---

2. For example, see the arguments of Robert J. Sternberg, James R. Averill, or Kurt Danziger.

complexity than existent literal language might and increase the chance that the ineffable is heard, if not negotiated.

The claims of enthymeme, problem setting, and epistemic access suggest that metaphors might allow us to achieve better understandings and a more unified process of deliberation, one that would avoid a press to a final end and consensus and yet allow sufficient direction and commonality for a community to move toward an action. Metaphors might provide a shared discursive moment, a site where purposes and motives could be transfigured. But of course there is no such easy solution. While disciplinary metaphors, such as Wittgenstein's form of life and language-games, are setting problems, generating new ideas, and creating new relationships among the ideas, some readers struggle to control the direction of disciplinary expansion and the choice of which theories get articulated: the intentions of different audiences affect the meaning that they find in a metaphor. The missing middle term of the enthymeme becomes subject to debate. Hence, in addition to solutions to set problems and complex articulations of conceptual relationships, metaphors also generate contestatory fields, fields that reveal conflicts about directions within a discipline. The contestatory fields are in some ways indicative of disciplinary divisions, and the resulting arguments about metaphors often demonstrate the underlying motives that a disciple brings to a metaphor and show how a disciple's purposes interact with metaphoric form.

Problem setting and epistemic access premise significant control of meaning to the form itself. If, however, metaphoric meaning is situationally determined, the motives and purposes, in both inventing and interpreting the metaphor, must also be seen as significant; any transformative power of metaphors results from interactions among form, motive, and purpose. Since the nature of intentions (as recognized in form, motive, and purpose) depends on context, then the history, connections, and extensions of the metaphor all add to the generativity of two terms. With this understanding, it is not the single use, but rather both the repetition of the metaphor itself in various texts and contexts as well as the evolution of its conceit over time that make meaning and determine the deliberative effects of metaphor.

I

In Wittgenstein's *Philosophical Investigations,* there are many startling metaphors that still resonate in the humanities and social sciences—

language-games, form of life, the tool box, the fly in the bottle, the old city and suburbs. Each image is demonstrably vivid enough to set a problem and generate answers; in fact, we all know them—the literature on these images is massive. How then did Wittgenstein create such generative images? Was it poetic genius that made his words so memorable, so essential to contemporary thought? Is poetry part and parcel of *poesis?* Or is *poesis* part and parcel with social setting?

Wittgenstein was from a large, literate Viennese family who valued and used metaphor and parable. In her memories of Wittgenstein, his sister Hermine observes that all the Wittgenstein children used "analogy" to communicate, and she shows this with the following example. Finding it difficult to understand his decision to teach elementary school after World War I, she told him that using his philosophically trained mind for elementary school teaching resembled "somebody wanting to use a precision instrument to open crates." Wittgenstein responded, "You remind me of somebody who is looking out through a closed window and cannot explain to himself the strange movements of a passerby. He can not tell what sort of storm is raging out there or that this person might only be managing with difficulty to stay on his feet." And Hermine understood (4). From this memoir, one might think that since Wittgenstein was raised in a family that valued linguistic play, he was able to take that poetic experience and manipulate it in disciplined ways, but this is unlikely. While his familial experience with analogy may have helped him to create some of his metaphors and examples, at least two—language-games and form of life— appeared in earlier philosophical and popular literature with which he was familiar. The generative power of the metaphors and their incorporation and prevalence in disciplinary discourses do not innately arise from their original use and their original interactivity, but from the context of Wittgenstein's arguments at Cambridge, the motives of his philosophical culture, and purposes of his audience. Their spectacular generativity lies in his intentional use of them in a specific context to an audience of his disciples, not in their initial creation.

Two philosophers who influenced Wittgenstein, Gottlob Frege and Fritz Mauthner, already had compared symbol systems to games. Mauthner in *Contribution to a Critique of Language* (1901) wrote, "Language is only a convention, like a rule of a game: the more participants, the more compelling it will be" (quoted in Janik and Toulmin 126). Frege also used the game metaphor—though he used it to explore mathematics. In *The Foundations of Arithmetic,* Frege distinguished the theory of math from the practice of math with a comparison to rules of a game (theory) and the object of the game (practice) (remarks 107-9). While I know of no explicit response to Mauthner's game by Wittgenstein (though of course he read Mauthner), Wittgenstein did respond to Frege's mathematical formulations—including the game metaphor—when he was meeting with members of the Vienna Circle in the early thirties. Waismann transcribed Wittgenstein's response to Frege, and while most of what Wittgenstein says at this time is related to the philosophy of mathematics and its relationship to logic, he extends the game metaphor to logic: "Now the rules of chess are the pieces of my game and the laws of logic for instance are the rules of the game. *In this case I have yet another game and not a metagame*" (121). When Wittgenstein calls logic "*yet another game,*" he starts to generate the concept of multiple games within language; he is making *game* a conceit that extends beyond Frege's passing analogy. While this is a small extension of Frege—from mathematics to logic—and a small denial of metatheorizing, with this statement Wittgenstein begins to move the word *game* from Frege's small analogy in mathematics to the start of a conceit involving other symbol systems and their relationships. Over time—a decade or more—through manipulation of this borrowed metaphor,[3] Wittgenstein begins to articulate a complex relationship between games and the multiple ways we use language.

Wittgenstein's metaphor form of life also is borrowed—though its sources and their relationship to Wittgenstein are more speculative because the metaphor was so very common, so very dead. As Janik and Toulmin observe, Wittgenstein "was in no more a position to *invent* the term 'forms of life' than one could today invent the phrase 'territorial imperative'" (230). Janik and Toulmin identify one of the metaphor's early sources as Eduard Spranger's popular 1922 book on characterology (*Lebensformem* or *Forms of Life*), but Rudolf Haller identifies even earlier sources for the metaphor, W. Fred's *Lebensformem* (1911) and Otto Stoessl's *Lebensform und Dichtungsform* (1914). Arguing for a more likely conceptual influence on Wittgenstein, G. P. Baker and P. M. S. Hacker identify a passage in Oswald Spengler's *Decline of the West* (1932) that identifies "culture-language," a concept that occurs in Wittgenstein's *The Blue and Brown Books;* they see the terminological shift to form of life as a shift in emphasis to "the underlying consensus of linguistic and prelinguistic behavior which is presupposed by a language" (*Understanding* 137). Regardless of its original source or meaning, Wittgenstein resurrected this dead metaphor in a scant *five* uses within the *Investigations!* With just five uses, he reconceives and recontextualizes the metaphor in

---

3. Farhang Zabeeh provides the details of the genesis of language-games prior to the *Investigations* (331-33).

such a way that it becomes the subject of philosophical papers and books even forty-five years after its first publication in a Wittgensteinian context. He manages to create a non-reference-fixing (Boyd) metaphor whose meaning is significant to interpreters who share, or believe they share, with Wittgenstein the values and purposes revealed in the interactions of the metaphor's two terms. They believe they share a motivational system.

These borrowed metaphors, language-games and form of life, became prominent in philosophical discourse only after Wittgenstein had recontextualized them and created a coterie of interpreters through conversations and lectures at Cambridge. Alone on the page, form of life and language-game do not generate insight for the uninitiated (ask a sophomore), nor did they generate much language theory in their original use at the start of the century. Wittgenstein manipulated the metaphors, their context, and their interpreters to have them represent his problems, and answers. For example, having cut the attendance of his 1933-34 lectures from thirty or forty students to five favorites, Wittgenstein allowed them to transcribe his ideas as the *Blue Notebook,* which introduced language-game to Cambridge philosophy (Monk 336-37). His close disciples knew the motivations of his thinking, the purposes of his epigrams, and the problems that his metaphors set; they knew the missing term of the enthymeme.

Without an initiation to Wittgenstein's intentions, without an induction into the philosophical motives of his community, the reader has difficulty interacting with the metaphors' terms. Rather than the comfort of working with a familiar conceit, the naive reader—who does not share strategies of recognizing a metaphor, values for relating the terms, and a means of limiting the range of values (Searle)—must interpret from her frame of motives and purposes, aided only by textual context. Naive readers, however, are rare; a naive reading is the experience of the foreigner and the child, not of the disciplined reader (and obviously the alien response of the foreigner and the child is unlikely to be heard). The surrounding discourse that Wittgenstein created and the social structure of the discipline are virtually the complete source of the metaphors' contemporary meaning, and so the generative and revolutionary potential for his metaphors is limited. There is some space for individual problem setting and epistemic access, but mostly disciplined metaphors work to generate discussions that make purposes and motives explicit.

II

As already shown, many philosophers attend closely to the sources and history of these metaphors; this is indicative of a larger pattern, an unusual *need to secure meaning*. For complex reasons, they are returning to Wittgenstein's sources as a means of hermeneutic inquiry and are not allowing the metaphoric process of catachresis to direct research. This drive to authorize and control meaning is a part of making and owning aspects of the world. If non-reference-fixing metaphors interrogate motives, deep cultural assumptions and possibilities, then readers must articulate and defend those motives or risk having them changed. Certainly some philosophers, Stanley Cavell or Jean-François Lyotard, for instance, use the metaphors generatively in the sense described by Boyd (a nondefinitional reference, a conceit to be extended). However, other philosophers attack this strategy for theory building because it fails to recognize and so violates Wittgenstein's intentions—they claim to know his intentions. One can speculate that it is the attacker's intentions that are violated, but this speculation simply tends to create an infinite regression of unknowable intentions. More revealing are the attacks on theory building (catachresis) with these metaphors.

The attacks, maneuvers of the disciplinary police, are especially evident in discussions of language as a form of life. Given this metaphor's limited usage (only five times), one might think its extensions would be easily dismissed or avoided, but since it is particularly ambiguous and since the questions, values, and limits that it assumes are unclear, extensions of form of life become particularly controversial. To critique alternative values, questions, and meanings and to direct future disciplinary discourse, some philosophers argue against extensions of the metaphor—*based on Wittgenstein's intentions*. Because form of life is the metaphor least used by Wittgenstein, the least contextualized of the two metaphors, I focus the discussion there to demonstrate how important an author's purpose, correctly discerned or not, can become in a what is apparently a truth-seeking, knowledge-producing activity. That is, the history of concept (the motivational system) and its author's intentions (purposes) are used to control its future interpretations even if the new interpretations are insightful or productive of disciplinary discourse.

The metaphor form of life appears frequently in scholarship on Wittgenstein himself, but it also appears in work diverging from Wittgenstein's original arguments. Among the most prominent scholars who have used Wittgenstein as a starting point to their own thinking is Stanley Cavell. While Wittgenstein's ideas appear in all of Cavell's books to date, they are utilized in service of Cavell's thinking about thinking. His aim in critiquing skepticism and reclaiming the ordinary may overlap with Wittgenstein's, but Cavell has also developed recognizable purposes in ethics and aesthetics, and he is formulating a vigorous interdisciplinary agenda for contemporary philosophy in literary theory and film. The relationship of his thought to Wittgenstein's is complex, but as my concern here is only form of life, his utilization of the metaphor can be glimpsed through a few pages in *This New Yet Unapproachable America: Lectures after Emerson after Wittgenstein*.

In two lectures drawing on Emerson, Thoreau, Heidegger, and Wittgenstein, Cavell argues that philosophizing starts with skepticism or a loss of the sublime but must go on to find the everyday world (114). He writes that American philosophy is relatively free of the European tradition of foundations (108) and so can turn or return to the "practice" of language and the moral requirement of searching for the world (for Cavell this includes, among other actions, the interpretation of popular films). Cavell's intention for philosophy to seek worldly wisdom (somewhat aestheticized) differs from Wittgenstein's intention of a philosophy limited to denying the ideal—though Wittgenstein's clearing of the site of reified abstraction is necessary before Cavell's building.

In his philosophical building, Cavell adeptly elaborates Wittgenstein's form of life into a conceit that supports his intention to connect the human to the natural world. Cavell acknowledges that form of life usually is interpreted as "a conventionalized, or contractual, sense of agreement," what he calls an "ethnological" sense (41). He claims there is also a "biological" sense to form of life, a sense that "recalls differences between the human and socalled 'lower' or 'higher' forms of life" (42). This second sense emphasizes not "*forms* of life" but "forms of *life*." Cavell observes that the more prevalent interpretation emphasizing the social nature of language is read accurately as a significant rebuke to philosophy's emphasis on the individual and the inner rather than outer, but in limiting the conceit's interpretation to formal conventions, one risks developing a "*petit bourgeois* fear of change" (43). Cavell claims that his addition of a second interpretation allows a "mutual absorption of the natural and the social" and supplements "its sense of political or social conservatism" (44).

In *This New Yet Unapproachable America,* he suggests that this elaboration was given in his earlier *The Claim of Reason*, and in fact, it is present, but only in the sense that life has body (83). Quoting four passages from the *Investigations*—one about forms of life (p. 226), one about body and soul (p. 178), and two about sensation (remarks 281, 283)—Cavell argues that the skeptic's problem of knowing the existence of the other is not a false problem of "reaching to the other's (inner) life," but instead a problem of acknowledging the other's presence. This argument is removed from, though not inconsistent with, his later argument for a biological extension of form of life. Still, Cavell's reference to and conceptual evolution from his earlier writing reveals the pondering and cumulative acts of invention necessary to delineate possible relationships within a metaphor and develop knowledge from it, knowledge in excess of the normal cultural motives. Wittgenstein's statements that "to imagine a language is to imagine a form of life" (*Investigations* remark 19) or that agreement in language "is not an agreement in opinions but in form of life" (p. 241) do not innately support a biological reading. The biological reading is an invention of the conceit and Cavell. The purposes of a well-disciplined scholar privilege a specific meaning and transform the enthymeme's missing middle proposition. Cavell—because of his intention to return philosophy to the outer, the dynamic world, and the fleshy human—folds another meaning into the disciplinary conceit form of life. He can not erase the volumes that have read form of life as conventional behavior, merely the social, and so while he keeps that meaning, he acts and pushes the metaphor in a direction that substantiates his purposes.

This kind of generative activity, so often seen as the paradigmatic work in a discipline, is subject to critique, but not necessarily critique based on its intellectual use to the discipline. Instead interpretations of metaphors are read against the original use of the metaphor by Wittgenstein, the context as described by the critic, and the "jagged" nature of Wittgensteinian thinking; these criteria form the grounds for recognizing intentions. This concern with recognizing intentions suggests that in addition to answering research questions, a common practice in promoting one's own work is to police the direction of others' research.[4] In the policing, different criteria of knowing Wittgenstein's intentions are offered as evidence for the validity of the claim.

A very clear, introductory example of this is Lynne Rudder Baker's brief article, "On the Very Idea of a Form of Life." In the first two paragraphs, she defines her project as "discussing the most persuasive interpretation" and then showing how Hilary Putnam and Richard Rorty have "mistaken assumptions about Wittgenstein's idea of form of life" (277). To justify her reading of a "non-systemic character of form of life" based on communal and conventional agreement (278), she primarily appeals to the authority

---

4. This limited review should in no way suggest a limit to the number of theorists undertaking this practice. See, for instance, Nicholas F. Gier's *Wittgenstein and Phenomenology* or Michael Brearley's "Psychoanalysis: A Form of Life?"

of Wittgenstein's disciple, Anscombe, who wrote of Wittgenstein's thinking that "he preferred it left jagged." That is, Baker uses a disciple's opinion of Wittgenstein's intention as a primary criteria for supporting her argument that Wittgenstein intended form of life only to show, not to say, and that "little meaningfully can be said about" the metaphor (288). Baker then feels free to critique the specific claims about form of life made by Putnam (empiricist) and Rorty (arbitrary) and to dismiss their extensions and critiques of the metaphor.

The concern about alternative extensions of form of life also structures one chapter of Gertrude Conway's *Wittgenstein on Foundations*, a 184-page book on form of life. She argues that "with form of life, Wittgenstein is offering an account of what does provide restraints in application and interpretation of rules [the rules of language]" (39), and she reads the metaphor as *defining a new type of philosophical foundation*, the point at which justification must come to an end and we can only say, "That's how we do it" (Wittgenstein, *Mathematics* 74). To demonstrate the value of her interpretation, she identifies the inadequacies of four types of interpretations of form of life and then discusses the value and implications of her interpretation, for well over a hundred pages.[5] Since form of life is used *only* five times in the *Investigations*, her need to build a set of assumptions for her single, though "jagged" interpretation of form of life is particularly extreme, but it is indicative of the danger seen in the generativity of metaphors and the drive to define the assumptions between the interacting terms, assumptions that potentially change cultural motives. Conway's argument for the validity of her reading of Wittgenstein's intentions is based on the commentary of his disciples as well as "statements and related concepts developed in Wittgenstein's later works" (55); her criteria is largely interpretive best fit. She ranges over the possible history of the metaphor from Schopenhauer forward (57), even examining Wittgenstein's use of the single word *form*.

The third work examined here repeats many of the same moves to limit the extensions of the metaphor; however, Newton Garver appeals to slightly different criteria for recognizing Wittgenstein's intentions. Building on an earlier, briefer essay by J. F. M. Hunter, he also critiques three flawed interpretations of form of life.[6] Then Garver, like Hunter, argues for a single, biological or natural human way of *life*, one form common to us

---

5. The four interpretations connect form of life to (1) language-games, (2) biology, (3) cultural systems or networks, or (4) natural history without a simple biological basis. Conway finds the first indefensible and the last three too narrow.

6. Roughly speaking, each author describes the limitations of interpretations that (1) equate

all. Garver bases much of his critique on the invalidity of pluralizing form of life to forms of life. He argues that Wittgenstein, for the most part, used the singular form; this, according to Garver, demonstrates that Wittgenstein himself intended the metaphor to mean that human beings had "a common form of life" (188). He is not without sensitivity to the fact that his circumscription of meaning has "very meagre" worth. He writes that "its significance consists almost entirely in rebutting the kind of importance—mainly sociological and relativistic, and perhaps sceptical—that others have read into Wittgenstein's sparse use of this expression" (200-201). This statement against a relativistic interpretation of Wittgenstein is very revealing of the motives that he attacks and his reasons for refusing the metaphor's evolution. However, his insistence on an accurate (i.e., limited) interpretation of the metaphor is not just a reflection of his sense of its meaning; there are elements of simply demanding accuracy and taking pleasure in judging. In his campaign for purifying Wittgenstein's metaphors, Garver includes Cavell among the polluters; despite Cavell's similar concern with the natural or biological basis of human existence within form of life, Garver finds Cavell's casual pluralization of the metaphor intolerable (Wittgenstein only pluralized it once in his five usages).

Garver accepts no evolution of the metaphor away from authorial intention as he understands it, but he is concerned about the basis of misreading and examines three ways in which other philosophers have failed to realize Wittgenstein's intention of arguing for a common form of human life. They have failed to interpret in the best light. According to Garver, the first possibility for a misreading is that they create a false connection between form of life and language-games (180-83), the second is that they connect the concept to earlier, plural uses, such as Spranger's or Stoessl's (183-85), and the third is that they, mostly through Malcolm, think a form of life may be "a basic trait of character or temperament" based on conversations and a passage of the *Tractatus* (185-87). In all three varieties of "misreadings," Garver sees the philosophers as seeking a false coherence ("fit" and "best light") among Wittgenstein's texts (spoken and written). While it is noteworthy that Garver is concerned about the interpretive processes of others, committed to understanding their error and to offering evidence for his inference of intention, he does so by offering a modified New Critical approach to interpretation.

Baker's and Conway's appeals to evidence in other texts, history, and

---

language-games and form of life, (2) see form of life as a basic trait of temperament or behavior, or (3) see the metaphor as defining sociological connections, classes, or styles of life.

conversants would not be valid for Garver; he wishes to erase just that type of evidence to offer the opposing interpretation based on very specific words and passages. The difference in understanding intention and meaning is methodological. Even so, while the three philosophers differ on what constitutes access to authorial intention, they have explicit criteria for arguing knowledge of intentions. The concern with authorial intention shows that the metaphor form of life does not, by itself, generate new meaning through a simple interactivity of the two terms; the generativity of the metaphoric form is balanced with the disciple's intentions, disciplinary motives, and rhetorical readings. For many, the metaphor can only mean what Wittgenstein intended: Wittgenstein owns it, but of course, it is the Wittgenstein of their reading. This appeal to intention is particularly telling in critiques of Lyotard's appropriation of the metaphor language-games.

The language-games metaphor accomplishes many purposes for Wittgenstein. With it, he shows that language and games are both actions that can be based on either definite or arbitrary rules, both evolve with practice, they are solely human activities, and they are invented, require mastery, are social, often public, and depend on the frame around them for their meaning. Using this metaphor, Wittgenstein sets the problem of defining language; he creates epistemic access, again through non-reference-fixing definition. When one sets out to define either term, language or games, looking through all the activities that are language or all the activities that are games, one doesn't find a clear definition for either; the reader must deliberate on what is the weight and use of each term. Wittgenstein writes that, for each, "we see a complicated network of similarities overlapping and crisscross: sometimes overall similarities, sometimes similarities of detail" (*Investigations* remark 66). Within all the activities that we call games, we find only a "family resemblance": we find only a loose, intransitive resemblance among baseball, catch, and chess. Baseball may share a few features with both catch and chess, but not the same features. Baseball and catch use balls, but baseball and chess are played to win. The rules of baseball and chess are set; the rules of catch are arbitrary and negotiated. Catch and chess can be played by one or two; baseball requires eighteen and a few umpires—unless the players negotiate the rules. With the language-games metaphor, Wittgenstein argues that language is also a loosely related collection of activities: fluid, negotiated activities and rigid, rule-bound activities. While he develops the relationships between the metaphor's primary and secondary subjects, between language and games, Wittgenstein does not develop the relationships among language-games; their relationship is especially ambiguous. He does note that one can't understand English if one only knows German (remark 495), but he strongly resists defining the relationship in more detail than through family resemblance because "if you try to reduce their relations to a *simple* formula you go wrong" (p. 180).

Lyotard disregards this warning and also Wittgenstein's intentions (if he cared or was even aware of Wittgenstein's intentions). Lyotard has very different intentions in his appropriation of the metaphor, and his use of language-games in texts written far from Vienna and Cambridge decades after Wittgenstein's death demonstrates the evolution of the metaphor. In *Just Gaming*, Lyotard's dialogue with the literary editor JeanLoup Thebaud, Lyotard elaborates a theory of language-games to examine the problem of justice in postmodern culture. Wittgenstein's name does not appear in this text, but language-games, a conceit interpreted anew as fragmented discursive practices, sets Lyotard's problem. In *The PostModern Condition,* Lyotard argues that "we no longer have recourse to grand narratives" (60); ancient traditions of values are lost and only "little narratives," local stories, language-games remain. Since no metanarrative can exist, Lyotard argues that adjudication among different stories (including persuasion and the building of consensus) is a terrorist imposition of someone's will to power. In *Just Gaming*, he claims we must judge without criteria, that justice preserves "the purity of each game" (96). For Lyotard, "language games are not translatable, because, if they were, they would not be language games; it is as if one wanted to translate the rules and strategies of chess into those of checkers" (53). In so arguing, Lyotard extends the relationship between games and language to argue that language-games are pure and incommensurable and that speakers are trapped in their games; there is no game of catch evolving to baseball as members of the second team arrive.

Lyotard's extension of the metaphor is contrary to many of Wittgenstein's intentions. While both dismiss the grand narrative and high theory and use language-games as blood in that vein, Wittgenstein limits the metaphoric relationship at the point of relating games or language beyond family resemblances; he writes, "if you try to reduce their relations to a *simple* formula you go wrong" (p. 180). Lyotard creates this "*simple* formula" when he extends the relationship and sees language-games as separate and incommensurable sets of rules, criteria, and judgments. This formulation, while it violates Wittgenstein's intentions, suits Lyotard's. In arguing for a postmodern condition and a repudiation of Enlightenment ethics, Lyotard presents a fragmented world; he is aided in this by extending the conceit language-games into a series of separate, unrelated sets of rules, a direction that supports his argument that humans are so separated that criteria for justice and judgment are impossible. The motives of postmodern culture facilitate the promulgation of Lyotard's reading of language-games and its reception by the audiences who share his intentions.

Even so, the disciplinary police, or in this case the interdisciplinary police, come quickly.[7] Terry Eagleton, in critiquing Lyotard's call to judge "without criteria," protests "a travesty of the later Wittgenstein" and Lyotard's failure to *read* "Wittgenstein's insistence" that language-games are interwoven (397). Despite Lyotard's lack of reference to Wittgenstein, Eagleton feels it necessary to use language-games only with Wittgensteinian meaning. Lyotard may have extended the metaphor in ways that advance his philosophy, but the motives and purposes of his interpretation of the metaphor violate Eagleton's, and perhaps Wittgenstein's. The enthymeme's assumptions differ, and an extension of meaning is refused. Eagleton refuses Lyotard's rhetorical reading of language-games, justifying the refusal by appealing to the authority of an original author.

In these instances of interpreting metaphors, the enthymemic aspect of metaphors and the emphasis by individual disciples on Wittgenstein's purposes to fill in the missing middle term seem to determine meaning, not the form's generativity. While occasionally philosophers extend Wittgenstein's metaphors, the responses to the extensions are rarely further extensions. The free play of poetic conceits and the generativity often envisioned for metaphors are very limited for these two philosophical metaphors. They generate conversation and even occasional understanding, but the conversation tends to be forensic, clearly circumscribed by concern for authorial intention. Wittgenstein's ability to borrow first and then extend metaphors demonstrates the complex interactions of his divergent (and dialogic) thinking, his later adeptness at creating context, and the disciplining of his followers. Conceivably, he benefits from bor-

---

7. There are Anglo-American philosophy discussions about appropriate meaning and extensions of or restrictions on language-games. Rush Rhees in *Discussion of Wittgenstein* and Norman Malcolm in "Language Game (2)" discuss the implications of taking "speaking" as "language" and its relationship to "games" and "routines." Rhees argues that Wittgenstein saw the same language spoken in various games, that language is conversational and implies a complex culture. The builders who simply shout "block," "slab," "beam" are engaged in a routine and their shouts do not meet the criteria of a language or language-game. Malcolm defends the builders' shouts as language and language-game by appealing to Wittgenstein's intention as documented in other writings. While Malcolm acknowledges that Rhees is right based on "Wittgenstein's *explicit* description," he writes for "something in the background" (40), explaining that "Wittgenstein is supposing" (39) and "he was making an unspoken 'assumption'" (40). In this case the metaphor cannot be restricted, but based on Wittgenstein's intentions as revealed elsewhere, must be kept static.

rowing metaphors without acknowledgment of earlier contexts; he owns the metaphor. By presenting and developing form of life and language-games outside of their authorial history, Wittgenstein can extend the metaphors without the critique of original intention that circumscribes the extensions of philosophers such as Lyotard and Cavell.[8] He achieves a particularly strong type of authority in the privacy of his borrowing, the centrality of his text, and the development of a culture that supports his intentions as a defining moment in the significance of the metaphor.

It is startling that the internal dynamic of the metaphor solicits a return to context, the text, and the concepts of interpretive fit and best light: hermeneutics describes the activity of policing metaphors better than theories of rhetorical reading do. To protect their intentions, certain theorists call on their interpretations of Wittgenstein's intentions, and these intentions are presented as objective and/or risking of prejudice. The tension between the competing intentions of scholars solicits a return to meaning as demonstrable in the original intention of the metaphor, though that origin is in Wittgenstein's usage (not in earlier usages) and though intentions are especially hard to read in tropes (be they metaphor or irony). Given its escape from referentiality, metaphor is especially hard to paraphrase, let alone define given its generativity, interactivity, and large enthymemic aspect. Still, at the site and cite of Wittgenstein's metaphors,

---

8. Catachresis of philosophical metaphors may call forth a discussion of the metaphor's context, history, and authorial intention, a process that does not happen with scientific metaphors. Scientific metaphors are subject to few, if any attacks for inappropriate interpretation. I believe that there are several factors in this divergence. First and most significantly, scientists, unlike humanists, do not discuss metaphors. In the historical sciences they do tell stories and discuss the value of alternative stories, but metaphors per se are not discussed. Still, the assumptions underlying the unanalyzed metaphors of science should create tensions similar to those which control philosophy's discourse. While Richard Harvey Brown analyzes a social science, not a hard science, to demonstrate this point, he argues that the debate in historical sociology between evolutionary functionalism and experimental empiricism lies in their respective root metaphors, organism and mechanism, and in the culture that the metaphors sustain. Both sets of scholars, according to Brown, see their language as literal and consequently cannot critique their own or others' constructions as poetic constructions, a limit that allows them to get on with the business of making knowledge—perhaps.

If scientists are not evaluating authorial intention and systems of metaphor, one might assume that the empirical, experimental regulation of the laboratory directs the generativity of scientific metaphors. And certainly that could be a factor. The use of a disciplinary metaphor would be in its ability to generate useful experiments or to predict descriptions. However, the idea that metaphoric interactivity is generating copious ideas testable against reality violates the enthymemic model of metaphor for which I have been arguing. Still, it is not without value if the assumptions of scientists within any field are very similar. The nature of their textbook education, their agreement on facts and models, and their stratified pattern of citation limits the probability of alternative interpretations.

interpretations and work toward understanding often replace rhetorical readings; when two or more readings are on the table and responding theorists want justifications for their discursive actions, they turn to a hermeneutic to stop or slow the forward movement of others' disciplinary plans.

The hermeneutic turn implies a return to or stasis at the point of speaking the trope, but it is a stasis full of tension and exploration. Metaphors, where meaning becomes unstable, increase efforts to stabilize meaning, and at that moment, cultural motives are put in play. When scholars turn to study Wittgenstein's intentions articulated in a view diverging from theirs, they increase the possibility of deliberation over meaning and a dialectical means of finding justified action (Eugene Garver). This suggests that unstable cultures, which by definition have members with differing intentions, work harder to recognize intentions and, on occasion, may be forced into deliberations over authorial meanings and responsible hermeneutics. Still, mulling over intentions and meanings does not innately open a reader to alternative meanings or fields of action; it need not privilege the texts or interpretations of others. Recognizing alternative positions need not be a hermeneutics of risking prejudices, but rather may well be a hermeneutics of preserving prejudices. In reading metaphors, philosophers show an unusual flexibility in donning the various roles of interpreter, dialectician, and audience.

III

It is difficult to describe how we recognize authorial intention, and it is hard to credit agency, weigh the conventions, have criteria for understanding, and name intentions *outside the everyday dramas of life,* for "an 'inner process' stands in need of outward criteria" (Wittgenstein, *Investigations* remark 580). The various practices of intentionality—intending, desiring, believing—woven through and in our lives are less familiar on the page, more elusive in the sophist's speech, and frighteningly alien in terrorist acts. But even the most familiar practices of intending can paradoxically be difficult to recognize: we can recognize what is familiar, but if it is too familiar, we tend to overlook it, see it as self-evident, and may not even know how we recognize it. Hence the process of recognition may seem more inner, innate, and mystical. Despite all the complexities, partial engagements, negotiations, refusals, and ambiguities, people work at and manage to recognize each others' meanings and intentions, and as the philosophers of the last chapters have shown us, what is recognized is recognized by a variety of public, describable, outward criteria, and so subject to understanding, deliberation, and revision.

Speech act theory argues that any intention that can be understood must fall within a recognized range of actions, a pattern based in our experience and acumen (Austin). Within much of speech act theory, however, beliefs in identifiable, consistent conventions, a single intention as a irreducible concept, and a docile interpreter are too strong and need supplement. For example, in *Speech Acts* John Searle writes:

> In speaking I attempt to communicate certain things to my hearer by getting him to recognize my intention to communicate just those things. I achieve the intended effect on the hearer by getting him to recognize my intention to achieve that effect, and as soon as the hearer recognizes what it is my intention to achieve, it is in general achieved. He understands what I am saying as soon as he recognizes my intention in uttering what I utter as an intention to say that thing. (43)

This admittedly slim statement of intention in communication fails to recognize the ways in which (1) the forms of discourse, while part of the intention of the rhetor, in fact open the possibility of and even suggest interpretive moves beyond the cognizance of the rhetor or the audience, (2) cultural motives require specific actions, such as judging and justification or censorious silence, from the rhetor and the audience, and (3) degrees of differing purposes between rhetors and audiences can prevent clear recognition of intentions and meanings and instead foster sophistic writings and willful misreadings as well as simple misunderstandings, both productive and destructive. A slim (credulous) theory of intentions does not appreciate that our worlds are at stake in our speaking and hearing and in our writing and reading. Nor does it, given the potential dangers within all speech acts, appreciate that these are high-stake engagements subject to the great, ripping forces of everyday intentions and misunderstandings.

The supplements to speech act theory offered here make complicated any claim to know another's or one's own intentions, but they do not invalidate the claim that—through shared practices, conventions, expectations, and inventions—we acknowledge each other's intentions. Through the acknowledgments, often incomplete and inconsistent, we negotiate aspects of our worlds. Indeed, acknowledgment and negotiation are the only means we have for going on, for recognizing worlds, and for understanding and misunderstanding each other. The practices, conventions, expectations, and inventions of reading a metaphor may be very different than those of reading a narrative; the practices, conventions, expectations, and inventions of reading a metaphor in a discipline may be very different than those of reading a metaphor in a poem. Still, the techniques are describable ways by which we make and maintain human worlds; they are what makes us human and not infallible gods or logical machines.

What troubles me more is how one can distinguish between cultural motives, such as those embedded in practices accompanying forms and discourses, and those subjective intentions that supplement, subvert, and reiterate cultural intentions and allow each of us to speak and claim aspects of the world as "mine." This trouble may be in the nature of the question, the seeking of formula for a distinction between parts of a whole, since intention itself is dependent on culture, prejudice, discourse, topic, subject, situation, and moment. There will *necessarily* be jagged edges in the distinction between concepts that function and are recognizable only within a whole situation and through the larger concept of intention. Purposes are embedded in forms and discourses whose motives direct purposes. Intentions, cultural and subjective, are recognizable only within scenes, acts, agents, agencies, and purposes. Further complicating the interpretation and differentiation of subjective and cultural intentions, the prejudices of a rhetor or an audience—while not intentions in themselves—are knowable only in public appearances where they are manifest as intentional action, within the same speech acts that manifest subjective and cultural intentions.

In addition to the problem of knowing the single part of a reciprocal interaction, there is a further difficulty along the jagged edge: despite recognition of the subject-in-process (Kristeva) and while intentions are ongoing in speech acts (intention in) and in planning (intention to), interpretive scholarship tends to describe the subject and intention as forensic notions, the past in a recognizable pattern (and so in a coherent pattern of responsibility). The deliberating (intending in), future-creating (intending to) subject-in-process evades our methodologies as it evades our facile definitions. The subject-in-process has a trajectory, and that trajectory makes her reading of others and our reading of her more than simply readings for understanding. As the philosophers reading Wittgenstein have shown us, the subject-in-process reads to find a means to claim aspects of the world, to partake in the pleasure of judging others, to mentor and parent junior colleagues, and to interpret and re-present the misunderstood text. For these reasons and others, her prejudices, as evident in her language, fit her intentions since language works for a plethora of purposes besides understanding and communication.

In appreciation of (and in surrender to) the jagged edges of describing intentions, I ask somewhat different questions, questions less about differentiation and more about rhetor and audience: Whose intention is it that speaks, and to whom is that intention addressed? To answer these I buy a litmus test from Burke, who has guided us so far in theorizing intentions within rhetorical practices and certainly has never omitted space (small space) for an agent's choice among acts, within scenes. Hence my answer is dependent on motives, Burke's move to paradox that deconstructs the structured order of form and drama. Through the paradoxes of substance and action, the intentions of the speaker and the audience are structured and determined as well as ambiguous and self-deconstructing. Motives that are enigmatic and paradoxical particularly reveal the inconsistencies within, among, and between intentions, and so show the strategic ambiguities and fissures that allow the partial agents "the partial acts that but partially represent themselves and but partially conform to their scenes" (*Grammar* 83).

Consequently, Burke tells us that forms speak, as forms are a way of experiencing "situations beyond the tactics of expression" (*Philosophy* 92). Wittgenstein can write his chains of negations or pilfer his metaphors, but each form sets up describable interpretive patterns that audiences can manipulate to achieve their motives and purposes and so claim their world. The form allows audiences to proliferate meanings. While the negatives allow the audience to experience textual turns, the form also offers the audience tactics for refusing a turn. The writing of a narrative and its contextualization as either deliberative or forensic begins an accrual, a formal process that is subject to the speech acts of rhetors and readings of audiences, but one in which the repeated form of narration, in and of itself, sets patterns of experience, reflection, mimesis, interpretation, and degrees of opening or closure. Reading metaphors, the audience has the thrill of finding the missing middle term, but the term itself is not innate in the form and thus the cultural motives speak loudly in the metaphor, though the form be chosen by a rhetor and experienced by an audience.

The cultural motives speak, for "motives are shorthand terms for situation" and discourses are situated (Burke, *Counter-Statement* 29). What is possible in philosophy is different than what is possible in poetry, what is possible in Vienna is different than what is possible in Cambridge, what is considered in 1920 is different than what is considered in 1990. Despite all Wittgenstein's offerings of different methods, the fly will not easily leave the fly-bottle; philosophy will not leave, no, cannot leave the philosophy-bottle.[9] The situation of philosophical discourse defines and mediates among its motives and through its motives the possible horizons. Carnap would be hard-pressed to base logic on ethics. McDowell would be mad to address the APA and advocate misconception. Wright conceives his discipline as dialogic, but he would not mistake APA conversations for those of the parlor, for his other would be judged, and judged deficient. Baker, Garver, and Conway argue that the metaphor form of life denotes specific concepts, and they must have criteria for their conclusions because, within philosophy, terms are defined. A philosophical audience is likely to ignore or dismiss alternative speech acts; they would not understand the cultural motives.

While the distinction between them can be made, motives and acts are complexly interlocked. Cultural motives show us what a speech act is and is not. To discuss the motive behind a speech act and the society that authorizes the act is to imply that the agent is acted upon and does not have willful action, but to consider an agent's act in terms of its effect on cultural motives and the society created in the act is to consider motive and society as passively made by individual action. The motives of the society are dependent on, defined by, and developed in the agent's act, just as the agent and act, in turn, are dependent on, defined by, and developed in the cultural motive. The grammar of agency creates tautologies, tensions, and paradoxes that can undermine assertions of intention but do not invalidate the concepts contained in the grammar *given the criteria of everyday usage and describable practice.* Motives speak, but do not dictate.

Purposes also speak, though in occult ways and never in soliloquy. Burke writes that it is pathological to disassociate purpose from agent, act, agency, or scene; purpose is *not* itself an act or an agent, nor is it a single state or process (*Grammar* 288-89). Ordinary language philosophers would tell us purpose is not known as an inner state or a consciousness, but rather it is recognized as a grammatical expression, part of a symbolic action. Purpose is an enactment that does something in the world and to the world, and consequently, as it manifests itself in texts, it produces part of its own context. For these reasons, purpose is the term most susceptible to dissolution, but also for these reasons, purpose creates describable experiences and hence the sensible criteria that reveal purpose within and throughout the drama.

A purpose, a subjective intention, is placed within motives (shorthand for a situation), but as it is knowable in ratio with an agent or an act (a

---

9. "What is your aim in philosophy?—To shew the fly the way out of the fly-bottle" (*Investigations* remark 309).

scene, an agency), one can locate specific purposes within dramas. To write that three analytic philosophers at an APA symposium share the motives of judging and justification is to move toward defining cultural intention and possibility. To write that Wright's forgiveness of opposition has a different purpose than Goldfarb's dismissal or McDowell's banishment places their respective textual acts as arising in significantly different purposes (reflecting different beliefs, desires, scenes, rhetorical strategies, cultural engagements, etc.). Each subject-in-action claims and owns different aspects of the world, or the philosophical discourse. There are ways an analytic philosopher will speak; there are ways a particular philosopher will speak. Given experiences with a particular agent (as well as others), readers can learn to infer and predict some of his intentions, not just his purposes, but the relationship of those purposes to his motives and forms. In a drama, a set of actions (conventions, practices, inventions, and expectations) become identifiable with a particular agent; these particular acts, over time, demonstrate enough consistency to ascribe purposes in specific ratios.

Engaging with and being engaged by purposes is an inseparable piece of our experiences of language and our acumen with human relationships. I would premise that the ability to infer purposes is paradoxically the primary source of both suspicion and identification; for in the acts of inferring purpose, agents learn strategies for engaging with others and using those engagements to understand their own worlds, as well as the alien worlds of others. To recognize purposes is to learn to reflect on self-definition, difference, and congruent and divergent action. Whether we engage others' purposes—whether with suspicion or respect, as audience or interpreters—the evolution and richness of our own intentions depends on our recognition of those of others and our willingness to risk and to imagine, invent, and decipher worlds we do not own as well as our abilities to reject and critique alien and dangerous worlds. It is an odd double consciousness we practice in exchanging worlds, offering ours, glancing at theirs. We are always and never in the differend, for we always lack *rules* of judgment (having only guides) but are amply experienced in reciprocity and recognition, perhaps more accurate terms for what we achieve in communication than understanding is. Together we do not stand under anything, but we do give back and forth and know again. In the philosophical interchanges offered here, discursive interactions certainly seem far less about forming absolute knowledge and accurate interpretations and more about "going on."

Understanding cannot be simply a semantic overlap nor a shared system of reason; semantic and rationalist systems are not up to explaining the very fractured and incomplete interchanges between interlocutors. Discourse, subjectivity, and the rhetorical situation are too complex for those models. The impact of multiculturalism (Viennese and British), diversity, and power differentials—even in the disciplined discourse of philosophy—disrupts any simple convergence on a meaning. What we call understanding, a bridging of alterity, is achievable through a pragmatic process of recognition of difference and reciprocal adaptation and address. The difficulties of communication and acknowledging even disciplined intentions underline that the political erupts in speaking, for as Aristotle tells us, people are political animals because they speak.

We always communicate in diversity: selecting, reflecting, and deflecting worlds. Fears of identity politics and the excesses of multiculturalism are fears of human interactions and changing worlds, for identity politics and multiculturalism are simply two manifestations of the conflicting intentions that language necessarily declares. Community, understanding, and consensus—even in Aristotle's polis[10]—are ideals and models. Description, close reading, and interpretive theory demonstrate that *diversity is the norm*. Rather than continue to work with counterfactuals so thoroughly critiqued, rhetoricians need new models and discourses about what is rhetoric, models that reflect contemporary theories of language and politics.

Recognition of difference and reciprocity in adaptation and address—not the stasis of community, understanding, and consensus—are what make rhetoric possible, for rhetoric is not simply about conflict: in fact, deep division destroys the likelihood of discursive persuasion and increases the need for violent, economic, and socially disruptive strategies. Deep division obstructs ongoingness. Premised on struggle and the presence of alterity, rhetoric can work to maintain deep difference and clarify lines of conflict in the service of claiming recognition and demanding reciprocity.[11] Even so, rhetoric most often works to minimize conflicts

---

10. As discussed in the Introduction, there are a number of classicists and political scientists who read Aristotle as embracing diversity and writing to understand its nature. In addition, rhetorician Carolyn Miller argues that the polis is not an empirical structure but an ideological construction, and hence Aristotle was aware of the diversity.

11. There are times when it is rhetorically and politically advantageous to increase difference and force interlocutors to move toward you. As bell hooks reminds us in "Choosing the Margin as a Space of Radical Openness" (*Yearning*) an essay where the incantation is "Language is a place of struggle," the politics of location calls for lived experience in the margin for "the formation of counter-hegemonic cultural practices" (145). The margin can be a space of repression or resistance, creativity, and power. As well, in societies, there are multiple forces (economic, discursive, political, religious, educational) that necessitate engagements between different groups and compel conversation. The refusal of conventional conversation by one group, even a minority

and thus to multiply recognitions, increase reciprocal movement, and find *the dynamic means of justified action.* If the other's intentions and meanings are recognized imperfectly and suspiciously, if the differentiation between the subject speaking and the culture speaking is tenuous, this has never ended, in itself, the possibility of communication, association, practical reason, deliberation, and justified action, in part because the absolutes of conflict and consensus are both exceedingly rare and unhealthy states. But the acknowledgment of the partiality of our recognitions does require new ways of describing, explaining, and engaging the concepts of politics, persuasion, reason, deliberation, action, consensus, and citizenship, and all of these concepts are basic to rhetorical thinking.

The reconception of deliberative rhetoric cannot be tackled at the closing of a book on intentions, but its development would be helped by returning to my discussion of how we recognize aspects of each other's worlds. Rather than seeing contradiction, break, and blockage as the characteristics of struggle (be that struggle for either understanding or political position), the cases in this book suggest that a more diffuse and constant difference is characteristic of exchange: interlocutors may be networked in a discipline, but the degree of sharing is underdefined, and they are positioned differently as they analyze a variety of similar philosophical problems from disparate nodal points. In the end, however, despite the partiality of their overlaps, their struggle for recognition and reciprocity is one of composition, not one of opposition. They struggle with each other's meanings and go on to form a larger discourse.

The struggle across difference is constituting—though certainly not always constituting in comfortable ways or of things we necessarily want. It is the struggle across difference that forces the act, and as Robert Wess reminds us, an act is an invention, the constituting of something that wasn't there before.[12] Hence the importance of Burke's example of summation and convergence is our amendable U.S. Constitution (*constitution* being a member of the paradoxical *stance* family) (*Grammar* 324). As Burke notes, however, constitutions are formed in struggle, different clauses suiting different constituencies. Burke writes that "Constitutions are agonistic instruments. . . . For what a Constitution would do primarily is *substantiate an ought* (to base a statement as to *what should be*

---

group, may oblige the other group to shift discursive and material practices. The Montgomery bus boycott is a good example of this.

12. While appearing too recently to affect this book significantly, Robert Wess's *Kenneth Burke: Rhetoric, Subjectivity, Postmodernism,* with its insight into the place of constitution in Burke, should change Burkean scholarship.

upon a statement as to *what is*). And in our 'agonistic' world, such substantiation derives point and poignancy by contrast with notions of what should not be" (*Grammar* 357, 358). Speech acts, most explicitly in deliberative situations, are constituted and substantiated in response to shoulds and should nots. Their power is in their contrasting and reciprocating stances and their responsiveness to other acts, but since—at the cessation of deliberation or in the formation of a constitution—the speech acts or constitutional clauses must find "*merger* or *balance* or *equilibrium.*" Still, in the finished text or act, as court cases display, there remains "conflict among the clauses" (349). This vision reveals that states are conflicted, even if they are constituted as a whole; that communities are conflicted, even if they are constituted as a whole; that texts are conflicted, even if they are constituted as a whole. Burke may go too far in characterizing constitutions solely as responses to enemies rather than to others and as sites of conflict rather than discursive frictions, but even within his very agonistic view, the work of constitutions is composing. Certainly constitutions are the products of stylized struggles of material interest (389), and they suggest "the coordinates one will think by" (367).

If the usual pattern of our engagements, commitments, and disparities is closer to that of a game of hacky sack or to the experience of a city than to that of a bloody battle, it is troubling that the dominant metaphor for politics and argumentation remains war and that the dominant conceptualization of knowledge formation remains dialectic.[13] It, however, is explainable. Though he is prey to it himself, Burke warns us that we like to move from initial differences to opposites, writing:

> Polar otherness unites things that are *opposite to* one another; synecdochic otherness unites things that are simply different from one another. The beloved's house is not *opposite to* the beloved, but merely *different from* the beloved. Under dialectic pressures, however, (as in political alignments) any difference may come to be felt as an antithesis. (*Philosophy* 78)

The primary rhetorical problem is that difference becomes opposition under political conditions.[14] The push apart, whether the basis is as bio-

---

13. As I close this book, I can now imagine better what Iris Marion Young meant in her offering of city life as a metaphor for an alternative to the ideal of community. City life offers "social differentiation without exclusion," "variety" within shared social spaces, "eroticism" in offering the other as attractive, and the "publicity" of a variety of public spaces.

14. Despite a desire to equate the political simply with any power differential, I think a better

logical as having two symmetrical sides or as grammatical as the "not," moves diversity to opposition. However, one need not go as far as dialectical thinking to explain the rhetorical movement from small difference and friction to antagonism. Burke's fellow post-Marxists Laclau and Mouffe argue that ambiguity (the slippage of the signifier) is, in itself, "the formula of antagonism," "the limit of the social" (*Hegemony* 128). Ambiguity allows space for our intentions. Still, however many sources it has, the effect of antithesis (and the fantasy of synthesis) is to generate the constant possibility of false dichotomies and the endless potential to widen small difference into rupture.

The task for rhetoric then is to recognize and critique the discursive drive to dichotomy and opposition as well as the drive to identification and consensus. While acknowledging the theatrical possibilities of Hegelian dialectic, a pragmatic rhetorical theory would recognize that discursive ambiguity, grammatical paradox, and the subject's position subvert the fixity of ideology and open possibilities for claiming aspects of the world. In doing so, it would contribute to an acknowledgment that the rhetorical requirements of emancipatory politics—the politics of difference and distribution—are not alien to those of everyday speech practices. To speak is to negotiate alterity.

If alterity is a basic, inevitable, and productive as well as alienating and disruptive force in recognition and reciprocity, the real question then is what distinguishes who is recognized and what is reciprocated. For rhetorical equality among citizens is at the heart of a truly deliberative democracy. Rhetoricians who are concerned with deliberation should be asking questions, such as:

What text is written out?

In negotiations over meaning, what meanings dominate? Why? What meanings are heard? By whom? What meanings are not heard? Why?

Which narratives accrue, and which stand in isolation?

---

sense of the relationship between the political and the mechanisms by which diversity becomes opposition can be formulated by working with Laclau and Mouffe's definition of political action, quoted in the Introduction. They define political action as "a type of action whose objective is the transformation of a social relation which constructs a subject in a relationship of subordination" (*Hegemony* 153). The drive to make difference into opposition thrives where the difference is one of subordination and there are acts to transform that relationship. Here's the rub: the nature of interpretation, as interpretive theory has shown, is to transform. What is at issue here, in the case of moving diversity to opposition, is whether the objective of the transformation is to change a social relationship of subordination.

Who does not achieve presence?

What forms resist rhetorical readings?

How are recognition and reciprocity authorized and moderated by culture, institution, and social power?

What are the means to justified action?

A deliberative rhetoric that responds to contemporary theory must engage the voices not heard in and the texts not written for traditional rhetorical forums (the "public sphere"): that is, if it is to achieve a deeper understanding of the ways our intentions form worlds or fail. It would study deliberations where there is no pretense of common good (say, fights over election district boundaries) to understand the nature of discursive successes and failures; after all, given innumerable locations in the world, the claim of common good is power-laden and an evasion of politics. What is more likely, given innumerable locations in the postcolonial world, is the amending and augmenting of what is good and the proliferating of visions of the good.[15]

However much we might want community and understanding and a common good, we cannot escape the limits of our recognitions. Our recognitions, even if they are generous and grow to recognize other worlds, are finite. Our engagements with each other are partial, as are our claims on the world. Our intentions are not simply the purposes that we attribute to our speaking, but rather they include subjective purposes, cultural motives, and the forms of language that together dilute any simple control of what we say and how we are understood. Our audience may reciprocate, but their purposes, cultural motives, and forms situate them, and their most reciprocal interpretations transform our intentions. Knowledge, deliberation, and persuasion are exhausting, exhilarating pursuits, pursuits of recognition and reciprocity: they are not states; they are the pursuit of the many worlds created by the too-fertile forces of human intention.

---

15. See Robert M. Cover's "Nomos and Narrative," Drucilla Cornell's *The Philosophy of the Limit*, and Martha Minow's "Justice Engendered" for critiques of the notion of a single good and arguments for the recognition and acceptance of difference as a basis of the good.

Works Cited

Altieri, Charles. *Act and Quality: A Theory of Literary Meaning and Humanistic Understanding.* Amherst: University of Massachusetts Press, 1981.
———. *Subjective Agency: A Theory of First-Person Expressivity and Its Social Implications.* Cambridge: Blackwell, 1994.
———. "Toward a Hermeneutics Responsive to Rhetorical Theory." In *Rhetoric and Hermeneutics in Our Time: A Reader,* edited by Walter Jost and Michael Hyde, 90-107. New Haven: Yale University Press, 1997.
Anscombe, G. E. M. *Intention.* Oxford: Blackwell, 1963.
———. *An Introduction to Wittgenstein's Tractatus.* Philadelphia: University of Pennsylvania Press, 1971.
Arbib, Michael A., and Mary B. Hesse. *The Construction of Reality.* Cambridge: Cambridge University Press, 1986.
Arendt, Hannah. *The Human Condition.* Chicago: University of Chicago Press, 1958.
Aristotle. *Politics.* Translated by Ernest Baker. New York: Oxford University Press, 1995.
———. *The Rhetoric and Poetics.* Translated by W. Rhys Roberts. New York: Random House, 1984.
———. *Topica.* Translated by E. S. Forster. Cambridge: Harvard University Press, 1987.
Armstrong, Nancy, and Leonard Tennenhouse, eds. *The Violence of Representation: Literature and the History of Violence.* New York: Routledge, 1989.
Audi, Robert. "Deliberative Intentions and Willingness to Act: A Reply to Professor Mele." *Philosophia* 18 (1988): 243-45.
Austin, J. L. *How to Do Things with Words.* Cambridge: Harvard University Press, 1975.
———. *Philosophical Papers.* Edited by J. O. Urmson and G. J. Warnock. 3d ed. Oxford: Oxford University Press, 1961.
Averill, James R. "Inner Feelings, Works of Flesh, the Beast Within, Diseases of the Mind, Driving Force, and Putting on a Show: Six Metaphors of Emotion and Their Theoretical Extensions." In *Metaphors in the History of Psychology,* edited by David E. Leary, 104-32. Cambridge: Cambridge University Press, 1990.
Ayer, A. J. *Freedom and Morality and Other Essays.* Oxford: Clarendon Press, 1984.
———. *Wittgenstein.* Chicago: University of Chicago Press, 1985.
Baker, G. P., and P. M. S. Hacker. *Wittgenstein: Understanding and Meaning.* Vol. 1. Oxford: Blackwell, 1980.
Baker, Gordon. *Wittgenstein, Frege, and the Vienna Circle.* Oxford: Blackwell, 1988.

Baker, Lynne Rudder. "On the Very Idea of a Form of Life." *Inquiry* 27 (1984): 277-89.
Bakhtin, Mikhail. *Problems of Dostoevsky's Poetics*. Edited and translated by Caryl Emerson. Minneapolis: University of Minnesota Press, 1984.
Barber, Benjamin R. *Strong Democracy: Participatory Politics for a New Age*. Berkeley and Los Angeles: University of California Press, 1984.
Baron, Jane B. "Intention, Interpretation, and Stories." *Duke Law Journal* 42 (1992): 630-78.
Bataille, Georges. *Eroticism*. Translated by Mary Dalwood. New York: Marion Boyars, 1987.
Benoit, William. "A Note on Burke on 'Motive.'" *Rhetoric Society Quarterly* 26 (1996): 67-79.
Bernstein, Richard J. "Wittgenstein's Three Languages." In *Essays on Wittgenstein's Tractatus*, edited by Irving M. Copi and Robert W. Beard, 231-47. New York: Macmillan, 1966.
Bertelsen, Dale A. "Kenneth Burke's Conception of Reality: The Process of Transformation and Its Implications for Rhetorical Criticism." In *Extensions of the Burkean System*, edited by James Chesbro, 230-47. Tuscaloosa: University of Alabama Press, 1993.
Berthoff, Ann E., ed. *Richards on Rhetoric: I. A. Richards: Selected Essays (1929-74)*. New York: Oxford University Press, 1991.
Bizzell, Patricia, and Bruce Herzberg. *The Rhetorical Tradition*. Boston: Bedford, 1990.
Black, Max. *Language and Philosophy: Studies in Method*. Ithaca: Cornell University Press, 1949.
——. *Models and Metaphors*. Ithaca: Cornell University Press, 1962.
——. "Some Problems Connected with Language." In *Essays on Wittgenstein's Tractatus*, edited by Irving M. Copi and Robert W. Beard, 95-114. New York: Macmillan, 1966.
Blackwell, Kenneth. "Early Wittgenstein and Middle Russell." In *Perspectives on the Philosophy of Wittgenstein*, edited by Irving Block, 1-30. Oxford: Blackwell, 1981.
Blankenship, Jane. "Kenneth Burke on Ecology: A Synthesis." *Extensions of the Burkean System*, edited by James Chesbro, 251-68. Tuscaloosa: University of Alabama Press, 1993.
Booth, Wayne. *Critical Understanding: The Powers and Limits of Pluralism*. Chicago: University of Chicago Press, 1979.
——. *Modern Dogma and the Rhetoric of Assent*. Chicago: University of Chicago Press, 1974.
——. *Rhetoric of Irony*. Chicago: University of Chicago Press, 1974.
Bouveresse, Jacques. *Wittgenstein Reads Freud: The Myth of the Unconscious*. Translated by Carol Cosman. Princeton: Princeton University Press, 1995.
Bove, Paul A. *Intellectuals in Power: A Genealogy of Critical Humanism*. New York: Columbia University Press, 1986.
Boyd, Richard. "Metaphor and Theory Change: What Is 'Metaphor' a Metaphor For?" In *Metaphor and Thought*, edited by Andrew Ortony, 356-408. Cambridge: Cambridge University Press, 1979.

Bratman, Michael E. *Intention, Plans, and Practical Reason.* Cambridge: Harvard University Press, 1987.
Brearley, Michael. "Psychoanalysis: A Form of Life?" In *Wittengenstein Centenary Essays,* edited by A. Phillips Griffiths, 151-67. New York: Cambridge University Press, 1991.
Brown, Richard Harvey. "Rhetoric and the Science of History: The Debate Between Evolutionism and Empiricism as a Conflict of Metaphor." *Quarterly Journal of Speech* 72 (1986): 148-61.
Brown, Stuart C. "I. A. Richards' New Rhetoric: Multiplicity, Instrument, and Metaphor." *Rhetoric Review* 10 (1992): 218-31.
Bruner, Jerome. "The Narrative Construction of Reality." *Critical Inquiry* 18 (1991): 1-21.
Bulkin, Elly, Judith Keegan Gardiner, Rena Grasso Patterson, and Annette Kolodny. "An Interchange on Feminist Criticism: On 'Dancing Through the Minefield.'" *Feminist Studies* 8 (Fall 1982): 629-75.
Burke, Kenneth. *Attitudes Toward History.* Berkeley and Los Angeles: University of California Press, 1984.
———. *Counter-Statement.* Chicago: University of Chicago Press, 1957.
———. *A Grammar of Motives.* Berkeley and Los Angeles: University of California Press, 1969.
———. *Language as Symbolic Action.* Berkeley and Los Angeles: University of California Press, 1966.
———. "(Nonsymbolic) Motion/(Symbolic) Action." *Critical Inquiry* 4 (1978): 809-38.
———. *Permanence and Change.* New York: Bobbs-Merrill, 1965.
———. *The Philosophy of Literary Form.* Berkeley and Los Angeles: University of California Press, 1973.
———. *A Rhetoric of Motives.* Berkeley and Los Angeles: University of California Press, 1969.
———. *The Rhetoric of Religion: Studies in Logology.* Berkeley and Los Angeles: University of California Press, 1970.
———. "Words as Deeds." *Centrum* 3 (1975): 147-68.
Butler, Judith, and Joan W. Scott, eds. *Feminists Theorize the Political.* New York: Routledge, 1992.
Campbell, John Angus. "Reply to Gaonkar and Fuller." *Southern Communication Journal* 58 (1993): 312-18.
Carnap, Rudolf. "Ethics." In *Essential Readings in Logical Positivism,* edited by Oswald Hanfling, 205-6. Oxford: Blackwell, 1981.
———. "Intellectual Autobiography." In *The Philosophy of Rudolf Carnap,* edited by Paul Arthur Schilpp, 3-84. London: Cambridge University Press, 1963.
———. *The Logical Syntax of Language.* London: K. Paul, Trench, Trubner, 1937.
Cascardi, Anthony. *The Bounds of Reason: Cervantes, Dostoevsky, Flaubert.* New York: Columbia University Press, 1986.
Cavell, Stanley. "The Availability of Wittgenstein's Later Philosophy." In *Wittgenstein: The Philosophical Investigations,* edited by George Pitcher, 151-85. Notre Dame, Ind.: University of Notre Dame Press, 1968.

———. *The Claim of Reason*. London: Oxford University Press, 1979.
———. *This New Yet Unapproachable America: Lectures after Emerson after Wittgenstein*. Albuquerque: Living Batch, 1989.
Charland, Maurice. "Finding Horizon and Telos: The Challenge to Critical Rhetoric." *Quarterly Journal of Speech* 77 (1991): 71-74.
Chen, Kuan-Hsing. "Beyond *Truth and Method*: On Misreading Gadamer's Praxical Hermeneutics." *Quarterly Journal of Speech* 73 (1987): 183-99.
Chesbro, James W. "Epistemology and Ontology as Dialectical Modes in the Writings of Kenneth Burke." In *Landmark Essays on Kenneth Burke*, edited by Barry Brummett, 135-54. Davis, Calif.: Hermagoras, 1993.
Chicago Cultural Studies Group. "Critical Multiculturalism." *Critical Inquiry* 18 (1992): 530-55.
Chisholm, Roderick M. "Intentionality." In *Encyclopedia of Philosophy*, edited by Paul Edwards, 201-4. New York: Collier-Macmillian, 1967.
Clayton, Jay. "Narrative and Theories of Desire." *Critical Inquiry* 16 (1989): 33-53.
Cloud, Dana L. "The Materiality of Discourse as Oxymoron: A Challenge to Critical Rhetoric." *Western Journal of Communication* 58 (1994): 141-63.
Cocchiarella, Nino B. *Logical Studies in Early Analytic Philosophy*. Columbus: Ohio State University Press, 1987.
Conway, Gertrude. *Wittgenstein on Foundations*. Atlantic Highlands, N.J.: Humanities, 1989.
Copeland, Rita. *Rhetoric, Hermeneutics, and Translation in the Middle Ages*. New York: Cambridge University Press, 1991.
Corlett, William. *Community Without Unity*. Durham, N.C.: Duke University Press, 1989.
Corliss, Richard L. "Schleiermacher's Hermeneutics and Its Critics." *Religion Studies* 29 (1993): 363-79.
Cornell, Drucilla. *The Philosophy of the Limit*. New York: Routledge, 1992.
———. *Transformations*. New York: Routledge, 1993.
Cover, Robert M. "The Supreme Court, 1982 Term—Foreword: Nomos and Narrative." *Harvard Law Review* 97 (1983): 4-68.
———. "Violence and the Word." *Yale Law Journal* 95 (1986): 1601-29.
Danziger, Kurt. "Generative Metaphor and the History of Psychological Discourse." In *Metaphors in the History of Psychology*, edited by David E. Leary, 331-56. Cambridge: Cambridge University Press, 1990.
David, Henry. "Text and Theory in Critical Practice." *Quarterly Journal of Speech* 78 (1992): 219-22.
Davidson, Donald. *Actions and Events*. New York: Oxford University Press, 1980.
———. "Locating Literary Language." In *Literary Theory After Davidson*, edited by Reed Way Dasenbrock, 295-308. University Park: Pennsylvania State University Press, 1993.
de Lauretis, Teresa. *Alice Doesn't: Feminism, Semiotics, Cinema*. Bloomington: Indiana University Press, 1984.
Dennett, Daniel C. *The Intentional Stance*. Cambridge: MIT Press, 1987.
Derrida, Jacques. *Limited, Inc*. Evanston, Ill.: Northwestern University Press, 1988.
Diamond, Cora. "What Nonsense Might Be." In *Ludwig Wittgenstein: Critical Assess-*

ments, vol. 2, edited by Stuart Shankar, 125-41. Dover, N.H.: Croom Helm, 1986.
"Dissoi Logoi or Dialexeis." Translated by Rosamond Kent Sprague. In *The Older Sophists.* Columbia: University of South Carolina Press, 1972.
Dutton, Denis. "Why Intentionalism Won't Go Away." In *Literature and the Question of Philosophy,* edited by Anthony J. Cascardi, 194-209. Baltimore: Johns Hopkins University Press, 1987.
Eagleton, Terry. *The Ideology of the Aesthetic.* Cambridge, Mass.: Blackwell, 1990.
Eden, Katherine. "Hermeneutics and the Ancient Rhetorical Tradition." *Rhetorica* 5 (1987): 59-86.
———. *Poetic and Legal Fiction in the Aristotelian Tradition.* Princeton: Princeton University Press, 1986.
———. "The Rhetorical Tradition and Augustinian Hermeneutics in *De Doctrina Christiana.*" *Rhetoric* 8 (1990): 45-63.
Epstein, Barbara. "Why Post-Structuralism Is a Dead End for Progressive Thought." *Socialist Review* 25 (1995): 83-119.
Ermarth, Michael. "The Transformation of Hermeneutics: Nineteenth-Century and Twentieth-Century Moderns." *The Monist* 64 (1981): 175-94.
Fann, K. T. *Wittgenstein's Conception of Philosophy.* Berkeley and Los Angeles: University of California Press, 1969.
Farrell, Thomas B. "From the Parthenon to the Bassinet: Death and Rebirth along the Epistemic Trail." *Quarterly Journal of Speech* 9 (1990): 78-84.
———. *Norms of Rhetorical Culture.* New Haven: Yale University Press, 1993.
———. "On the Disappearance of the Rhetorical Aura." *Western Journal of Communication* (1993) 57: 147-58.
Fetterley, Judith. *The Resisting Reader: A Feminist Approach to American Fiction.* Bloomington: Indiana University Press, 1978.
Fischer, Michael. *Stanley Cavell and Literary Skepticism.* Chicago: University of Chicago Press, 1989.
Fish, Stanley. *Doing What Comes Naturally: Change, Rhetoric, and the Practice of Theory in Literary and Legal Studies.* Durham: Duke University Press, 1989.
———. *Is There a Text in This Class? The Authority of Interpretive Communities.* Cambridge: Harvard University Press, 1980.
———. *There's No Such Thing as Free Speech and It's a Good Thing, Too.* Oxford: Oxford University Press, 1994.
Fisher, Walter. *Human Communication as Narration: Toward a Philosophy of Reason, Value, and Action.* Columbia: University of South Carolina Press, 1987.
Fishkin, James S. *Democracy and Deliberation: New Directions for Democratic Reform.* New Haven: Yale University Press, 1991.
Foss, Sonja K., Karen Foss, and Robert Trapp. *Contemporary Perspectives on Rhetoric.* Prospect Heights, Ill.: Waveland, 1985.
Fraser, Nancy. *Justice Interruptus: Critical Reflections on the "Postsocialist" Condition.* New York: Routledge, 1997.
———. *Unruly Practices: Power, Discourse, and Gender in Contemporary Social Theory.* Minneapolis: University of Minnesota Press, 1989.

Frege, Gottlob. *The Foundations of Arithmetic: A Logico-Mathematical Enquiry into the Concept of Number.* Translated by J. L. Austin. Oxford: Blackwell, 1968.

Frow, John. "Foucault and Derrida." *Raritan* 5 (Summer 1985): 31-42.

Gadamer, Hans-Georg. "The Hermeneutics of Suspicion." In *Hermeneutics: Questions and Prospects,* edited by Gary Shapiro and Allen Sica, 54-65. Amherst: University of Massachusetts Press, 1984.

———. *Philosophical Hermeneutics.* Translated by David E. Linge. Berkeley and Los Angeles: University of California Press, 1976.

———. *Reason in the Age of Science.* Cambridge: MIT Press, 1981.

———. "Rhetoric and Hermeneutics." In *Rhetoric and Hermeneutics in Our Time: A Reader,* edited by Walter Jost and Michael Hyde, 45-59. New Haven: Yale University Press, 1997.

———. "Rhetoric, Hermeneutics, and the Critique of Ideology: Metacritical Comments on *Truth and Method.*" In *The Hermeneutics Reader,* edited by Kurt Mueller-Vollmer, 274-92. New York: Continuum.

———. *Truth and Method.* Translated by Joel Weinsheimer and Donald G. Marshall. 2d rev. ed. New York: Continuum, 1993.

Gaonkar, Dilip Parameshwar. "The Idea of Rhetoric in the Rhetoric of Science." *Southern Communication Journal* 58 (1993): 258-95.

Gardiner, Judith Keegan, ed. *Provoking Agents: Gender and Agency in Theory and Practice.* Chicago: University of Illinois Press, 1995.

Garver, Eugene. *Aristotle's Rhetoric: An Art of Character.* Chicago: University of Chicago Press, 1994.

Garver, Newton. "Form of Life in Wittgenstein's Later Work." *Dialectica* 44 (1990): 175-201.

Geras, Norman. "Post-Marxism?" *New Left Review* 163 (1987): 40-82.

Gier, Nicholas F. *Wittgenstein and Phenomenology: A Comparative Study of the Later Wittgenstein, Husserl, Heidegger, and Merleau-Ponty.* Albany: State University of New York Press, 1981.

Girard, Rene. *Deceit, Desire, and the Novel: Self and Other in Literary Structure.* Translated by Yvonne Freccero. Baltimore: Johns Hopkins University Press, 1965.

———. *Violence and the Sacred.* Translated by Patrick Gregory. Baltimore: Johns Hopkins University Press, 1977.

Goldfarb, Warren. "Wittgenstein, Mind, and Scientism." *The Journal of Philosophy* 86 (1989): 635-42.

Gorgias. "Encomium of Helen." In *The Older Sophists,* edited by Rosamund Kent Sprague, 50-54. Columbia: University of South Carolina Press, 1972.

Grayling, A. C. "Wittgenstein's Influence: Meaning, Mind and Method." In *Wittgenstein Centenary Essays,* edited by A. Phillips Griffith, 61-78. New York: Cambridge University Press, 1991.

Guinier, Lani. *The Tyranny of the Majority: Fundamental Fairness in Representative Democracy.* New York: Free Press, 1994.

Gutman, Amy, and Dennis Thompson. *Democracy and Disagreement.* Cambridge: Harvard University Press, 1996.

Habermas, Jurgen. *Moral Consciousness and Communicative Action.* Cambridge: MIT Press, 1990.
Haller, Rudolf. *Questions on Wittgenstein.* Lincoln: University of Nebraska Press, 1988.
Hancher, Michael. "Three Kinds of Intention." *Modern Language Notes* 87 (1992): 827-51.
Hariman, Robert. "Critical Rhetoric and Postmodern Theory." *Quarterly Journal of Speech* 77 (1991): 67-70.
Heidegger, Martin. *Being and Time.* Translated by John Macquarrie and Edward Robison. New York: Harper and Row, 1962.
Henderson, Greig E. "Aesthetic and Practical Frames of Reference: Burke, Marx, and the Rhetoric of Social Change." In *Extensions of the Burkean System,* edited by James W. Chesbro, 173-85. Tuscaloosa: University of Alabama Press, 1993.
Hennessy, Rosemary. *Material Feminism and the Politics of Discourse.* New York: Routledge, 1993.
Hintikka, Merrill, and Jaako Hintikka. *Investigating Wittgenstein.* New York: Blackwell, 1986.
Hirsch, E. D. *The Aims of Interpretation.* Chicago: University of Chicago Press, 1976.
———. *Validity in Interpretation.* New Haven: Yale University Press, 1967.
hooks, bell. *Yearning: Race, Gender, and Cultural Politics.* Boston: South End, 1990.
Hotopf, W. H. N. *Language, Thought, and Comprehension: A Case Study of the Writings of I. A. Richards.* Bloomington: Indiana University Press, 1965.
Hunter, Allen. "Post-Marxism and the New Social Movements." *Theory and Society* 17 (1988): 885-900.
Hunter, J. F. M. "'Forms of Life' in Wittgenstein's *Philosophical Investigations.*" In *Essays on Wittgenstein,* edited by E. D. Klemke, 273-97. Chicago: University of Illinois Press, 1971.
Hyde, Michael, and Craig R. Smith. "Hermeneutics and Rhetoric: A Seen but Unobserved Relationship." *Quarterly Journal of Speech* 65 (1979): 353-63.
Iglesias, Teresa. "Russell on Vagueness and Wittgenstein's *Tractatus.*" In *Wittgenstein and His Impact on Contemporary Thought,* edited by Elisabeth Lunfellner, Werner Lunfellner, Hal Berghal, and Adolph Hubner, 46-49. Vienna: Holder Picheler Tempsky, 1978.
Iseminger, Gary, ed. *Intention and Interpretation.* Philadelphia: Temple University Press, 1992.
Iser, Wolfgang. *The Act of Reading: A Theory of Aesthetic Response.* Baltimore: Johns Hopkins University Press, 1978.
———. *Prospecting: From Reader Response to Literary Anthropology.* Baltimore: Johns Hopkins University Press, 1989.
Jackson, Bernard S. "Narrative Theories and Legal Discourse." In *Narrative in Culture: The Uses of Storytelling in the Sciences, Philosophy, and Literature,* edited by Cristopher Nash, 23-50. New York: Routledge, 1990.
Jameson, Frederic. *The Political Unconscious: Narrative as a Socially Symbolic Act.* Ithaca: Cornell University Press, 1981.
Janik, Allan, and Stephen Toulmin. *Wittgenstein's Vienna.* New York: Simon and Schuster, 1973.

Jarratt, Susan. *Rereading the Sophists: Classical Rhetoric Refigured*. Carbondale: Southern Illinois University Press, 1991.
Jost, Walter, and Michael Hyde, eds. *Rhetoric and Hermeneutics in Our Time: A Reader.* New Haven: Yale University Press, 1997.
Journet, Debra. "Ecological Theories as Cultural Narratives." *Written Communication* 8 (1991): 446-72.
Juhl, P. D. *Interpretation: An Essay in the Philosophy of Literary Criticism*. Princeton: Princeton University Press, 1980.
Kingwell, Mark. *A Civil Tongue: Justice, Dialogue, and the Politics of Pluralism*. University Park: Pennsylvania State University Press, 1995.
Kintgen, Eugene, Barry M. Kroll, and Mike Rose, eds. *Perspectives on Literacy*. Carbondale: Southern Illinois University Press, 1988.
Klemke, E. D., ed. "Preface." In *Essays on Wittgenstein*, edited by E. D. Klemke, ix-xi. Chicago: University of Illinois Press, 1971.
Knoblauch, C. H., and Lillian Brannon. *Rhetorical Traditions and the Teaching of Writing*. Upper Montclair, N.Y.: Boynton/Cook, 1984.
Koelb, Clayton. *Inventions of Reading: Rhetoric and the Literary Imagination*. Ithaca: Cornell University Press, 1988.
Kolodny, Annette. "Dancing Through the Minefield: Some Observations of Theory, Practice, and Politics of a Feminist Literary Criticism." *Feminist Studies* 6 (1980): 1-25.
Kristeva, Julia. *Desire in Language: A Semiotic Approach to Literature and Art*. Translated by Thomas Gora, Alice Jardine, and Leon S. Roudiez. New York: Columbia University Press, 1980.
———. *Revolution in Poetic Language*. Translated by Margaret Walker. New York: Columbia University Press, 1984.
Lacan, Jacques. *Ecrits*. Translated by Alan Sheridan. New York: W. W. Norton, 1977.
LaCapra, Dominick. "Reading Exemplars: Wittgenstein's Vienna and Wittgenstein's *Tractatus*." *Diacritic* 9 (1979): 65-82.
Laclau, Ernesto. *New Reflections on the Revolution of Our Times*. New York: Verso, 1990.
———. "Politics and the Limits of Modernity." In *Universal Abandon? The Politics of Post-Modernity,* edited by Andrew Ross, 63-82. Minneapolis: University of Minnesota Press, 1988.
Laclau, Ernesto, and Chantal Mouffe. *Hegemony and Social Strategy: Towards a Radical Democratic Politics*. London: New Left Books, 1985.
Landau, Misia. *Narratives of Human Evolution*. New Haven: Yale University Press, 1991.
Landry, Donna, and Gerald MacLean. "Rereading Laclau and Mouffe." *Rethinking MARXISM* 4 (1991): 41-60.
Law, Jules David. *The Rhetoric of Empiricism*. Ithaca: Cornell University Press, 1993.
Lawrence, Roy. *Motive and Intention: An Essay in the Appreciation of Action*. Evanston, Ill.: Northwestern University Press, 1972.
Leff, Michael. "Hermeneutical Rhetoric." In *Rhetoric and Hermeneutics in Our Time: A Reader,* edited by Walter Jost and Michael Hyde, 196-214. New Haven: Yale University Press, 1997.

———. "The Idea of Rhetoric as Interpretive Practice: A Humanist's Response to Gaonkar." *Southern Communication Journal* 58 (1993): 296-300.
———. "In Search of Ariadne's Thread: A Review of the Recent Literature on Rhetorical Theory." *Central States Speech Journal* 29 (1978): 73-91.
———. "Things Made by Words: Reflections on Textual Criticism." *Quarterly Journal of Speech* 78 (1992): 223-31.
Lentricchia, Frank. *Criticism and Social Change*. Chicago: University of Chicago Press, 1985.
———. "Reading History with Kenneth Burke." In *Representing Kenneth Burke*, edited by Hayden White and Margaret Brose, 119-49. Baltimore: Johns Hopkins University Press, 1982.
Lummis, Douglas C. *Radical Democracy*. Ithaca: Cornell University Press, 1996.
Lunsford, Andrea, Helene Moglen, and James Slevin, eds. *The Right to Literacy*. New York: Modern Language Association, 1990.
Lyon, Arabella. " 'The Good Man Speaking Well,' or Business as Usual." In *(Inter)views: Criticism, Philosophy, and Rhetoric*, edited by Gary Olson, 220-26. Carbondale: Southern Illinois University Press, 1994.
Lyotard, Jean-François. *The Post-Modern Condition: A Report on Knowledge*. Translated by Geoff Bennington and Brian Massumi. Minneapolis: University of Minnesota Press, 1984.
Lyotard, Jean-François, and Jean-Loup Thebaud. *Just Gaming*. Translated by Wlad Godzich. Minneapolis: University of Minneapolis Press, 1985.
MacIntyre, Alasdair. *After Virtue*. South Bend, Ind.: University of Notre Dame Press, 1982.
MacKinnon, Catherine A. *Toward a Feminist Theory of State*. Cambridge: Harvard University Press, 1989.
Mailloux, Steven. "Articulation and Understanding: The Pragmatic Intimacy Between Rhetoric and Hermeneutics." In *Rhetoric and Hermeneutics in Our Time: A Reader*, edited by Walter Jost and Michael Hyde, 378-94. New Haven: Yale University Press, 1997.
———. *Interpretive Conventions: The Reader in the Study of American Fiction*. Ithaca: Cornell University Press, 1982.
———. "Language Games (2)." In *Wittgenstein: Attention to Particulars*, edited by D. Z. Philips and Peter Winch, 35-44. London: Macmillan, 1989.
———. *Rhetorical Power*. Ithaca: Cornell University Press, 1989.
Malcolm, Norman. *Dreaming*. Boston: Routledge & Kegan Paul, 1967.
———. "Thinking." In *Wittgenstein and His Impact on Contemporary Thought*, edited by Elisabeth Leinfellner et al., 411-19. Vienna: Holder Pichler Tempsky, 1978.
Martin, Emily. "The Egg and the Sperm: How Science Has Constructed a Romance Based on Stereotypical Male-Female Roles." *Signs* 16 (1991): 485-501.
McDowell, John. "Wittgenstein and the Inner World." *The Journal of Philosophy* 86 (1989): 643-44.
McGuinness, Brian. "Editor's Preface." In *Ludwig Wittgenstein and the Vienna Circle*, 11-31. New York: Blackwell, 1979.

———. *Wittgenstein: A Life*. Berkeley and Los Angeles: University of California Press, 1988.

McKerrow, Raymie E. "The Centrality of Justification: Principles of Warranted Assertability." In *Argumentation Theory and the Rhetoric of Assent*, edited by David Cratis Williams and Michael David Hazen, 17-32. Tuscaloosa: University of Alabama Press, 1990.

———. "Critical Rhetoric in a Postmodern World." *Quarterly Journal of Speech* 77 (1991): 75-78.

Mele, Alfred R. "Against a Belief/Desire Analysis of Intention." *Philosophia* 18 (1988): 239-42.

Miller, Carolyn. "The *Polis* as Rhetorical Community." *Rhetorica* 11 (1993): 211-40.

Minow, Martha. "The Supreme Court, 1986-Foreword: Justice Engendered." *Harvard Law Review* 101 (1987): 10-95.

Monk, Ray. *Ludwig Wittgenstein: The Duty of Genius*. New York: Free Press, 1990.

Moore, Michael. *Act and Crime*. New York: Clarendon Press, 1993.

Mouffe, Chantal. "Hegemony and New Political Subjects: Toward a New Concept of Democracy." In *Marxism and the Interpretation of Culture*, edited by Cary Nelson and Lawrence Grossberg, 89-101. Chicago: University of Illinois Press, 1988.

———. *The Return of the Political*. New York: Verso, 1993.

Mueller-Vollmer, Kurt. *The Hermeneutics Reader*. New York: Continuum, 1992.

Mulvey, Laura. *Visual and Other Pleasures*. Bloomington: Indiana University Press, 1989.

Nelson, Cary. "Writing as the Accomplice of Language: Kenneth Burke and Poststructuralism." In *The Legacy of Kenneth Burke*, edited by Herbert W. Simons and Trevor Melia, 156-73. Madison: University of Wisconsin Press, 1989.

Nussbaum, Martha C. *The Fragility of Goodness: Luck and Ethics in Greek Tragedies and Philosophy*. New York: Cambridge University Press, 1986.

O'Banion, John D. *Reorienting Rhetoric: The Dialectic of List and Story*. University Park: Pennsylvania State University Press, 1993.

Okin, Susan Moller. *Justice, Gender, and the Family*. New York: Basic Books, 1989.

Overington, Michael A. "Kenneth Burke and the Method of Dramatism." In *Landmark Essays on Kenneth Burke*, edited by Barry Brummett, 91-114. Davis, Calif.: Hermagoras, 1993.

Palmer, Richard E. *Hermeneutics*. Evanston, Ill.: Northwestern University Press, 1969.

Pateman, Carole. *Participation and Democratic Theory*. Cambridge: Cambridge University Press, 1970.

Pears, David. *The False Prison*. Vol. 1. Oxford: Clarendon Press, 1987.

Pitcher, George. "Wittgenstein, Nonsense, and Lewis Carroll." *Massachusetts Review* 6 (1965): 591-611.

Plato. *Phaedrus*. Translated by R. Hackforth. New York: Cambridge University Press, 1952.

Pratt, Mary Louise. "Ideology and Speech-Act Theory." *Poetics Today* 7 (1986): 59-72.

Proust, Joelle. "Formal Logic as Transcendental in Wittgenstein and Carnap." *Nous* 21 (1987): 501-20.

Pullman, George. "Of Thieves and Liars, or Why Hermeneutics Is Rhetoric Carried Out by Other Means." *Studies in the Literary Imagination* 28 (1995): 1-11.
Rhees, Rush. *Discussion of Wittgenstein.* London: Routledge & Kegan Paul, 1970.
Richards, I. A. *Beyond.* New York: Harcourt Brace Jovanovich, 1974.
———. *Coleridge on Imagination.* London: K. Paul, Trench, Trubner, 1934.
———, *The Philosophy of Rhetoric.* New York: Oxford University Press, 1965.
———. *Practical Criticism.* New York: Harcourt, Brace and Company, 1929.
———. *Principles of Literary Criticism.* New York: Harcourt, Brace and Company, 1925.
———. *Speculative Instruments.* Chicago: University of Chicago Press, 1955.
Richards, I. A., and C. K. Ogden. *The Meaning of Meaning.* New York: Harcourt, Brace and Company, 1923.
Rooney, Ellen. *Seductive Reason: Pluralism as a Problematic of Contemporary Literary Theory.* Ithaca: Cornell University Press, 1989.
Rorty, Richard. *Philosophy and the Mirror of Nature.* Princeton: Princeton University Press, 1979.
Rowland, Robert C. "Purpose, Argument Evaluation, and Crisis." In *Argumentation and the Rhetoric of Assent,* edited by David Cratis Williams and Michael David Hazen, 119-34. Tuscaloosa: Alabama University Press.
Rueckert, William. "Kenneth Burke and Structuralism." *Shenandoah* 21 (1969): 19-28.
Russell, Bertrand. *Autobiography.* London: Unwin, 1971.
———. Introduction to *Tractatus Logico-Philosophicus,* by Ludwig Wittgenstein. Boston: Routledge & Kegan Paul, 1922.
Russo, John Paul. *I. A. Richards: His Life and Work.* Baltimore: Johns Hopkins University Press, 1989.
Salkever, Stephen G. *Finding the Mean: Theory and Practice in Aristotelian Political Philosophy.* Princeton: Princeton University Press, 1990.
Salmond, John William, Sir. *Jurisprudence.* 7th ed. London: Sweet & Maxwell, 1924.
Saxonhouse, Arlene W. *Fear of Diversity: The Birth of Political Science in Ancient Greek Thought.* Chicago: University of Chicago Press, 1992.
Schleiermacher, Friedrich D. E. *Hermeneutik.* Translated by H. Kimmerle. Heidelburg: Karl Winter, 1959.
Schlick, Moritz. "What Is the Aim of Ethics?" In *Essential Readings in Logical Positivism,* edited by Oswald Hanfling, 207-23. Oxford: Blackwell, 1981.
Schon, Donald A. "Generative Metaphor: A Perspective on Problem-Setting in Social Policy." In *Metaphor and Thought,* edited by Andrew Ortony, 254-83. Cambridge: Cambridge University Press, 1979.
Schwartz, Joseph M. *The Permanence of the Political: A Democratic Critique of the Radical Impulse to Transcend Politics.* Princeton: Princeton University Press, 1995.
Scult, Alan. "The Relationship Between Rhetoric and Hermeneutics Reconsidered." *Central States Speech Journal* 34 (1983): 221-28.
Searle, John R. *Intentionality: An Essay in the Philosophy of Mind.* New York: Cambridge University Press, 1983.

———. "Metaphor." In *Metaphor and Thought,* edited by Andrew Ortony, 92-123. Cambridge: Cambridge University Press, 1979.

———. *Speech Acts: An Essay in the Philosophy of Language.* New York: Cambridge University Press, 1969.

Selzer, Jack. *Kenneth Burke in Greenwich Village: Conversing with the Moderns, 1915-1931.* Madison: University of Wisconsin Press, 1996.

———, ed. *Understanding Scientific Prose.* Madison: University of Wisconsin Press, 1993.

Siebers, Tobin. "Language, Violence, and the Sacred: A Polemical Survey of Critical Theories." In *To Honor Rene Girard,* edited by Stanford French and Italian Studies, 203-19. Saratoga, Calif.: Anma Libri, 1986.

Smith, Barbara Herrnstein. *Belief and Resistance: Dynamics of Contemporary Intellectual Controversy.* Boston: Harvard University Press, 1997.

Smith, Paul. *Discerning the Subject.* Minneapolis: University of Minnesota Press, 1988.

Southwell, Samuel B. *Kenneth Burke and Martin Heidegger with a Note against Deconstruction.* Gainesville: University of Florida Press, 1987.

Spanos, William V. "The Apollonian Investment of Modern Humanist Education: The Examples of Matthew Arnold, Irving Babbitt, and I. A. Richards (I)." *Cultural Critique* 1 (1985): 7-72.

Spender, Dale. *Man Made Language.* Boston: Routledge & Kegan Paul, 1980.

Spolsky, Ellen. "The Uses of Adversity: The Literary Text and the Audience That Doesn't Understand." In *The Uses of Adversity: Failure and Accomodation in Reader Response,* edited by Ellen Spolsky, 17-35. Cranbury, N.J.: Associated University Press, 1990.

Stamp, Glen H., and Mark L. Knapp. "The Construct of Intent in Interpersonal Communication." *Quarterly Journal of Speech* 76 (1990): 282-99.

Sternberg, Robert J. *Metaphors of Mind: Conceptions of the Nature of Intelligence.* Cambridge: Cambridge University Press, 1990.

Stewart, Susan. *Nonsense: Aspects of Intertextuality in Folklore and Literature.* Baltimore: Johns Hopkins University Press, 1978.

Swearingen, Jan C. *Rhetoric and Irony: Western Literacy and Western Lies.* New York: Oxford University Press, 1991.

Thomason, Richard H. "Accommodation, Meaning, and Implicature: Interdisciplinary Foundations for Pragmatics." In *Intentions in Communication,* edited by Philip R. Cohen, Jerry Morgan, and Martha E. Pollack, 325-63. Cambridge: MIT Press, 1990.

Toulmin, Stephen. *Human Understanding.* Princeton: Princeton University Press, 1972.

Travers, Ann. "Radical Democracy's Feminist Potential." *Praxis International* 12 (1992): 269-83.

Waismann, Fredrich. *Wittgenstein and the Vienna Circle.* New York: Barnes and Noble, 1979.

Walzer, Michael. *Spheres of Justice: A Defense of Pluralism and Equality.* New York: Basic Books, 1983.

Warnick, Barbara. "Leff in Context: What's the Critic's Role?" *Quarterly Journal of Speech* 78 (1992): 232-37.

———. "The Narrative Paradigm: Another Story." *Quarterly Journal of Speech* 73 (1987): 172-82.
Warnke, Georgia. *Gadamer: Hermeneutics, Tradition, and Reason*. Stanford: Stanford University Press, 1987.
———. *Justice and Interpretation*. Cambridge: MIT Press, 1993.
Warnock, G. J. *English Philosophy Since 1900*. London: Oxford University Press, 1958.
Wells, Susan. "Richards, Burke, and the Relation Between Rhetoric and Poetics." *PRE/TEXT* 7 (1986): 59-75.
———. *Sweet Reason: Rhetoric and the Discourses of Modernity*. Chicago: University of Chicago Press, 1996.
Wess, Robert. *Kenneth Burke: Rhetoric, Subjectivity, Postmodernism*. New York: Cambridge University Press, 1996.
West, Robin. *Narrative, Authority, Law*. Ann Arbor: University of Michigan Press, 1993.
White, Hayden. *Tropics of Discourse*. Baltimore: Johns Hopkins University Press, 1978.
Wiggins, David. "Deliberation and Practical Reason." In *Essays on Aristotle's Ethics*, edited by Amelie Oksenberg Rorty, 221-40. Berkeley and Los Angeles: University of California Press, 1980.
Williams, David Cratis, and Michael David Hazen, eds. *Argumentation Theory and the Rhetoric of Assent*. Tuscaloosa: University of Alabama Press, 1990.
Wimsatt, W. K., and Monroe C. Beardsley. "The Intentional Fallacy." In *The Verbal Icon*, edited by W. K. Wimsatt, 3-18. Lexington: University of Kentucky Press, 1954.
Wittgenstein, Hermine. "My Brother Ludwig." In *Recollections of Wittgenstein*, edited by Rush Rhees, 1-11. New York: Oxford University Press, 1981.
Wittgenstein, Ludwig. *Letters to Russell, Keynes and Moore*. Edited by G. H. von Wright. Oxford: Blackwell, 1974.
———. *Notebooks 1914-1916*. Edited by G. H. von Wright and G. E. M. Anscombe. Translated by G. E. M. Anscombe. Oxford: Blackwell, 1961.
———. *On Certainty*. Edited by G. E. M. Anscombe and G. H. von Wright. Translated by Denis Paul and G. E. M. Anscombe. New York: Harper, 1969.
———. *Philosophical Investigations*. Translated by G. E. M. Anscombe. New York: Macmillan, 1958.
———. *Remarks of the Foundations of Mathematics*. Edited by G. von Wright, R. Rhees, and G. E. M. Anscombe. Translated by G. E. M. Anscombe. Cambridge: MIT Press, 1956.
———. *Tractatus LogicoPhilosophicus*. Translated by C. K. Ogden. Boston: Routledge & Kegan Paul, 1922.
———. *Tractatus LogicoPhilosophicus*. Translated by D. F. Pears and B. F. McGuinness. London: Routledge & Kegan Paul, 1961.
———. *Zettel*. Edited by G. E. M. Anscombe and G. H. von Wright. Translated by G. E. M. Anscombe. Berkeley and Los Angeles: University of California Press, 1967.
Wright, Crispin. "Wittgenstein's Later Philosophy of Mind: Sensation, Privacy, and Intention." *The Journal of Philosophy* 86 (1989): 622-34.
Yack, Bernard. *The Problems of a Political Animal: Community, Justice, and Conflict in Aristotelian Political Thought*. Berkeley and Los Angeles: University of California Press, 1993.

Young, Iris Marion. *Justice and the Politics of Difference*. Princeton: Princeton University Press, 1990.

Zabeeh, Farhang. "On Language Games and Forms of Life." In *Essays on Wittgenstein*, edited by E. D. Klemke, 328-73. Chicago: University of Illinois Press, 1971.

Zaretsky, Eli. "Identity and Democracy: A Critical Perspective." In *Radical Democracy: Identity, Citizenship, and the State*, edited by David Trend, 140-56. New York: Routledge, 1996.

Index

act
   in Austin, 90 n. 11, 106-8, 170 n. 1
   in Burke, 89-92, 95-97, 187-90
action (political), 18, 44, 55, 71, 191-95. *See also* drama
aesthetic texts, 5, 27, 28-29, 32, 36, 43-46, 53-54, 55, 165, 177
aesthetics (in *Tractatus*), 23, 115, 117-18, 121, 133, 136-37, 177
agency, 22, 28, 34, 57-59, 84 n. 1, 90, 96, 152, 187-90
agent, 22, 84 n. 1, 96-100, 187-90
Altieri, Charles, 11-12, 65, 69 n. 15
ambiguity, 102-4, 194
analytic philosophy, 6-7, 143-45
Anscombe, G. E. M., 11, 129, 146, 150, 150 n. 13, 154, 179
argument, 1-2, 14-15, 71, 74-75, 81, 87-88, 38, 53-4, 129-41. *See also* persuasion
Aristotelian rhetoric, 13-17, 42-43, 83
Aristotle, 5, 13-18, 191
assent, 29, 41-45, 64
audience intentions, 1-2, 11-12, 14-19, 49-51, 58, 84, 105-11, 131-37. *See also* intention
audience, 1-2, 7, 11-12, 15, 38, 49-51, 58
Augustine, 151-54, 155, 164-65, 165 n. 22
Austin, J. L., 8, 90 n. 11, 106-8, 169-70, 186
authorial intentions
   access to, 1-2, 5, 82-83
   as constraint, 32-32, 42-44, 46, 49, 58-59, 86 n. 6, 87
   constructed, 9-11, 12, 49-51, 39-40, 101
   ignored, 130-41
   in metaphor, 176-85
   in narrative, 49-54, 155-58, 160-64. *See also* intentions
authority, 29, 64-66

Baker, Lynne Rudder, 178-79, 189
Beardsley, Monroe, 9, 27
belief, 6-7, 42, 47, 143-46, 151
Booth, Wayne, 16, 21, 40-48, 53-54
Burke, Kenneth, 22, 82-104, 106, 108
   constitution, 192-93
   drama, 89, 96-101, 130-33, 140, 161-65, 167, 187-90
   narrative, 147 n. 6
   negation, 116-18, 125
   opposites, 193-94
   purpose, 22, 86-87, 96-101, 126-40, 152, 170-72, 176, 186-90

Carnap, Rudolf, 23, 115, 128, 134-37, 149 n. 12, 189
catachresis, 171, 176-84
causality, 98, 124, 144
Cavell, Stanley, 49 n. 15, 176-78, 180, 184
coherence of text, 133, 179, 180, 184, 187
communication, 31-36, 89, 93, 98, 170, 187-95
communitarianism, 16, 16 nn. 15 and 16, 37, 138
community, 16-20, 35, 47, 48, 51-53, 99, 114, 138, 190-93
conflict, 15-16, 18-20, 41-47, 65, 83-86, 92, 95, 191-95
consensus, 16-17, 47, 62, 100, 191-95
conversation, 42-43, 65, 70, 83-84
Conway, Gertrude, 179, 189
culture, 63, 89, 92-93, 185

de Lauretis, Teresa, 159-60, 164
deliberation
   Aristotle, 13-20
   Burke, 85, 102-4
   defined, 5 n. 3

deliberation (*continued*)
  going on, 187-95
  interpretive rhetorics and, 4-5, 53, 70, 71, 81
  metaphor and, 24, 176-85
  narrative and, 151-55, 157-58, 171-72
  negatives and, 115, 130-34
  See also action (political); democracy; public discourse; pluralism
democracy, 12-13, 18-20, 85, 103, 194
desire
  intentionality, 6-7, 11, 143-46
  narrative, 24, 144-67
  negative, 116-17
  psychoanalytic theory, 144, 146, 159-60, 164
  and purpose, 99-101
dialectic processes, 62, 85, 103-4, 156-60, 159 n. 20, 185, 193
dialectical materialism, 84-85, 90-92, 95, 194
dialogue, 61, 64, 80, 84-85
difference, 17-20, 45, 58-59, 63-69, 95, 99-100, 103-4, 146, 191-95
disciplinary discourses, 105, 113-15, 147-67
dissent, 42, 45-47
drama, 22, 96-101, 130-33, 140, 161-64, 165, 167. *See also* Burke, Kenneth

Eagleton, Terry, 183
education, 31, 37, 39, 46, 70
ethics
  in rhetoric, 14-17, 29
  in *Tractatus*, 112, 117-18, 121, 128, 131, 133, 136-37
experience and language, 87-89, 94-95, 101, 107-11

Farrell, Thomas, 12 n. 10, 52 n. 16, 56, 147 n. 7
Fish, Stanley, 21, 48-54, 82, 99, 114
forensics
  metaphor and, 183-85
  narrative and, 151, 157-58, 160-67
  past orientation, 5, 20, 187-88
form, 22, 86-89, 115-24, 186-89. *See also* structure; narrative; negative; metaphor
formalism, 37-38, 40, 71-72
Fraser, Nancy, 12 n. 10, 19 n. 22

Frege, Gottlob, 113, 115, 128
Freud, Sigmund, 127 n. 8, 146, 167

Gadamer, Hans-Georg, 21, 58-71, 82-83, 95
Gaonkar, Dilip, 3, 56-57
Garver, Eugene, 13-15, 185
Garver, Newton, 179-81, 189
going on, 50 n. 15, 109-11, 119, 130-37, 140, 186, 190, 192
Goldfarb, Warren, 162
good, 16, 195
Guinier, Lani, 5 n. 3, 16

Hancher, Michael, 9-11, 12, 88. *See also* intentions (active, final, programmatic)
Heidegger, Martin, 59-60, 95 n. 13
hermeneutics
  ontological, 21, 58-70, 184-85
  relationship to rhetoric, 55-57, 69-80
  romantic, 21, 58-59
  suspicion and, 68-69, 101, 190
Hirsch, E. D., 28, 56 n. 2
history
  conditions of, 27
  desire and, 159 n. 19
  of a discourse, 28-29, 33-35, 71, 71 n. 18, 75
  historical consciousness, 56
  mode of being, 60, 63
hooks, bell, 16 n. 17, 67, 191
horizons, 62, 68, 75, 87, 139

idealism, 43, 100-101, 106, 177
identification, 82-83, 85, 88, 103, 190, 194
incommensurability, 16, 49 n. 15, 94, 99, 114, 133-34, 182-83
instrumental discourse, 3-4, 8, 32-33, 37-38, 51, 74, 83-86, 119
intention, 3-4, 6-7, 8-12, 30-31
  active, 9-11, 50
  audience intentions, 1-2, 11-12, 14-19, 58, 84, 105-11, 131-37
  final, 9-11
  legal theory and, 145, 165-67
  programmatic, 9-11, 50, 58, 87, 88
  public nature of, 105-11, 143-45, 160-67, 185-92
  rhetoric's assumption of, 3-5. *See also* authorial intention and audience intention
intentionality, 6, 11, 143-46

interpretative rhetorics, 4, 8-9, 12-13, 55-58, 95-96. *See also* rhetorical criticism
interpreter, 36, 39, 60-69
  difference from audience, 45-47, 64-69, 156
intersubjectivity, 46, 55, 81, 84
invention, 62, 74, 76-79, 110-11, 124, 149, 157-58, 170-85
irony, 27, 44, 48-49
Iser, Wolfgang, 124-26
Janik, Allan, and Stephen Toulmin, 128, 134-35, 173
judgment, 47, 61, 64-65, 157, 159-67, 186, 190

kairos, 4, 20, 28
Koelb, Clayton, 79
Kristeva, Julia, 123 n. 7, 125, 146

Laclau, Ernesto, 18-20, 194
Leff, Michael, 8-9, 56-57, 69 n. 15
limits of language, 116-18, 123, 127, 131, 144, 148-49, 151
literacy, 12, 65 n. 12, 153
literary criticism and theory, 5, 27, 32, 35-37, 89, 124-26
logic, symbolic, 114-15, 117-18, 121, 127-30, 135-36
Lyotard, Jean-François, 176, 182-84

Mailloux, Stephen, 22, 56, 71-76, 83
Malcolm, Norman, 23-24, 155-58, 163, 183 n. 7
McDowell, John, 163-64, 189
mental (inner) processes, 108-10, 163, 177-78, 185-87
metaphor, 22, 24, 38, 170-85, 188
  as transformative, 170, 173-75, 176-85
misunderstanding, 30, 37, 46-47, 103, 108, 113-15, 186, 169 n. 1
modernism, 41-47
motive, 22, 87, 89-96
  cultural, 94-96, 127-40, 170-85, 186-90
  universal, 94-96
Mouffe, Chantal, 18-20, 194
multiculturalism, 31, 36-37, 61, 128, 140, 191. *See also* pluralism
Mulvey, Laura, 159-60, 164
mysticism
  purpose and, 98-99, 106, 109

Wittgenstein on, 115, 117-18, 129, 132-33, 136-37

narratives, 22, 23-24, 182, 188
  accrual, 148-58
  characters in, 130-32, 161-64
  deliberative, 24, 151-55, 157-58
  forensic, 24, 151, 157-58
  legal, 165-67
  metanarrative as theory, 111-12, 182-84
  rationality, 147-49, 159
narrators, 152-53
negation, 116-18, 124-26
negatives, 22, 23, 115-26
  reading negatives, 126-41
  revolutionary potential, 116-17, 124-26, 134, 139-40
negativity, 116, 125-26, 139-40
negotiation of difference, 4, 7-8, 24-25, 28, 59, 85, 190-95
negotiation of meaning, 32-5, 58-59, 101, 113-14, 129-41
nonsense, 118-24

Ogden, C. K., 31-32, 46
opposites, 193-95

paradox, 84 n. 1, 90-93, 102-4, 188
  of action, 90-92
  of definition, 102-3, 116-17, 118
  of substance, 102, 192-93
performance, 97, 106-11, 170 n. 1
persuasion, 1-2, 14-15, 50, 68, 191
  refused by audience, 25, 45-47, 64-69, 66 n. 13, 83-84, 191 n. 11
  refused as rhetorical, 37-38, 43, 45, 56
philosophy's relationship to rhetoric, 3-4, 5-7, 11-12, 32, 37-39, 43, 69-70
Plato, 29, 37, 42, 43, 50-51, 118
Platonic rhetoric, 42-43, 70-71
pluralism, 12-13, 16-20, 16 nn. 16 and 17, 19, 28, 37, 47, 53, 58, 82, 103. *See also* multiculturalism; power differentials
poetics, 28, 36, 84
positivism, 115, 134-37
postmodernism, 2, 17-20, 26, 42, 63 n. 11, 98, 182-83
power differentials, 21, 36-37, 40-48, 64-68, 81, 114, 128-24, 140, 191, 193 n. 14, 194-95

prejudices, 21, 61-69, 106, 114, 126, 127, 130-33, 138, 184-85
production, 4-5, 21, 28, 62-63, 69-80
psychoanalytic criticism, 24, 144, 146, 159-67
public discourse, 5, 12-20, 31-32, 87. *See also* democracy; multiculturalism; pluralism; power differentials.
purpose, 22, 86-87, 96-101, 126-40, 152, 170-72, 176, 186-90

reading
 ethics of, 28
 feminist, 45, 159-60
 instrumental, 119
 rhetorical, 79, 124-26, 131, 150-54, 183
realism, in *Tractatus*, 117-18
reality
 experienced, 86 n. 5, 87-89
 narrative, 147-49, 153-54, 165-67
 in radical democracy, 18
 real life, 70
 relationship to text, 125-26
rhetor, 14-15
rhetoric
 assumptions about intention, 3-5
 defined, 5, 14, 30, 37, 39, 43, 52-53, 69-76
 literary, 27, 37-41, 43-45
 relationship to hermeneutics, 55-57, 69-80
 relationship to philosophy, 3-4, 5-7, 11-12, 32, 37-39, 43, 69-70
 sophistry and, 14-5, 29, 84, 186
 See also deliberation
rhetorical criticism, 8-9, 13 n. 11, 56-57. *See also* interpretive rhetorics
rhetorical hermeneutics, 71-76
rhetorical situation, 2, 4, 8, 12, 15, 20, 22, 58, 61, 187
 desire and, 145-46, 146 n. 5
 as motive, 89-96
Richards, I. A., 21, 29-40, 49, 54, 70, 82-83
Rooney, Ellen, 16 n. 17, 67
Russell, Bertrand
 as modernist, 41, 44
 Wittgenstein and, 113-14, 126-36, 149 n. 12

sadism, 24, 158-67
Schleiermacher, Friedrich D. E., 58-59, 63

Schlick, Moritz, 134-36
Searle, John, 144, 170, 175, 186
skepticism, 41, 42, 49 n. 15, 106-11, 177-78
sophistry
 Gorgias, 1-2, 10, 50-51, 118
 mental states and, 143
 rhetoric and, 14-5, 29, 84, 186
speech act theory, 186. *See also* Austin, J. L.; Searle, John
Stewart, Susan, 120-23, 134
subjectivity, 13, 187, 190. *See also* agent; agency

tautology, 117, 120 n. 5, 133, 135
textual coherence, 133, 179, 180, 184, 187
textuality, 8-9, 35, 55-58, 60-61
Toulmin, Stephen, 133-34, 150
tradition, 61-64, 87
transformation (social), 18-20, 38-39, 41-43, 51-53, 67-68, 72, 92-94, 120-24
transformation (symbolic), 85, 102, 103, 120-24, 170-72, 185
translation, 33-34, 56, 63, 72-73, 80, 102, 151, 155-56
truth, 3-4, 41, 43-44, 60, 69

understanding
 Booth, Wayne, 42, 46-47
 going on, 184-95
 hermeneutical, 58-63, 67, 70-76, 80
 inventing, 78-80
 limits of, 138-41
 ordinary language philosophy, 106-11, 113-15
 Richards, I. A., 31

Vienna Circle, 126, 134-37, 174

Warnke, Georgia, 62, 63 n. 11
Wells, Susan, 38, 71 n. 18, 146 n. 5
Wess, Robert, 86 n. 5, 192 n. 12
Wimsatt, W. K., 9, 27
wishes, 143, 167
Wittgenstein, Ludwig
 Carnap and, 134-37
 going on, 50 n. 15, 109-11, 119, 130-37, 140, 186, 190, 192
 metaphors, 172-75, 177-78
 narratives, 101, 149-58, 162

negatives in *Tractatus Logico-Philosophicus*, 23, 113-18, 149-50, 180
nonsense, 118-24
performance and understanding, 108-11

Russell and, 113-14, 126-36, 149 n. 12
on theory, 111-12, 174
Wright, Crispin, 189

Young, Marion Iris, 47, 193 n. 13

www.ingramcontent.com/pod-product-compliance
Lightning Source LLC
Chambersburg PA
CBHW031550300426
44111CB00006BA/249